CAMBRIDGE LIBRARY COLLECTION

Books of enduring scholarly value

Polar Exploration

This series includes accounts, by eye-witnesses and contemporaries, of early expeditions to the Arctic and the Antarctic. Huge resources were invested in such endeavours, particularly the search for the North-West Passage, which, if successful, promised enormous strategic and commercial rewards. Cartographers and scientists travelled with many of the expeditions, and their work made important contributions to earth sciences, climatology, botany and zoology. They also brought back anthropological information about the indigenous peoples of the Arctic region and the southern fringes of the American continent. The series further includes dramatic and poignant accounts of the harsh realities of working in extreme conditions and utter isolation in bygone centuries.

Fur-Clad Adventurers

Z.A. Mudge (1813–88) was an American pastor, author and Arctic exploration enthusiast. After the success of his popular books *North Pole Voyages* and *Arctic Heroes*, he wrote this book on the Western Union Telegraph Expedition. In the mid-nineteenth century the Western Union Telegraph Company decided to create a telegraph line that would run from San Francisco, California to Moscow, Russia. The line was to run through Alaska and Siberia, and although the project was abandoned in 1867, a large amount of Arctic exploration had been achieved in the meantime. This book, first published in 1880, is Mudge's compilation of the accounts of some of the explorers who were involved in different stages of the expedition, including the naturalist W.H. Dall during his exploration in Alaska. Mudge goes on to include the Siberian experiences of George Kennan and W.H. Bush (whose own account is also reissued in this series).

Cambridge University Press has long been a pioneer in the reissuing of out-of-print titles from its own backlist, producing digital reprints of books that are still sought after by scholars and students but could not be reprinted economically using traditional technology. The Cambridge Library Collection extends this activity to a wider range of books which are still of importance to researchers and professionals, either for the source material they contain, or as landmarks in the history of their academic discipline.

Drawing from the world-renowned collections in the Cambridge University Library and other partner libraries, and guided by the advice of experts in each subject area, Cambridge University Press is using state-of-the-art scanning machines in its own Printing House to capture the content of each book selected for inclusion. The files are processed to give a consistently clear, crisp image, and the books finished to the high quality standard for which the Press is recognised around the world. The latest print-on-demand technology ensures that the books will remain available indefinitely, and that orders for single or multiple copies can quickly be supplied.

The Cambridge Library Collection brings back to life books of enduring scholarly value (including out-of-copyright works originally issued by other publishers) across a wide range of disciplines in the humanities and social sciences and in science and technology.

Fur-Clad Adventurers

*Or, Travels in Skin-Canoes, on Dog-Sledges,
on Reindeer, and on Snow-Shoes,
through Alaska, Kamchatka, and Eastern Siberia*

ZACARIAH ATWELL MUDGE

CAMBRIDGE
UNIVERSITY PRESS

CAMBRIDGE UNIVERSITY PRESS

Cambridge, New York, Melbourne, Madrid, Cape Town,
Singapore, São Paolo, Delhi, Mexico City

Published in the United States of America by Cambridge University Press, New York

www.cambridge.org
Information on this title: www.cambridge.org/9781108050005

© in this compilation Cambridge University Press 2012

This edition first published 1880
This digitally printed version 2012

ISBN 978-1-108-05000-5 Paperback

Dog-Sledging.

See page 270.

FUR-CLAD
ADVENTURERS

Or, Travels in Skin-canoes, on Dog-sledges, on Reindeer, and on Snow-shoes, through Alaska, Kamchatka, and Eastern Siberia

By Z. A. Mudge

Author of "Arctic Heroes," "North-Pole Voyages," Etc.

FOUR ILLUSTRATIONS

NEW YORK: HUNT & EATON
CINCINNATI: CRANSTON & CURTS

PREFACE.

THIS work is a complement of "Arctic Heroes" and "North-Pole Voyages," in that it carries its readers into the Arctic regions; but it is not repetitional of the matter of those volumes in the incidents related, nor in the character of the information given. It conveys its readers to other lands, and into those little known. This last remark is especially true of Alaska, the newly acquired territory of the United States.

We are indebted for the materials from which we have wrought this volume to "Alaska and its Resources," by W. H. Dall, of the Smithsonian Institution; "Tent Life in Siberia," by George Kennan; "Reindeer, Dogs, Sledges, and Snow-Shoes," by R. H. Bush; and F. Whymper's "Travels in Alaska." All of these works resulted from explorations in the interest of the Russo-American Telegraph Company, whose operations closed in 1867, so

that the information they developed. is fresh
and valuable.

We remark, as we have in effect in our relative volumes, that the spelling of the proper
names belonging to the Arctic regions is an Art
which no man seems yet to have learned; the
aim of authors in this line appears to have been
originality, as few agree with any other, and
not every one agrees with himself.   We have
aimed at the simplest form having any credit-
able authority.

CONTENTS.

8   CONTENTS.

Illustrations.

FUR-CLAD ADVENTURERS.

CHAPTER I.

A START.

MANY years ago Shakspeare's fairy was made to say, "I'll put a girdle round about the earth." What was then imagined, modern enterprise proposed to do in sober earnest. Iron wires first ran from city to city in many countries, climbing the mountains, spanning the rivers, and often stretching across desolate regions, all to bring populous centers together. Finally, men of science said, "We will lay our telegraphic cable across the Atlantic, and bind the Old World to the New." This was tried and failed. More money was expended; brains and labor were laid under heavy contribution, and new efforts were made; but for a time the best only *almost* succeeded. Men began to say, "It cannot be done."

While these efforts were being made they were watched by the "Western Union Telegraph Company." *They* had been for several years thinking of putting a girdle round the earth. But their plan was to keep the wires on the land as much as possible. So when they thought the Atlantic

Cable would fail altogether, they formed the "Western Union Extension Company," with a capital on paper of ten millions of dollars, which brought them promptly five hundred thousand in cash to begin operations. The company intended business, and soon some of the best business and scientific men of the country were secured to their service, exploring corps were organized, composed of men after the Arctic-hero stamp, ships were set afloat, and an energy was breathed into the enterprise which went far to assure success.

Of course, we need not tell the reader that the Atlantic Cable did finally succeed, and that the new company's heroic work was not needed, and therefore, was stopped. But its operations had continued two years, three millions of dollars had been expended, and those in its service had explored nearly six thousand miles of unbroken wilderness, met and conquered difficulties, experienced thrilling adventures, faced cold the most intense, waded through the deepest snows, and studied men and nature under extraordinary, if not absolutely new, circumstances.

We propose to turn the hands of time back about ten years on their dial-plate, and put ourselves in the company of several, in turn, of the parties of these explorers; go with them, see, so far as possible, what they saw, and hear what they heard. We do not propose to experience what they at times experienced, for we shall travel leisurely, and, if we please, in dressing-gown and slippers.

Captain Charles S. Bulkley, U. S. A., took command of the exploring expedition, with his headquarters at San Francisco, California. It was proposed to run the telegraph wire from San Francisco to the mouth of the Frazer River, thence through British Columbia, Russian America, across Bering Strait, and through North-eastern Siberia to the mouth of the Amoor River, on the Asiatic coast. The hearty sympathy of the Czar of Russia was secured, and he proposed to extend his telegraph system to the mouth of the Amoor, thus directing the electric current from America through Asia and Europe. A communication sent by this route from New York to London would travel twenty-five thousand miles, a distance equal to the circuit of the earth.

From the Amoor there would, it was thought, open up eventually a splendid telegraph business with Peking, and the Celestial Empire generally, and John Chinaman would sip his tea and talk the while with Brother Jonathan about the silk and tea market! Would not all this be a fine thing to do? Well, the Western Union, or, as it is generally called, the Russo-American Company, set about doing it.

Commander Bulkley made a pioneer visit, in the early spring of 1865, to Sitka, capital of Russian America. Returning after a few weeks to San Francisco, three expeditions were sent out. One to British Columbia, one to Siberia, and one to Russian America, now *our* Alaska. We propose to visit the last-named country first, though our narrative of adventure there is mostly a year later in time than that to Siberia. In the independent way in which we go we can accommodate ourselves in the time and order of our visit.

Let it be understood that our place of embarkation is San Francisco; our vessel the clipper-ship " Nightingale ; " our companion of travel Mr. Dall, a Bostonian, and naturalist, in the employ of the Smithsonian Institution, to collect scientific facts and specimens concerning our *now* national estate, the Alaska Territory; and the port where we would land is St. Michaels, a trading station of the Russian Fur Company, on an island of the same name in the south-western part of Norton Sound.

Our last North-Pole voyage was so disastrous, and our "*drift*" on the floe with the Captain Tyson party so decidedly disagreeable, that we propose to "skip" the sea voyage in this narrative. We will, therefore, take the reader at once to the harbor of St. Michaels.

It was September 24, 1866, when the " Nightingale " arrived. She was greeted in the true arctic manner. A blustering north wind hurled a cloud of snow in the faces of her men, and covered her deck with an inch or two of half-melted snow and hail. A year previous a preliminary exploring party had been left here, under the direction of Robert Kennicott, chief of the scientific corps. Kennicott had been trained to the hardships of this position by large experience in the service of the Hudson Bay Company. Much was expected of him and his party in obtaining the informa-

tion necessary to determine the exact line on
which to erect the telegraph poles. No word had
been heard from him during the year. The al-
most-unknown region into which he had plunged
with his heroic men had hid him from the civilized
world, and therefore great anxiety was felt concerning him.

The storm prevented the ship's approach that
night to the landing. A boat was sent ashore, but
its return was not expected until the morning.
Dall's anxiety to hear from his friend Kennicott
was so great that he could not sleep. He accompanied the officer of the deck in his dreary night-
watch, pacing the deck in the rain and sleet. The
wind howled through the rigging, a dismal fore-
boding of the morrow's news. It was not until
four o'clock in the afternoon of the next day that
a boat could come from the shore.

"Where's Kennicott?" said Dall, pressing forward to the gangway, and addressing the first man
who left the boat. "Dead, poor fellow, last May,"
was the sad reply.

The stormy greeting given to the "Nightingale" made her captain desire to leave as soon as
possible. So the next morning our explorers were
in readiness to go ashore. They were put for this
purpose on board a scow loaded with coal. A
steamer called the "Wilder," brought from San
Francisco on the deck of the "Nightingale," un-
dertook the task of taking this scow in tow. This
little steam craft was an effort of Yankee skill,
and was intended for river exploration especially.

It was "flat-iron" shaped, strongly but clumsily constructed, and was confidently expected to do its part in forwarding the great enterprise. This, its first effort, did not promise well for the future, but our party reached the landing safely, though not without some fears that their part of the exploration would end somewhere between the shore and the anchorage of their vessel.

The Russian trading-port gave them shelter. Mr. Dall, after filling his pockets with provisions, sought a back room, selected "a soft plank," rolled himself in a blanket, and attempted to sleep. Success in the effort required some skill and more perseverance, for the rain dripped through the roof, the dogs howled, and so did the Russians, who were made drunk by the liquor just landed from the vessel. As the death of Kennicott was the first lesson to our explorer in bitter disappointment, so this night's experience was the first trial of physical discomfort. Both were emphatic declarations that the enterprise undertaken was, as had been known to all concerned, no pastime.

We shall not desire to leave St. Michaels without looking at the fort, the people, and the surroundings. However the *explorers* may have felt, *we* are in no hurry.

The people here are a mixed race, and decidedly peculiar. They include pure Russians, Aleuts from the adjacent islands, natives of Eastern Siberia, Finlanders, natives who belong to the great Esquimo family, and a race which has come from the intermarriage of the Russians with the natives.

When we remember that many of the *employés* of
the fur company were men convicted of various
crimes in Russia, and given their choice to come
into this region or spend their lives in prison, we
may form some idea of the moral tone of the community. Their governor is Stepanoff, of four
years' experience in this position, a middle-aged
man of great energy, having a soldier's contempt
for small gains by petty trickery, generous in his
bearing to strangers, and a consistent friend of
the explorers. He loves good cheer and bad
liquor—it's all bad—and gambles and drinks in
the most democratic way with his workmen. On
these occasions he often gets into a fight with
them, receiving a black eye in the encounters.
All this he takes good-naturedly, as Stepanoff *the
boon companion.* But woe to the man who swerves
a hair's breadth from the discipline of Stepanoff *the
governor!* His argument with such a one is his
strong arm and bony fist, the knuckles of which
are his chief disciplinary weapons.

Mr. Dall was accommodated with comfortable
quarters after the first night. The room contained a Russian stove, a pattern in use generally
throughout Alaska. They are a box-like article,
built of fragments of stones cemented with a clay
mortar. A wood fire is built in them, and a lib-
eral supply of fuel is added until the thick walls
of the stove are intensely heated. The coals and
ashes are then carefully removed, a closely-ad-
justed damper is put across the chimney-flue, so
as to prevent the escape of the heat, and then

your cooking and heating apparatus is in order
for twenty-four hours. A good amount of cooking can be done on a large one. If more is needed,
it is done in a cook-house.

The bed of the fort was equally simple. The
sleeping-place was a platform against the side of
the room, a few feet from the floor and seven feet
wide. The lodger had just to take his reindeer
skin with the hair on and sewed up at one end, so
as to make a kind of bag, jump in, lay his head
on a feather pillow, draw over himself a pair of
blankets, and sleep. Sheets, counterpanes, un-
der-beds, and that sort of bed arrangements, are
deemed in this region unnecessary articles.

The fort is made by arranging log-buildings
with plank roofs in the form of a square. The
space between the buildings is filled up by setting
stakes in the ground, ten feet high, and pointed at
the top. Outside of the stakes or stockade are
two heavy earthworks, behind which are several
old-fashioned, rusty pieces of artillery, and two
modern brass howitzers. All this would be no
great defense against an attacking war-ship, but is
quite sufficient to warn off the enemies belonging
to this region. As this is the head-quarters of the
fur trade, and a large amount of wealth is in store
in the business season, there must needs be a military air about the place, which is increased by
the flag which floats in the breeze, and the watch-
man on duty night and day, who paces back and
forward, tolling a bell hourly to keep all reminded
of his presence. Beyond the inclosure are store-

houses, a shed where boats are kept in winter, a blacksmith's shop, and a church.

For wood and lumber the fort is dependent upon Alaska's great river, the Yukon, which bears on its mighty waters a full supply from the far inland country, dropping it almost at the door of the people of the coast. With this father of Alaska waters we shall become well acquainted.

A narrow channel of water, called the canal, separates the island on which the fort stands from the mainland. The country, as it gradually rises from the shore, is rocky and barren.

On the island, half a mile from the fort, is a native village, consisting of a few houses. We will just look round these a little before leaving the vicinity for our inland journey, though the men are away in their boats hunting the white whales. An old lady, by no means attractive in form or countenance, who keeps one of the houses, will let us satisfy our curiosity by examining the premises. You see that roof, fifteen feet square, whose eaves are about four feet from the ground, from the center of which, through a hole, the smoke is pouring out? Well, that is a native house, but no door or window does it contain; you may go all round it and find only solid ground, above which the spruce logs rise which make the unbroken sides of the house. There must be a door, or some mode of entrance; so let us look round and find it. Here is a shed a few yards from the house. Going in, we find a hole in the ground; get down now on your hands and knees, and crawl in. A singular

2

and dirty way of entering a house, this crawling through an underground passage. But it is the way they make winter huts in this country. We finally reach the end, push away a bear-skin or seal-skin with which it is closed, and enter the hut. All that goes in or out of the house goes by this passage, though we think from the sights and odors that there is much that ought to go out that does not. But we must not be critical if we do not find the old lady the most tidy of housekeepers.

Here where we have entered is the middle one of three equal sections into which the floor is divided. This is solid earth, in the center of which, directly under the square hole in the roof, a few stones are laid, and fire is built, the hole alone being the outlet of the smoke, and the inlet of air and light. Spruce logs on the sides of this middle section mark its separation from the other two. These have the ground covered with spruce branches, over which woven grass mats are spread. Here the inmates sit, and here they eat and sleep It will not be difficult for the reader to infer that a short call will be more agreeable to a stranger than a long one.

CHAPTER II.

FIRST DOG-SLEDGING.

THERE are two objects of interest near the fort, which we cannot stop now to examine, the Greek church and the dance-house. We shall meet both elsewhere. We must leave immediately, and commence our inland explorations. To understand better where we are to go and what we are to do, let us take a glance at a good map of Alaska; a large one of North America, even, will do. Notice the large river, whose sources rise in the Rocky Mountains, flow north, join and make a river which looks as if it intended to empty into the Arctic Sea, but which returns and runs south and west until it seems near the sea-coast; then goes south nearly parallel with the shore through many hundreds of miles, turns west and north, and pours into Bering Sea through a beautiful delta. This river is the Yukon, on whose waters we purpose to voyage. In length and volume of water it ranks among the greatest rivers of the earth; it is the mighty Amazon of the north. Run your eye south-east from Norton Bay; note where the Yukon turns south; just there is a trading port called Nulato; we wish to strike the river at that point.

Our party left on October 8, having been at

2

the fort a little more than two weeks; it consisted
of Mr. Dall, Captain Ketchum, of the Kennicott
explorers, and in command of them since Kennicott's death, and Mr. Westdahl, the astronomer
of the expedition. With these were a company of
native laborers. The boats in which they sailed
were the native oomiaks, a flat-bottomed, light
craft made by stretching properly-prepared seal
skins over a wooden frame, and fastening them
by walrus-skin lines.

The noon on which they embarked was sunny,
the sea calm, and the wind fair. They coasted
north, arriving at the mouth of Unalaklik River,
on which was a trading port of the same name.
But soon the wind increased and blew in their
faces, and they were glad to scud into a little cove
under a rocky shore, draw up their boats, and seek
a shelter. They had sailed about twenty-two
miles from the fort. Fortunately, there was a native village near, and its people, in the true Esquimo style, came running to the shore, shouting
"Chammi! Chammi!" which was their salutation
of welcome. Instead of shaking hands, some
greasy old fellows hugged the strangers like brothers. As they are famous for raising on their persons curious little specimens of natural history,
this kind greeting was repelled.

In the middle of the village there stood, after
the custom of these native villages, a kind of
town-hall, called a casine. It was larger than the
private houses, and, as it was not used as a common house, was cleaner. It was built in the gen-

eral style of the one we have described, partly under ground, with a subterranean passage into it.
It was used as a common bath-house, a dance-
room, and a lodging-house for strangers. To this
our explorers carried their traveling conveniences,
built a fire, set on their copper teakettle and made
their refreshing tea. The natives squatted round
in a happy mood, for they loved good "chy," that
is, tea, and deemed it all the better if biscuits
were crumbled into it. All this they received,
sharing, as a matter of course, with the strangers.
They did not charge any thing for the lodging,
but they expected to be boarded. Not the most
generous hospitality, we should think. But the
stormy night was spent comfortably by the visitors, who rolled themselves in their furs and blankets, and lay down on a platform raised against the
walls of the room.

The next two days were stormy, after the arctic
fashion. On the second day a company of the
natives came to the casine, intimating that they
wanted to bathe, and, of course, our visitors
moved out for the time. The bath is taken in
this way: A fire is built on the ground under the
hole in the roof. When the wood is burned to
coals, the hole above is closed with a dried skin,
and the inmates proceed to bathe in a liquid we
need not name, which they have carefully saved
for this purpose. Though offensive to our ideas
of propriety, it really answers a good purpose to
these heathen people. It makes a kind of soap
when united with the grease of their bodies, and

cleanses them nicely when they have finished off
with clean water. Having bathed, they roll themselves in their furs and tuck themselves away for
awhile on shelves under the roof.

Our party, being cold in the private quarters to
which they had fled, returned as soon as possible,
and quite soon enough to be almost driven out
again by the offensive odor.

Thursday morning our friends were in their
boats again. They soon came against a line of
the shore where there was a narrow shelving
beach backed by a perpendicular sandstone wall
from twenty to a hundred feet long. They were
only ten miles from the Unalaklik, and the wind
was fair and gentle, so Dall lay down and snoozed
an hour or two under a deer-skin. Ketchum, who
was more experienced in the ways of arctic winds
and ice, and whose ears and eyes were open,
caught the sound of crushing ice. He gave the
alarm, for the arctic foe was upon them. Dall
seized the paddle and prepared for the assault.
Cakes of ice, four inches thick, covered the surface
of the water, bent on *nipping* their frail boat, which,
of course, would go under in the first encounter.
All hands were kept on the alert, for it was a fight
for life. Soon the lights of the trading-post came
in sight. The imperiled boats fired several guns,
but it was night and the wind was blowing off
shore, and they were not heard. A landing was
finally effected a mile above the fort, the boats
drawn out of the ice, and the men, stumbling over
the drift-wood of the beach, reached the trading-

post. The inmates were soon roused, the gates opened, and supper prepared, with steaming tea. This over, a Russian gave Mr. Dall his bed, the title to which was disputed by whole families of wide-awake cockroaches. A canvas tent, with a good supply of furs, was prepared afterward, and occupied by Dall in preference to this too-numer ously occupied tenement.

Unalaklik is like St. Michaels, only on a smaller scale. Kennicott's men had, the previous winter, put up a rude house of earth and logs. Now that the telegraph company had increased to about forty, all hands engaged in putting up one equal to their necessities. The natives looked on with astonishment at the skill and energy of the stran-gers. Some of the officers put up for their own use a two-roomed house, well earthed round, with an open fire-place in one room, and a Yankee cooking-stove in the other. " Not wanted " was the card sent to the cockroaches, and the place was a marvel of comfort.

A stirring trade was now started with the natives for a full supply of fur-clothing for the expedition. Prices went up 200 per cent.! These heathen had learned a Wall-street acuteness in making prices according to the demand. These garments are, a fur frock, with a hood attached, fur pants, socks, and boots. The women's dresses do not differ much from the men's, except in the frock, which is longer, and rounded at the bottom in front.

Having rested a few days. Captain Ketchum

proposed, with a party of nine persons, to push on to the Yukon, and make the most that could be made of the winter for exploration, while the rest of the men remained at Unalaklik, getting ready poles for the line already surveyed. The Ketchum party consisted, beside the captain, of Mr. Dall; Mr. Francis, engineer of the little steamer; Lieutenant Michael Lebarge, who had been with Ketchum in the summer's exploration; and Mr. Whymper, a generous Englishman, who had joined the service as an artist; besides a Mr. Pickett, and three natives. With Mr. Whymper we shall become somewhat intimate, as he has afforded us, in a published volume, a chance to see through his eyes.

The dogs and sledges being ready, our party started about noon of October 27. Dogs were not plenty, and so those who were caught at large were pressed into the service. This brought, in one case, an old lady down upon them, who howled fearfully to the captain her complaint for her stolen dog. She was, however, abundantly satisfied by the gift of a little tobacco.

The party started, cheered on by shouts and salutes from the firearms of their friends who remained behind. They found the frozen surface of the Unalaklik River, over which they drove, covered with snow, making the sledging heavy, and compelling the men to trot behind their teams. Soon after leaving the fort they found the banks of the river covered with spruce-fir and birch-trees, with now and then a pile of drift-wood

brought down by the spring flood. Of course,
there were some mishaps to start with. Some of
the sleds lost a part of the bones with which they
were shod, making them drag heavily. This provoked the dogs, who were no better behaved than
those of their relatives which we have met on our
North-Pole voyages, and two of them gnawed
their harnesses and returned home. Well wearied
as the light of day began to fade, a clear spot on
the banks was found and a camp-fire was started,
bacon cooked, and refreshing tea made. Invigor-
ated by a good supper, they started off again by
starlight, hoping to reach an Indian village which
they knew lay at no great distance ahead. They
had not traveled far before they came to open water the whole width of the river. They took to the
banks, of course, but they were shelving, the sledges
in danger of being rolled over, with their loads,
into the water below, and the way at best was uncertain. To add to their embarrassment, the night
became very dark; so they unloaded the sledges,
tied up the dogs, made a cheerful log-fire, spread
branches on the snow, rolled themselves up in
their fur robes, and lay down and slept, with nothing above them but the branches of the trees and
the canopy of the sky.

The party awoke refreshed, but four of the dogs
had slyly gnawed their harness and returned to
the fort, thus showing their masters that vigilance
was the price of dog-service. The breakfast eaten,
a narrow strip of shore-ice was found, on which,
with great caution, they passed the open water,

and arrived at noon at the village of Iktigalik. The villagers were Indians, one of the many tribes of the territory, related more to our Indians than to the great Esquimo family, and having a language of their own. Our travelers found a few summer-houses on the left bank of the river, mere huts, built by driving spruce logs into the ground, and covering the roof with birch bark. There were behind the houses *caches*, that is, small houses about six feet square and high, elevated ten feet above the ground on four upright posts. They are simply store-houses for furs, fish, and other valuables, and are thus perched in the air, like an old-fashioned corn-house, to keep them from mice, dogs, and other depredators. Frames are also erected, where snow-shoes, boats, sleds, and harness can be safe from the rapacious dogs.

On the other side of the river were two winter-houses, like that we entered at St. Michaels, except that the square hole in the ground was merely covered by a dome-shaped roof. Into one of these our explorers entered. The underground passage-way was little better than a sewer. Through this they crept, finding the welcome given by the owners quite equal to the accommodations of their home. The fire in the center was burning low, and, to keep in the warmth, the hole above had been closed. The smoke thus retained, the stale-fish smell, and the odor of a group of dogs, mingled with the general perfume of filth of various kinds, made a sickening place. The hole was uncovered, the fire rekindled, and cooking operations commenced. The atmosphere was becoming purer, when some dogs, which were fighting and scrambling on the roof, tumbled through the hole. The pots were upset, and the room filled with a suffocating smell of burned hair, while the dogs beat a hasty retreat. The inmates were busy at this time making baskets, fish-traps, snow-shoes, and sleds. The children were fat and happy, one little fellow having a stick of ice in his fingers, which he sucked as if it had been sugar-candy.

The owner put a part of his platform at the disposal of the strangers, which they cleared of dirt, covered with their furs, and proceeded to do their own cooking, and make themselves at home. Fresh reindeer meat and wild fowl were procured, which, with the hot tea and biscuit, gave them no occasion for unappeased hunger.

As nearly all the dogs had decamped, the party were detained here several days, while Dall and Francis returned to the fort to bring back the fugitives. We will, in the meantime, study Indian home life with Mr. Whymper. These Indian men and women use tobacco, but they have some notions of their own in the manner of using it. In smoking, for instance, it is allowed, we suppose, that in the ordinary practice much of the esteemed article goes off in smoke into the open air. Now these Indians *swallow* the smoke, and so lodge about the stomach and lungs what would otherwise be lost. The snuff-takers pound the dry tobacco leaf in a mortar, put it into a wooden or bone snuff-box, then thrust into the box a wooden tube through which they sniff the pounded tobacco into their nostrils.

Of course our visitors were regarded with much deference by these natives. An Indian man was sick at one time and applied to the surgeon of the expedition for aid, saying, "I much pain here," laying his hand on his chest. The doctor applied a powerful blister. The next morning the man was in high spirits at his improved condition, and the doctor expected to find his breast raw. But the blister had only left a clean place on his skin of its exact dimensions. The man was cured, and the doctor's reputation was established.

The children of this people eat enormously. At one time a small boy, with large frontal protuberance, received an accidental gash on the cheek from a playmate. The doctor closed it with sticking plàster, and ordered quiet and abstinence. The little fellow starved himself for a week, the cut healed and his health improved, and the doctor's skill was deemed amazing. Our party pushed on up the river, tarried at a small Indian village, where several warm springs kept the water free from ice through the coldest weather. Here the most elegant salmon abound, and, where all other food failed, gave support to many natives. A stick thrust into one, as he came writhing from the water, was held over a good fire, and without further "fixings," he was roasted, and the delicious morsel was fit to be set before the king.

Leaving the Unalaklik at a point nearest the Yukon, our explorers were soon on its broad surface. It seemed indeed a sea, for its opposite shore was three miles away, with many intervening islands. Over its snow-covered, hummocky surface they cautiously proceeded, and arrived at Nulato in the early winter.

CHAPTER III.

A SAD STORY.

NULATO is a fair specimen of an inland fur-trading post of Alaska. Here Dall and Whymper, with their companions, spent the winter. We cannot fail to be interested in their account of it.

The commander may sit for his portrait. He is a short, thickset, strong-built man, born of a Russian father and Indian mother, and belongs to a class of people of whom we have spoken, known as creoles. He is legally married to an Indian wife by whom he has a large family of children. He cannot write, so he may be set down as a very ignorant man; but he can drive a sharp bargain with the natives for furs in the interest of the company, and that is why he holds the important office of commander at this station. The Russians despise him as they do all half-breeds, and he cringes to them, but he makes up for this humiliation by causing the natives to cringe to him. He is very hospitable and accommodating to our party, but gets terribly drunk and is then a demoniac. The fur company have found him honest in the business intrusted to him.

The fort is much the same as that we saw on the sea-shore. It is composed on three sides of houses built of round logs, the cracks chinked with moss, and the almost flat roofs covered with earth. The fort is made of posts set in the ground close together and sharpened at the top. Two of the houses have small turrets on the roof, armed with small, rusty cannon.

Our men were permitted to occupy one of the houses, with a shed for wood, a small store-house, and a kitchen attached. The people of the place are few, and composed of Russians, Indians, and half-breeds. The quarters of our party were hardly as comfortable as an Esquimo snow-hut. The raised bench about its walls for sleeping was full of cracks, up which the cold air rushed in freezing currents. The fire in the stone oven in the center of the room made little impression, as the heat rushed out at the eaves where the thermometer sometimes stood at 90 degrees, and on the sleeping bench was at the same time below zero. Calking with moss, lining the walls with fur, and various expedients were resorted to to keep out the cold.

Being well settled at Nulato for the winter, the explorers gave a dinner-party to Ivan, the commander, and his clerk, Iagor. The fare consisted of baked wild fowl, fried ham, Yankee "flap-jacks," served with molasses, which the men called "long-tailed sugar." For drink they had coffee and tea; the first the guests liked well, but the tea was not in quality up to their standard. All the natives of Alaska use the very best tea, and inferior qualities they will not taste though given

to them. The banquet pleased his excellency,
and as the demon Alcohol was not admitted, we
presume his happiness as well as the interest of
his entertainers were advanced by the omission.

One of the amusements of the winter was the
continuance of a famous discussion between
Whymper and Francis, the engineer. The debate
was begun on the trip to Nulato, and involved
the momentous question of the relative merits of
beans and rice as food. Francis had been in
China, and was well informed in reference to his
side of the subject. Whymper, who had traveled
extensively among the miners of the Pacific coast,
had the latest and most reliable information on
the esteemed qualities of beans. He dwelt elo-
quently upon beans fried, beans baked. In reply,
Francis urged, with amazing acuteness, the un-
equaled nutritious properties of rice with just
about no cooking at all. Again and again during
the journey of the spring, around camp-fires and
while sailing on the mighty waters of the Yukon,
did they return to this broad, profound, instructive
discussion, while the companions of their waiting
and toil were beguiled of many otherwise tedious
hours. It is reported that each disputant was, at
every step in the progress of the debate, more
deeply convinced of the merits of his own cause,
and so both, in the upshot, were delighted. One
thing, at least, was proved—the excellence of pleasant companionship under circumstances which
tend to despondency.

The tedious waiting was relieved, too, by the

coming to the fort of an Indian chief and a few followers, from two hundred and forty miles up the river. He brought eight robes made of twenty-four marten skins. Of course, he was welcomed by Commander Ivan, as these furs are very valuable. Captain Ketchum had seen him before, and immediately bargained with him to have in readiness plenty of deer and moose meat on the arrival of the white men at his village in the summer. Our explorers made him a present of a coat and some trinkets, and he began at once to harangue his men in a high-toned, vociferous manner, making with every sentence the most violent gesticulations, which seemed like an effort to stimulate them to deeds of valor on the war-path. But he was impressing upon his followers the great virtues of the white strangers, as shown in the presents, especially as seen in the gift of a plug of tobacco which he flourished in his hand.

Ou Christmas our party tried to be merry, but the effort was only tolerably successful. Thoughts of home and other Christmas days spent under different circumstances would create a back-current to the flow of good feeling. They decorated their room with flags and trading-goods, made it green with spruce-fir bush, paraded the newest and brightest of their tin plates and pewter spoons, raised a big fire of logs in their oven, and Mr. Dall went vigorously at work to make gingerbread, pies, and cranberry dumplings. A piece of reindeer meat took the place of English roast beef, and a brace of wild fowl represented Yankee tur-

3

keys. Green peas, tomatoes, and other preserved vegetables were added from their stores. The commander and his secretary were invited. After dinner, several original literary productions were read, and the occasion was one which left pleasant memories.

New Year's day was celebrated by raising the first telegraph poles in the division of the Yukon. A fine spruce-tree was brought from the woods, trimmed, cut the right dimensions, and peeled. After breakfast all went out, attached to it the stars and stripes, and the flags of the various departments of the expedition, and set and saluted it with cheers and thirty-six guns.

Mr. Dall was busy during the winter in collecting rare specimens of natural history, and Mr. Whymper in taking and working up his sketches, while Captain Ketchum and Mr. Lebarge—Mike, as he was familiarly called—was maturing their plans for a daring winter trip many hundred miles up the Yukon to Fort Yukon, the extreme western trading-post of the Russian company. Many incidents broke the monotony of the slow-moving days. A Russian *employé*, being offended at one of the Americans, showed his ill-temper by beating without provocation his offender's Indian servant. Ketchum seized and thrashed the Russian on the spot, without appeal to the commander, and thereby greatly increased the credit of the Americans with the Indians.

But the Indians were greatly annoying in one way; they were sure to come in a body, at meal time, squat round under feet, and watch every motion of the white men until they had retired from the table. They seemed to judge this a favorable occasion to study the character and habits of these specimens of the white race. They were well pleased, too, to eat what was left on the table.

Naturally our explorers were deeply interested in listening during their leisure hours to stories connected with the history of the fort. And sad stories some of them were. Here is an illustration of this fact:

In 1851, in the early winter, an English ship, in search of Sir John Franklin, touched at St. Michaels, and left Lieutenant Barnard, with a surgeon and seaman. They were to seek of the natives and fur-traders information concerning the lost ones. During the winter Lieutenant Barnard came to Nulato. The Koyukun Indians, the fiercest, most warlike, and feared of all the tribes dwelling by the waters of the Yukon, were at that time holding an annual fast, about twenty-five miles from Nulato. There was among them an old chief whose wealth, as Indians reckon wealth, and strong lines of character gave him great influence. His name rendered into English was Humpback Nose, he having a large Roman nose. Barnard remarked, in his simplicity, that he intended to *"send* for" this chief, to obtain from him, if possible, the information he was commissioned to obtain. This remark was repeated to the chief by an Indian who happened to hear it. Now Humpback Nose's idea of official dignity required that he

should be *sought*, not *sent for*. He called a coun
cil of his braves, and they voted the remark an
insult. The *shamans*, that is, the sorcerers—
medicine men—were consulted, and they declared
that the words of the white chief meant mischief.
In their heat the warriors were at first inclined to
go at once to Nulato and demand satisfaction.
But they waited for some days, and with time their
wrath subsided, and they were about to return
home when a single dog-sled appeared on the
river. It contained Bulegin, a Russian messenger, accompanied by a Nulato Indian, whom Barnard had sent to make inquiries of the chief, and
perhaps to request him to visit the fort for further
conference concerning Franklin. Bulegin drew
his sled upon the bank, sent his companion after
some water, and in the meantime fell asleep. A
Koyukun, with a true savage bravery, stole upon
the sleeping, unoffending man, and killed him instantly with a blow from his war-club. The Nulato Indian, returning from the spring, and seeing
what was done, turned to flee. "Stop!" the murderers shouted, "you are one of us; we will not
hurt *you*." He returned and witnessed the strip-
ping, cutting up, and the preparations to eat the
Russian. Seeing the Nulatoman did not enter
cordially into their horrid business, one of them
crept softly up behind him, and struck him dead.

Having tasted blood, the warriors, with demon
fury, armed with their deadly weapons, started for
Nulato. About half a mile from the trading-post
were three large winter-houses, crowded with In-

dians of the Nulato tribe—in all, men, women and children, not less than three hundred. It was a midnight in February. The assailants stole quietly to the houses of the unsuspecting sleepers, stopped the underground passage-way with the dry material of broken snow-shoes and sledges, piled fragments of canoes over the smoke-holes of the roofs, set all in a blaze, and raised their terrifying war-whoop. Nearly all the inmates perished in the flames and smoke. When the men, with axes, attempted to cut through the roof, and escape, they were shot down with arrows. One man only was missed by the archers, and, being a famous runner, escaped to the mountains. A few women were spared as captives, and one or two children were overlooked and fled to the woods.

As the Koyukuns had no guns at this time, but little noise was made, and the Russians at the fort slept on. As the murderers approached, the morning light was breaking, and they were seen by two women who were up early preparing the morning meal, who, instead of alarming the men, ran stupidly into the cook-house, and fastened the door. There was no picket-fence, or " stockade," as now at the fort, and the log-houses were some rods apart. They first approached the commander's house, and found him sitting behind it, not suspecting that a foe was near. Having met Ivan, one of their own people, employed at the fort as an interpreter, they said to him : " Steal up to the 'bidarshik' and kill him, or we will kill you." Ivan obeyed, and Derabin, the commander, fell to

rise no more. The Russian interpreter appeared
at the door at that moment, and was instantly
pierced by seven arrows. Rushing over his prostrated body, they entered the house. Barnard
was lying on a bed reading. As the foe opened
his door he seized his gun and leveled it at the
foremost Indian, a medicine man whom the Russians had christened Larriown. The savage struck
the barrel upward, and its contents entered the
ceiling, and the Englishman received a mortal
wound in the abdomen. Somehow in the scuffle
Larriown received a terrible wound in the lower
part of his body.

The assailants added to their other victims a
mother and three children, and left the commander's house and attacked that of the workmen. By
this time the men were alarmed and on the defen-
sive; as their enemies approached, a Koyukun was
shot dead, and the rest immediately took to their
heels, carrying away their booty and captives.

Larriown was left, suffering an agony of pain, in
an outer room of the commander's house. A Russian who had not been noticed by the Indians was
in an inner room, helpless of a fever. His Nulato
wife brought him a loaded pistol, and held him up
while he fired at the medicine-man. But his hand
trembled, the ball missed, and Larriown dragged
himself out to the river bank, where he found a
Koyukun mother who had been staying at the fort.
She was dragging her babe on a sled. He threw
the babe into the river, took its place, and ordered
her to drag him to a place of safety. She refused,

and Larriown stabbed her to the heart and escaped, no one ever knew how.

A messenger was hurried off to St. Michaels for the surgeon, but when he arrived he found his friend Barnard dead. Neither the Fur Company nor the Russian Government took any notice of this Indian massacre, except to conciliate Humpback Nose and his men by special presents. This was their established policy in such cases.

Ivan, the interpreter, who, under constraint, killed the commander, and the wicked old sorcerer, Larriown, with his equally hately wife, were all at Nulato during the sojourn of our party; the interpreter still held that office, and the sorcerer and his family were comfortably housed just outside the inclosure.

No wonder, in view of the shocking occurrences we have just narrated, that the Indians about Nulato were in a state of nervous fear of their repetition. During the winter a sensational story was started that old Larriown had planned to surprise and destroy in the spring one of our exploring parties. Careful inquiry by our men convinced them that it had no foundation. One incident of Indian suspicion proved quite amusing. In talking over the scarcity of provisions, one of our party remarked jocosely, that if pinched for food they could eat Paspikoff's baby, a recent addition to the population of the fort. This remark was repeated among the Indians, and threw them into a fear of excitement. They sent Ivan, the interpreter, to inquire if the strangers were cannibals. He

remarked with deep seriousness, in making the inquiry, that since poor Bulegin's case, no Indian
had been known to eat human flesh. After a
hearty laugh the explorers fully satisfied the ignorant natives of their mistake, and resolved to be
more guarded in their talk.

On the eleventh of March Captain Ketchum and
Mr. Lebarge started up the Yukon. Let the
reader take the map and find the point where the
Yukon, coming from the south, turns short toward
the west. Just there the Porcupine River flows
into it from the east, and at this juncture is Fort
Yukon, the most eastwardly trading-post of the
Russian company. To this point, six hundred
miles from Nulato, Ketchum and Lebarge proposed to go, with four sledges, twenty-two dogs,
and two Indian servants. It was a desperately
bold undertaking. A soft snow covered the surface of the river on which they proposed to travel.
The ice was treacherous in many places, as the
season was getting late. They could not carry
food enough for either themselves or dogs, and so
must live most of the way by their guns, or perish.
The Russians and natives shook their heads
at the undertaking. At the last moment the Indian servants backed out. Having by Ivan's influence secured two other Indian men, and two
boys, one of the latter Ivan's son, they started.
All Nulato turned out to see them off. The rusty
cannon on the turrets nearly shook the buildings
down in their noisy demonstration at the event;
and all the guns and pistols united in a sharply-

expressed good-bye, while their fellow-explorers shouted, " God bless you!" though with difficulty suppressing the fear that they would perish by the way.

Having secured a site, about a mile from Nulato, for a station-house of the Telegraph Company, and arranged with a Russian to build it, the remaining party of explorers began to perfect their preparations to follow Ketchum and Lebarge up the river to Fort Yukon. They only waited for the ice to break up to make good boating.

CHAPTER IV.

IN SKIN-CANOES.

ON the twenty-sixth of May, 1867, the party started up the Yukon. They had been watching the ice since the early days of the month, as little by little it gave way before the swollen waters, until the general crash came, and it swept like an avalanche toward the sea. Even now its scattered fragments, mingled with trees and logs from the banks, made navigation dangerous.

Mr. Dall and Whymper were in a moderate-sized skin-boat, attended by Kurilla, a skillful Indian steersman, and two Indian servants, "Tom" and "Beetle." The commander of Nulato, Ivan, the same name as that of his interpreter, accompanied them in a larger skin-boat, with a crew of seven persons—Indians and Russians. Both boats were somewhat heavily laden. Dall and Whymper used paddles, while Kurilla steered, and the other Indians rowed. Of necessity the boats hugged the shore, except when compelled to cross, as they often were, to avoid projecting or lodged ice and drift-wood. It was in these crossings, when the swift current, with its icy and woody freight, toyed with their frail boats, that their skill and courage were put to the test. After about six hours' rowing the Russian boat, which took the lead, drew up under the shelter of a high, rocky point; the other boat followed, a fire was built, and all hands took a lunch, with hot tea. While thus resting they observed that the ice-cakes and drift-wood were sweeping round the projecting point at a fearful rate. When the boats started, Ivan's boat struggled awhile in the midst of this danger, and then gave up the contest, drifted down a little way, and landed again. Kurilla sneered at this retreat, exclaiming: " Me no go back ! " A man stood in the bows with an iron-pointed pole, pushing the ice and logs to the right and left. Sometimes a heavy tree would go *under* the boat, lifting it as it rolled along fairly out of the water. Ice and logs were constantly scraping harshly over the bottom, reminding our voyagers that not a plank but a skin only, not more than an eighth of an inch thick, was between them and death. All worked vigorously in silent and painful suspense, until comparatively quiet and smooth waters were reached on the east side of the river. The Russians, who had " poohed " at the boating of our explorers, came on with a higher respect for the strangers. At an early hour all camped on an island. A small fleet of Indian canoes had kept in their wake, and their owners, now thoroughly wet by the fearful venture through the current, squatted round the camp-fire. It rained freely, and supper was obtained and eaten under difficulties, after which our explorers gathered round them rubber blankets, and lay down on the mud, covered with a few willow branches, and slept. The Indians bent down the tops of small willows, spread over them a great sheet of *drill*, thus making a sort of tent, crept under, huddled together and slept, without the rubber blankets.

The attending fleet of canoes increased in number as our voyagers proceeded, the Indians being on their way to the annual gathering for trade farther up the river. Their canoes are made of birch-bark, drawn over a light but well-constructed frame of birch and willow. The seams of these little crafts are sewn with the fine roots of spruce-fir, and are calked with spruce-gum. When a leak occurs they put ashore, build a fire, turn the canoe bottom upward, warm the gum, of which they are careful to have a good supply, repair damages, and proceed on their way.

The Indians were, of course, wide-awake for trade with our explorers. They had reindeer meat, ducks, geese, fish, and other articles of food to exchange for ammunition and various fancy and useful articles; but ammunition and tobacco were most eagerly sought. Strong drink the explorers did not sell, and Mr. Dall had before this found it necessary to poison the alcohol he carried for the preservation of his specimens of natural history, and to make this fact known to prevent it from being stolen and drank.

One of the sights along the banks which attracted the attention of the explorers was that of occasional graves of the natives. The dead were inclosed in a box; this was attached several feet from the ground to four upright poles. On the top of, or otherwise fastened to those poles, were articles belonging to the deceased. In one case there was a hut near a grave of a man, and it was said that his widow occupied the hut alone, and spent most of her time in watching and ornamenting the box containing the sacred dead.

The incidents of the voyage were at times intensely exciting. At one time, coming to a point round which the water rushed with great rapidity, the fleet of canoes first attempted to pass it. They scarcely entered the current, when, swift as an arrow, they were shot down the river a long distance. Kurilla proceeded very cautiously, keeping close to the shore, and the moment the boat touched the current, the paddles and oars were used with desperate energy, and the safer waters above were reached. On the first of June they entered one of many magnificent openings in the river. This one was five miles wide and eight long. It contained many beautiful islands, and appeared like a quiet lake. Soon after passing this lake they met an Indian from the upper waters who brought the glad news that Ketchum and Lebarge had arrived safely at Fort Yukon, and taken boats and pushed on still farther.

Our party's next halting-place was a native village, at the mouth of a small river flowing into the Yukon. Here the fur-traders came to secure furs in exchange for assorted articles. The huts were poor, and the people a wretched-looking group. When the explorers pitched their tent and tried to get a little rest and sleep, they came and lifted the bottom of the canvas and peered in, as curious as country boys at a newly-arrived circus. The tyone or head-man drove them away but was equally annoying and inquisitive. The voyagers soon made themselves at home, and opened a brisk trade. A large canoe was purchased, deer and moose meat, with many specimens of natural history were obtained, and two natives engaged for the further voyage. The tyone, in his close watching of the strangers, had seen with apparent surprise the use of water on the face and hands, and the use in the same connection of soap, brushes, combs, and other articles of the toilet. At his request Whymper gave him a towel and soap. Thus encouraged he tried to beg a comb and tooth-brush; not succeeding further in the begging line, sundry articles of the explorers, such as shirts, socks, pocket and sheath-knifes disappeared not to return.

On the evening of the second day Larriown and his wife, who accompanied our party, were called upon to practice their arts, as shamans, over a sick man. A fire was built, and the patient was wrapped in a deer-skin and laid on the ground near it. The natives then squatted about him in a circle, and the sorcerers commenced their ceremony. Dressed in a fantastic attire, they began to march round the circle in opposite directions. They gazed into the fire or into vacancy, he leading in a low, hoarse muttering, to which she responded on a higher key, both quickening their pace, and at times stopping suddenly and shuddering convulsively from head to foot; their strains now became wilder and more measured, the whole circle breaking in at intervals with a startling chorus. The sick man groaned, the lurid flames of the fire just revealed in the darkness the swarthy forms of the savage shamans, lighting up their ghostly features, which they drew into horrid contortions. The eyes of Larriown glared with fiendish wildness, as he paused at times, and made passes with his hands over the sick man. He then feigned to draw the evil spirit from the patient, wrestling with it as if nearly overpowered, and then throwing it into the fire. This done he started back, shrieked, frothed at the mouth, and ran back in terror, as if the fiend, leaping from the fire, was pursuing him. He finally desisted from sheer exhaustion, the circle broke up, and the sick man was removed, *not* restored. Some of the natives laughed and sneered at the whole performance as a cheat, while others seemed impressed with a solemn fear.

As the voyagers were gliding along up the Yukon the next day they saw a fire near the bank, at which the natives of the party were much frightened, fearing it indicated a camp of hostile Indians. But Dall and Whymper landed and found a deserter from the Hudson Bay Company and an Indian drying themselves by the fire. They had come down the river thus far, when they upset, and just escaped with their lives, losing guns, blankets, food, and every thing. The coming of our party was, of course, a most timely deliverance. They were fed, and supplied with the means of continuing their voyage to Nulato.

Soon after our fleet again started, the river spread out into a vast seeming lake filled with islands. They entered the channel between one of these islands and the shore; the passage-way was at times narrow and the banks high, and they sailed on and on, until they began to think that they had entered a small tributary of the Yukon, and seriously proposed to turn round. But they at last came out into the broad river; they had passed an island fifteen miles long, and the lake had extended twenty-five miles!

At one time the men went on shore to draw the boats round a point in the river with drag ropes. In doing so they disturbed the nests of young sea-fowls. This the mother birds resented in a furious way, making long circuits in the air, and sweeping down upon them, and buffeting them with their wings. The men were obliged to stop and beat them off with clubs. The fight was continued until the men were a fourth of a mile from the nests.

The next camping-place was a beach near which a river emptied into the Yukon; the sand-bar near its mouth had for ages been gathering the drift-wood until it had amounted to an immense pile. Some of it had long bleached in the sun, and dried in the warm winds until it had become quite marketable. What a pity that it should lie here wasting, when the people of our old Esquimo friend, Kalatura, of the far north, and even the

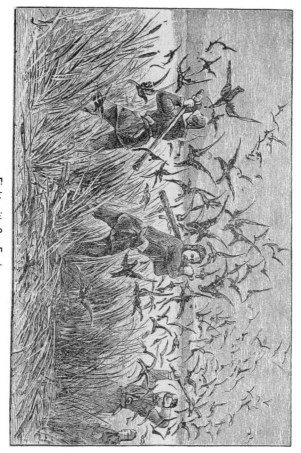

Fight with Sea-Fowls.

shivering families of some of our own northern cities, would be so pleased to take it away! Our voyagers could use only a little of its many hundred cords for their camp-fire. Another day's sail brought them to an important trading town. It bore the hard Indian name of Nuklukahyet; we might as well call it Nukluk for shortness, as each of our explorers make a greater difference in spelling it. Nukluk is two hundred and forty miles above Nulato, and is the most distant point on the river to which the Russians ascend for trade. Of late, the men of the Hudson Bay Company from the far east have come down here for furs, as the two great companies are thus brought in direct competition, to the advantage, no doubt, of the Indian traders.

The representatives of many tribes gather here from various directions, sometimes numbering about six hundred. On this occasion as our explorers, accompanied by the Russians and native boats, quite a fleet in all, approached the town, they were saluted by the large gun, and the whole population flocked to the landing. The Indians of the crowd yelled, as only Indians can, brandished their guns, and made the most intimidating gesticulations. But all this was only made for the same reason that some dogs bark at strangers whom they are glad to see. The guns were fired in the air, and were answered by volleys from the fleet.

The dress of the Indians here was much more of the North American Indian style than that of

4

the tribes nearer the mouth of the Yukon. It was
very gay, and mixed with some white men's fash-
ions. They filled their long, coarse, black hair
with flashy-colored feathers; on the back of their
head they stuck into their hair a ball of clay which
they covered with small, downy feathers of fancy
colors. This clay would, after awhile, crumble
off, of course, bringing the down with it, and leaving the dirt. Whymper once saw an Indian's head
in this plight, and he gave him a small piece of
soap, suggesting that it was good to wash one's
head with. He grinned his thanks, but did not
go and wash.

These Indians are fond of ornaments, some of
which are such delicate things as bear's claws and
teeth, sable tails, and wolf ears, all which they use
for necklaces. Then they have bands, embroid-
ered work of pretty devices, hawk and eagle feathers; some of the women wear hoops of birch round
the neck and wrists. Of course, they have ear
ornaments, and have even progressed a little beyond the women of civilization, and put bone and
shell ornaments in the nose. The baby's nose is
bored in time, so that it may grow up in fashion.
The village was short of provisions, but the Indians danced and pow-wowed all the same on
empty stomachs, waiting for the fish catch and
moose hunt. The head-man did what he could
for the strangers, and their fleet soon left, under a
farewell salute from the rusty old cannon of the fort
and the muskets of the Indians. Several canoes
from Nukluk joined the fleet of men wishing to

accompany the white men to Fort Yukon to trade.

The river soon began to narrow, and a range of rocky hills to rise on either side, and as they now voyaged mostly while the sun was down, it seemed almost like sailing under ground, so dark and overshadowing were some of the towering cliffs. The birch-bark canoes of our party had a hard time of it where a sharp rock came near to the surface. Once they leaked so badly that they were taken on shore, and the Indian women employed to sew up the damaged place, and gum it carefully. This they did with dispatch for a few trinkets.

The dogs belonging to the fleet ran along the shore, swimming in the inlets and round the cliffs which jutted into the river. When the canoes crossed the river, as they often did, the mettle of the dogs was severely tested in breasting the rapid current, so as not to be carried down stream. They all proved equal to the obstacles of the trip. and seem to enjoy it. They had been half-starved at the settlement, but now found fine foraging, and grew fat on the game. At one time they started a moose and kept him at bay until their masters came ashore and shot him.

"The Ramparts," as the white men called the cliffs, crowded more and more upon the river, causing the waters to be deeper and the current swifter until they came to "the rapids." The explorers had received fearful accounts of these from the Russians and natives. They found

the waters in the middle of the river seething like
a caldron over a sunken, rocky island; but on
either side was a smooth water, though running
about seven miles an hour. Several of the native
canoes boldly struck into this rapid, powerful current. With strong, quick strokes of the paddle
they ascended for awhile, seemed nearly to have
triumphed, then paused for a moment, yielded to
the mightier stream, and were launched like an
arrow from a bow, far down into the quiet waters.

The white men took matters more coolly. They
were not the equals of the Indians in muscle, but
their superiors in brains. They sent men ashore
who clambered over the rocks, with long track-
ing lines, dragging the canoes easily up the rapids,
except in few places where the jutting rocks compelled the trackers to jump into the boats; in
such cases they paddled vigorously, passed the ob-
struction, and then returned to the ropes. There
was really no great difficulty in the ascent, and the
great fleet was soon gliding smoothly. The deep
channels worn in the rocks beneath by the current
on each side of the island will make navigation
easy when the steam whistle and the splash of paddle-wheels shall be heard along the "Ramparts."

The day at this time, in the closing days of
June, had swallowed up the night. The sun disappeared only three fourths of an hour, leaving
his glow the while on the horizon. The camp-
fires where our excursionists stopped to eat were
made of drift-wood, of which there was plenty.
"The Ramparts" melted away into broad plains

which stretched away into the north, until they are washed by the Arctic Sea. They were now covered by a variety of flowers, whose perfume filled the air. But before leaving the overhanging terraces of the river lying between the Ramparts and the plain, some touching incidents occurred. The moose make this vicinity a favorite resort. The mosquitoes were tormenting them, so that to escape their stings they swarm out into the river. Late in the evening of a hot day the dogs started up one which the hunters soon shot. His meat proved delicious, better than that of the deer or reindeer. Soon after, as the fleet were gliding along, a cow moose and calf were seen swimming across the river toward a bank, past which the canoes were to pass. Though the boats made much noise the animals did not seem to mind them, but kept steadily on. Mr. Whymper seized his gun, landed, and ran along the shore to give them a cruel greeting when they touched the land. The mother was too quick for him, for she scrambled up the bank, and ran away before he could bring his gun to bear on her; but her dear child came to a sad end. Whymper declared that it grieved him to shoot it, but nevertheless it was, when cooked, exceedingly tender and good.

There was another incident of this kind which, as the white men were not concerned in eating, hurt their feelings much more than did the killing of the calf. A moose was seen swimming for dear life. An Indian glided swiftly after him in his canoe; shooting alongside, his knife flashed in the sunlight, and the next moment was buried in his neck just above his shoulders. The frightened moose looked so innocent and helpless as he yielded to the fatal stroke, and the blood gushed so freely from his wound, that even the savage hunter seemed moved to pity.

A black bear appeared occasionally on the bank of the river and grinned, and a lynx now and then showed himself, and *eyed* the curious-looking strangers; but, as all parties in such cases voted the let-alone policy, nothing further came of these incidents.

On the twenty-second of June the sun was below the horizon only forty-five minutes; vegetation put on a luxuriance which expressed its consciousness of the long arctic winter soon to follow, and the mosquitoes, innumerable, large, and ferocious, plied their vocation with a diligence which plainly spoke of the coming frost, in which no mosquito can either buzz or sting.

The Upper Yukon Indians were seen encamped on the bank, showing, in their manners, style of dress, better guns, and better homes, their long contact with the Hudson Bay Company; yet they remained savages still. On the next day the mouth of the Porcupine River was passed, which flows from the far east, and at noon the white houses of Fort Yukon appeared in sight. All hands loaded their muskets, and as they neared the fort blazed away. The people of the place, who crowded the shore, replied in the same noisy manner, while the flags of both parties fluttered in the wind. An old French Canadian and two Scotchmen greeted our adventurers cordially, and installed them in a room in the fort. The commander and his interpreter, with all the other keepers of the fort, were daily expected from the La Pierre House, two hundred miles away on the Porcupine River, where they had gone to bring down the annual supply of trading goods. Our men shook hands in a friendly way with the crowd of Indians, and then rested from their voyage of six hundred miles, which they had made in twenty-nine days, including three of rest. They were the first Americans to reach Fort Yukon from the sea.

CHAPTER V.

AT FORT YUKON.

WHILE waiting for the commander and his party, we will leisurely study the situation. The first trading post of this vicinity was built in 1847, a mile farther up the river; this was located on a steep bank, and the spring freshets washed it away. The present station was established in 1864, and is yet unfinished as a fort. There are some six or eight buildings, including a large one for the commander, smaller ones for the men, store-houses, and a block-house pierced for musketry, to which the defenders of the place could flee in case of Indian hostility. The houses are built of heavy logs, the roofs covered with sheets of spruce bark, confined to their places by long poles, and the windows are of parchment, except those of the commander's house. A fur-press stands in the fort, looking a little like a New England cider-press, only its compressing power is the wedge instead of a screw and bar; its purpose is to bring bales of furs into the smallest possible compass.

Just outside the grounds of the fort are the encampments of the Indians, who are waiting to exchange their furs for tobacco, guns, and ammunition, with a few other articles of less value. Such

luxuries as tea and sugar are not common among
the Indians, the expense of transportation causing
the prices of all the importations to be enormous.
The reader will appreciate this if he takes a map
of North America, and traces the distance through
which they come. First by ship they are brought
from the Atlantic through Hudson Strait into
Hudson Bay to Fort York, on its south-western
shore; there they are passed along through the
lakes and over the rivers, the route bearing north-
west, until they nearly reach the tide-water of the
Arctic Ocean, on the Mackenzie River; then going up the Peel River, which flows from the Rocky
Mountain Range, to Fort M'Pherson, they go on
the dog-sledges, and at times in small packages on
men's shoulders, fifty miles through rough mountain passes, to the upper waters of the Porcupine,
to the La Pierre House. Here, as we have stated,
they are transferred to boats for the Yukon River
and the fort. They are two years on the way from
Fort York. Of course the savage pays the expense, for what mission have fur companies but
gain! His flint-lock musket—he dislikes percus-
sion caps—costs forty marten skins. The gun
costs the company five dollars, and the forty skins
aggregate in the same market one hundred and
fifty dollars, or thirty hundred per cent. above
first cost. But this may not be an unreasonable
advance, as the furs, to reach their market, return
through the long route by which the goods came.

There were, during the stay of our explorers,
six tribes of Indians represented at the fort. They

were essentially alike in character, language, and dress, the modifications being the result in part of the localities they inhabited. None of them have settled villages, but all carry their skin tents, and camp where food is most abundant. The Tananah Indians, who inhabit the mountains, are the least known, and the most feared by the other tribes. Their country was never visited by white men. They do not, like other natives, bring their women when they come to trade. They live chiefly by hunting the deer over their rocky hills, and are as free and untamable as the prey they pursue.

These Indian traders, about five hundred at the time of our visit, were encamped outside the fort. Their skin tents and camp-fires, with groups of men and women here and there, made a peculiar and impressive picture. They seemed happy, talking away in their various dialects, or running and wrestling like children on a holiday, but it was the happiness more of well-fed beasts than men of immortal souls. They need the church and the school to expand the mind and lead to purer hearts.

On the twenty-sixth of June a shout was heard in the fort; the commander was approaching, with his fleet of boats laden with trading goods. The commander, M'Dougall, and M'Donald, the missionary of the station, soon landed, and were for the day made the guests of our explorers. They brought later news from the outside world, and were withal good-hearted Scotchmen, who knew

how to do their part in making a pleasant inter-
view. They were accompanied by Antoine, an
Indian-Frenchman, who acted as interpreter in
their business with the natives.

The next day a fleet of twenty-five canoes of
Tananahs were seen approaching the fort; they
came on in several orderly lines, keeping perfect
time with their paddles, skimming lightly over the
water, and seeming as much at home on its surface as a flock of ducks. As they neared the
landing, those on the shore welcomed them with
a volley of musketry, which they returned.
These Tananahs were every inch the savage.
They wore shell nose ornaments, and long, black
hair. Their mode of dressing their hair was original, but we hardly expect it will be adopted by
our ladies. When grown to its full length, and
parted in the middle, they smeared it with a mixture of grease and red ochre, until each lock looked
like a pipe of red mud; they were then brought
together behind the head, and bound with a fillet
of shells. A smaller bunch of hair hung on each
side of the face. When all is thus arranged, they
powder the whole with swan's down cut very fine.
The effect is decidedly sensational, and should one
with the head thus fashionably arrayed appear in
the thoroughfare of any of our large cities, he
would attract general attention. The grease and
ochre are renewed from time to time, but the arrangement is never marred by soap and water.
In hot weather intercourse with these gentlemen
is pleasantest in a windy day, and in a breeze

which blows full in their faces as they stand be·
fore you.

The Indians about Fort Yukon and within the
range of its trade, are, as a whole, milder and less
warlike than those of the United States territories.
Yet the number of their treacherous attacks on
the *employés* of the Hudson Bay Company are not
a few, nor less cruel.

The trade now commenced, and the lofts of the
store-rooms were soon crowded with choice furs;
many thousands of sables and beaver skins were
purchased, some hundreds of fox skins of all kinds,
with a few otter, mink, and silver-fox skins.
Dressed moose and bear skins were in great abundance.   The silver fox skins brought fancy prices,
so the savages, fortunate enough to have them,
adopt fancy tricks to increase their number.   They
have a way of smoking a less valuable fox skin,
and, by slipping it into a package of the genuine
articles, pass it off at many times its real value.
As the company make their *employés* responsible
for the kind of goods purchased, this trick seldom
succeeds.

When the trading was over, furs worth at home
fifty thousand dollars had been stored.

During the stay of our explorers they attended
several religious services held with the Indians by
the missionary of the English Church, Mr. M'Donald.   The missionary's reputation as a Christian
man was excellent, and he, no doubt, did his best
to benefit these wild men.   But they, being of different tribes, very imperfectly understood each

other, and none of them well understood him. When he spoke, as he did at times through an interpreter, the case was not much better. But they learn to sing Christian hymns, and may have received some seeds of Christian truth. What they need was such a man as their missionary to be with them all the time, instead of making a few visits two or three times a year. There is one thing greatly in the favor of missionary work at the fort. There is no intoxicating drink brought there. Mr. Dall very truthfully says: "One fact may be unhesitatingly avowed—if the Indian can obtain intoxicating liquors he is lost."

One day a shout was raised among the Indians, and our explorers rushed out of their house to see what was the matter, when they were made glad by the sight of the canoes of Ketchum and Labarge. It will be recollected that they started from Nulato in the winter, and had ascended the Yukon to the fort on the ice. They were now returning from a long, bold, and perilous voyage to Fort Selkirk, several hundred miles further up this river. Their safe return was greeted with great joy by their companions, and their stories of adventure listened to with deep interest.

On the eighth of July our party, including Ketchum and Labarge, started down the river. They took a good supply of specimens for friends, of the work of the Indian. Whymper and Mike took the bidarra—the large flat-bottomed skin boat—and others took each a skin canoe with Indians to manage them. A farewell salute was given

them by the musketry of the fort. It proved easy
going down stream, and they floated pleasantly on
both night and day, landing only twice a day to
build a camp-fire and make their tea. They slept
and ate on board, at times lashing all the canoes
together and making a merry time. A fresh breeze
usually attended them, and clouds of their tormentors of the upward voyage—mosquitoes—were
seen vainly attempting to follow them; they would
pursue the canoes for awhile with bloodthirsty
vigor, but, slowly falling in the rear, they retired
from the race amid the jeers of the men.

As they glided by the Ramparts large fires were
burning in the forests and on the side of the hills,
giving a wild grandeur to the scenery. On entering the rapids they were surprised to find in
the center a long-rocky island many feet out of the
water. When they were here on the upward trip
the angry waters rushed over it, but now they
ran in smooth, swift currents on either side.

Below the rapids a fleet of salmon-fishermen
were having a merry time. They sailed along in
line, each canoe-man raising his net high in the
air; at a given signal they all plunged them beneath the water, and as they rose with the struggling salmon they joined in derisive laughter, followed by a monotonous chorus. The shore at the
numerous camps of the fishermen was red with
this luscious fish as they were spread to dry.

Our voyagers had much fun in chasing the
young geese, whose wings were not grown sufficient-
ly for flight; the poor things could only dive, when

overtaken, and keep under water until nearly drowned. Many of them were taken and proved excellent eating. There could not have been a particle of fun in the chase to these little geese.

On the thirteenth of July our party arrived at Nulato. They had made the six hundred miles from Fort Yukon in six days, which had taken twenty-six in ascending.

CHAPER VI.

INDIAN AND INNUIT TRAITS.

OUR voyagers' stay at Nulato was short, but *we* may pause long enough to tell an incident or two illustrative of the character and manners of the people.

One of the men, in the absence of Mr. Dall, stole some of his alcohol into which he had put arsenic, the mixture being used to preserve his specimens of natural history. As the thief was liberally disposed, he treated his Russian friends, and they all drank freely. The result was far from giving the party a merry time. The large quantity they took prevented the liquor from staying on their stomachs and killing them, but agonizing gripes and fearful colics deeply impressed them that it was inexpedient, if not wicked, to steal a scientific man's liquor.

There was at Nulato an exile by the name of Shabounin, banished for crime from Archargel. This man was in a house one day with Tekunka, an Indian chief; the exile, for some reason not very apparent, insulted the chief and struck him a violent blow on his face, causing it to bleed freely. An outcry was made, and Mr. Dall ran in and found the room occupied by a crowd of armed Indians, the chief's own men, and a company of Rus-

sians cowering down in a corner. Tekunka was
standing on one side, wounded and bloody, but
hurling defiant words in good Russian, at his assailants. His men stood with their hands on their
guns, ready to do his bidding; but the savage chief
seemed for the moment satisfied with stinging them
with his tongue. "A word," he scornfully shouted, "and my men wash this floor with your blood!
You call us Indian dogs! We know what *you* are
—murderers, thieves, wretches, driven from Russia for your crimes. You come to our country
and abuse us without reason, take away our daughters, and pay us with a leaf of tobacco for furs
which you cannot trap yourselves! Why should I
not avenge this unprovoked insult? Why do I
not order my men to exterminate you like vermin?
Because I had rather stand here and tell you in
your own house that I *hate, despise,* and *defy* you!"

The Russian commander of the fort came in
and quelled the disturbance in a sullen and reluctant way. He rebuked the offending Russian, gave
the chief a present of tobacco and ammunition,
which he took disdainfully, and slowly retired with
his men.

It is well these Indians are generally inoffensive and quiet, for the Russians show neither courage nor wisdom in dealing with them.

These Indians have a few traits distinguishing
them from those further south. One of these
seems to be a more delicate ear for music, especially among the women. Those accompanying
our explorers on their Yukon voyage caught the

5

airs sung by the white men, so that they hummed
continually "Tramp, tramp, tramp, the boys are
marching," and " Marching through Georgia," and,
no doubt, these songs were passed along through
the tribes of the whole Yukon valley. The women
hum airs of their own while sewing or soothing
their children to sleep. Some of the ditties thus
warbled are quite tender and impressive. The
following is a part of one which Mr. Dàll heard
sung by a Koyukun woman, freely translated and
preserving the original measure :

"The wind blows over the Yukon.
My husband hunts the deer on the Koyukun Mountains.
Ahmi, Ahmi, sleep, little one, wake not. . . .

Long since my husband departed. Why does he wait in the
    mountains?
Ahmi, Ahmi, sleep, little one, softly.

"Where is my own ?
Does he lie starving on the hill-side ? Why does he linger?
Comes he not soon I will seek him among the mountains.
Ahmi, Ahmi, sleep, little one, sleep.

"The crow has come laughing.
His beak is red, his eyes glisten, the false one.
'Thanks for a good meal to Kuskokala, the shaman.
On the sharp mountain quietly lies your husband.'
Ahmi, Ahmi, sleep, little one, wake not.

"'Twenty deers' tongues tied to the pack on his shoulders ;
Not a tongue in his mouth to call to his wife with.
Wolves, foxes, and ravens are fighting for morsels.
Tough and hard are the sinews ; not so the child in your
    bosom.'
Ahmi, Ahmi, sleep, little one, wake not !

" Over the mountain slowly staggers the hunter.
Two bucks' thighs on his shoulders, with bladders of fat be-
    tween them.
Twenty deers' tongues in his belt. Go, gather wood, old
    woman
Off flew the crow—liar, cheat, and deceiver!
Wake, little sleeper, wake, and call to your father!

He brings you back fat, marrow, and venison fresh from the
    mountain.
Tired and worn, he has carved a toy of the deer's horn,
While he was sitting and waiting long for the deer on the
    hill-side.
Wake and see the crow hiding himself from the arrow!
Wake, little one, wake, for here is your father! "

Some of these songs attain a wide popularity,
and are heard every-where, as are the nursery songs
of other lands.

While at Nulato our explorers were startled by
the news that the whole of Russian America had
been bought by the United States; and a still
more startling word was the command to transfer
all the movable property of the Telegraph Company without delay to the fort at St. Michaels.
The Russians did not like the rumor that *they* were
sold out. "Perhaps," said one of their officers to
Mr Dall, "it is the *Americans* who are about to
march! "

Our explorers proceeded at once to obey orders. They purchased a *bidarra*—a large skin boat
—into which the specimens of natural history and
other valuable property was put, and six men were
hired to accompany them to the coast. About

midnight of July fifteenth they started, full of per-
plexity inspired by the strange order. The camp-
fires of the fishermen burned cheerfully along the
banks of the river, and in its waters were numerous
leopard seals which, no doubt, had ascended the
river for the purpose of fishing; even a white
whale ventured at one time on the same business
nearly to Nulato, at least four hundred miles from
the coast, his long swim being stimulated probably by the good eating on the way.

As our voyagers proceeded the river widened
until it spread out like a lake, filled with beautiful
islands. They landed at a small native village
where there was a Russian mission and a Greek
church; it was, however, a nearly deserted place,
as the natives were away salmon fishing, and most
of the Russians with their priest, or, as they call
him, pope, were at St. Michaels; so our party
pushed on. As we have stated, the Yukon, as it
approaches the coast, divides into many streams,
which flow through a vast plain into Norton Sound.
Down one of these to the open sound, along the
coast, into the narrow waters between the mainland and the island of St. Michaels, called the
Canal, to the fort, our explorers sailed safely.

Here they found many of the explorers and constructing parties of the Telegraph Company ready
to receive them. The story they told was short
and emphatic. The United States had completed
arrangements for the purchase of Russian America;
the Atlantic Telegraph was a success, and conse-
quently the overland project in which they were

engaged was wrecked, and with it the Union Telegraph Company; the bark "Clara Bell" was expected at the fort to take its men and property
to San Francisco.

While waiting for the vessel, which will not
come for a whole month, we will take the opportunity to become better acquainted with that portion of the Alaska people near the sea-coast which
belong to the Esquimo family. They are divided into several tribes, but all have the family
look and traits of character. They are the same
easy-going, small-brained, bestial sort of folks with
which we became acquainted on our "North-Pole
Voyages;" the only modifications observable in
their habits are such as come easily from the difference of their surroundings.

They have no marriage ceremonies; children
are greatly prized, if boys; girls are not welcome
at the paternal homes. If daughters come in an
undue proportion, and often if there is only one,
the little innocents are carried into some by-place,
their mouths stuffed with grass, and they are left
to perish. But their death cries in the ears of
God, and to Christian lands, for the Gospel of
Him who took little children in his arms and
blessed them.

Yet it is said that these Innuit men and women
are generally kind in the family-relation, seldom
guilty of violence where the white man's "fire-
water" does not come in to inspire it, and that
the children are kind and obedient to their parents. Plainly, however, this family happiness is

such *in their way*, which, in a truly Christian family, would be only a very poor way.

These people are fond of dancing, which is much
after the Indian sort.   They have several festivals,
two of which are rather rare and quite peculiar.
One is this: The man who proposes to give the
feast commences to work with intense earnest-
ness to get rich in furs of all valuable kinds, in
beads, and other esteemed things.   He patiently
toils on for many years—one was known to the
governor at the fort who toiled fifteeen years—
saving, with a miser's care, all his acquisitions.
When his ambition is satisfied his call is made,
and all the Innuits of the vicinity crowd to the
feast, not one beginning to make excuse.   The
festal exercises begin with dancing, in which each
is expected to do his "level best," and there is
never a lack of a becoming effort so to do.
Among the man's preparations, is the largest possible store of provisions, of which all are invited
to partake, the feast lasting as many days as do
these provisions.   On the last day the host and
his wife dress in their best attire, welcome the
crowd in his house, where his accumulated treas-
ures are spread before them, and they each receive
whatever gift they desire.   When the store of gifts
is exhausted the host and his wife strip themselves
of their fine apparel, put on ragged garments, and
give the good ones to those who may not pre-
viously have received any present.   The guests put
on their new clothes on the spot and in silence.
The host then assures his friends he has nothing

left, and laments that his gifts have been so few and valueless. The guests are then dismissed, and the entertainer is from that moment great and honored—a member for life of the upper circle of Esquimo society. One man gave away at such a feast ten guns, two hundred beaver and a hundred seal skins, fifty deer skins, five hundred sable, ten wolf skins, two hundred fathoms of strung beads, ten suits of clothing, and ten woolen blankets.

This is the Innuit way of making a "spread," and seems to be. prompted by the same elevated and refined ambition as that which inspires some in our own fashionable world. The result of the Innuit spread is poverty with great esteem ; ours often results in poverty without any esteem at all.

Mr. Dall witnessed one of the other peculiar festivals. A man had provoked a quarrel, and, "coming to himself" as the sinner in the case, sent a messenger seventy miles to the wronged man. The messenger was gayly dressed in a new suit, and carried a wand in his hand, ornamented with feathers. The coming of such a messenger was by arrangement made known to the offended. The messenger found him at work, approached him chanting, touched him with the wand, then suddenly seized him by the neck, and flourished over his head a murderous-looking knife. The man thus handled, understanding the programme, made no resistance. The messenger next inquired what restitution was required. The offended named the price of reconciliation, and was

informed when and where it would be given. Some
weeks later the feast was ready. The offended
and the offenders appeared, each in a new suit of
clothes; the latter received the required gifts and
much more, and then the two danced together.
Finally, they exchanged clothing, and the reconciliation was complete. The receiver of the gifts
distributed some presents to the spectators, and
the happy company departed. "Blessed are the
peacemakers," whatever we may say of this *way*
of bringing it about.

At the end of a tedious month the "Clara
Bell" arrived. It took home the forlorn hope of
the explorers, except Mr. Dall, who had in the
waiting arranged to stay another year, to complete his plan for scientific investigations in the
country. The results of his observations during
this prolonged visit we have in part anticipated.
We will now bid adieu to Alaska, and, in oui
own independent way, go back about two years,
and accompany another party of the Telegraph
Company's explorers.

CHAPTER VII.

A SEA-GIRT TOWN.

HAVING followed the Russian-American party, and through their eyes looked at Alaska, we propose to visit the opposite shore of Bering Sea. But let us start with the explorers from San Francisco. Our party was under the command of Major Abasa, a Russian gentleman of high standing and eminent qualifications for his position. He was accompanied by Captain J. A. Mahood, civil engineer; Captain R. J. Bush, who had just returned from three years' service in the "Carolinos;" and Captain Geo. Kennan—four persons in all.

This was a small number to survey some two thousand miles of a wild, unknown region ; but they were young, and full of a noble ambition to dare and do great things. They sailed from San Francisco in the Russian trading vessel "Olga," July 3, 1865, bound for the mouth of the Amoor River, on the western coast of the Ochotsk Sea. On the twelfth of the same month a party, under Lieutenant C. L. Macrae, sailed for the mouth of Anadyr River, far up the Siberian coast of Bering Sea, where he was to co-operate with our party. We shall meet Macrae by and by, but in the meantime will follow the Abasa party.

The farewells to the explorers as they left the wharf were full of pleasantry and sadness.

"Send us back," said one, "a piece of the North Pole and a specimen of the Aurora Borealis." "Take care of my dear brother," whispered a sister pleadingly to her brother's companion." "Good-bye, George! God bless you!" said the enthusiastic naturalist, Mr. Dall, to Kennan; "Keep your eye out for land snails and skulls of wild animals."

Thus, with the blessing of all and the prayers and tears of friends, our explorers left the shore, passed through the Golden Gate, and sailed over the storm-tossed waves of the Pacific northward, until, after about seven weeks, they were thrilled with joy by the cry from the mast-head, "Land ho!" Looking far above the hazy horizon, they saw, sharply cut against the dark blue sky, the snowy peaks of two lofty volcanic mountains of Southern Kamchatka. The sea-birds in great numbers had, for many days, hovered about them, and screamed their wild, but joyous, welcome. The first glimpse of land was a signal for a general stir on shipboard. In the cabin trunks were over-hauled, clean linen was placed at hand, boots took an extra luster, beards were trimmed, and all other becoming preparations made for a first appearance in a Kamchatka port. On deck the sailors plied their scrubbing brooms with vigor, and put things in general in the nicest trim. An Irish tar showed his high appreciation of the importance of cleanli-ness by scrubbing, with a hearty good-will, two young pigs. The pigs, however, were too ignorant to rightly estimate the benefit thus conferred. "Och! ye spalpeens, stop your squallin'! the gentlemen will think yer bein' murthered! Will yees be asy, I tell yees; it's all for yer own good!"

The voyagers soon saw the long, dark, craggy shore line, answering well to their long-cherished ideas of Kamchatka barrenness. A fog suddenly shut out every object a cable's length away; the vessel's head was put seaward, and a long, dreary night was spent in disappointment and suspense. The morning came, and the rising sun dispelled the fog-bank. The opening into Avatcha Bay was soon made, within which, on its northern shore, is situated Petropavlovsk, the extreme southern part of the peninsula. A sight now greeted our explorers which surprised and pleased them. As they glided under easy sail through the narrow mouth of the bay, the long array of beetling cliffs was lighted up by a shower of brilliant sunlight. The cliffs ranged from one hundred to four hundred feet in height. They were crowned with beautiful green slopes, dotted by a rich foliage, and down their sides, winding through the vegetation, rivulets reached the brink of the precipice and bounded over in silent, silvery threads, ending in tassels of spray midway of their descent to the foamy billows below.

At the bottom of the cliffs the sea has worn a succession of cavities, greatly varied in form and size. Over some of these cavities massive rocks were suspended, ready at any moment to go crash-

ing into the sea; others were supported by splen·
did arches ; and still others by slender pillars.
Here and there stood tall, jagged, or symmetrical
shafts, like some lightning-scathed giant of the
forest, shorn of its branches and ready to fall at
the first bidding of the storm king. Into these
caverns the sea rolled its waves with a thundering,
dismal sound.

In and around those caverns myriads of water-
fowl made their homes, including the sea-parrots,
with their beautiful plumage and unmusical voices,
and ducks, with their vociferous quack. There
was a thrilling interest attending the sight of
the wild freedom of those birds. Here they
huddled together on some projecting crag, as
cozily as doves in their cot, and looked con-
tentedly down upon their fellows, who were busily engaged in appeasing their hunger from the
abundance of the sea; there a noisy company were
buffeting each other from the sharp points of a
tall, rocky shaft, as hilarious as boys in a scuffle at
school recess. At times a cloud of them ascended
from the surface of the sea, alarmed at the approach of the vessel, flapping the water with their
wings as they rose and sailed off in a wide circuit
over the bay, its glossy surface mirroring their flying shadow.

The sea-washed base of these rocky projections
and the lower platforms of the caverns wêre black
with seals, which mounted them to bathe in the
warm sunlight, and then to clumsily slide over
each other and go splashing into the sea; they

kept up the while a hoarse bellowing, evidently most melodious to their own ears. So the sea-birds and the seals held daily concerts, to which there must be sublime additions when the tempest winds roar and the sea lifts up its voice.

As the "Olga" approached the bay, the cliffs on both sides diminished, and grassy slopes came down to the shore, indented by sheltering harbors. Sailing two or three miles through a widening opening, the voyagers entered Avatcha Bay, a beautiful sheet of water some twenty miles in extent, coasted along its northern side awhile, and then suddenly rounding a projecting headland, they were in the small, land-locked harbor of Petropavlovsk. A hundred Esquimo dogs saluted them with their wild howlings as they reached the shore. The whole town was soon astir to see the strangers. The children, though poorly clad and nearly as wild looking as the dogs, touched their caps and bowed respectfully to the new-comers. A German merchant, by the name of Fluger, who spoke English, courteously introduced himself to our explorers, and guided them in a short walk about the town. It was but a log-village, bearing some resemblance to a pioneer town of our own Western frontier. They found but one street which could properly be called such, and on this the better class of houses were located; around these were shaded grounds and ornamental gardens, through some of which streams of water were made to run. The roofs of the houses were covered with bark or thatched with straw, a few being tinned and painted red. The houses away from this street were located without the least regard to order and were scattered like a flock of birds which had suddenly alighted.

The strangers were at once shown through the Greek church, which was evidently "the lion" of the town. The dome, a necessary part of these sacred buildings, was a cheap affair, painted green. From the dome, low shed-like appendages extended in the shape of a cross. But an odd-appearing arrangement was a shed or belfry, several feet from the main building, in which was a chime of eight bells. These were now pealing out their not over-harmonious music in honor of their arrival.

After visiting Mr. Fluger's own house, our party were introduced by him to the captain of the fort. At his residence they found the evidence not only of comfort but of some refinement. Native and foreign flowers, and a rippling stream, adorned his grounds. In his parlor was a large Russian-made piano, and on the center table was a handsome stereoscope, with a large collection of photographic views. The walls of the room were ornamented with choice paintings and lithographs. The elegant Russian tea-urn was at hand, and at short notice the callers were treated to a cup of tea, said to be superior to any ever sipped in the States. We wish we could add that the visitors were not treated to any thing stronger.

This principal trading port of Kamchatka, with its hard name, Petropavlovsk, which no two authors spell in the same way, is made somewhat important by its furs. Its name, "the village of St. Peter and St. Paul," was given it in honor of the ships which sailed from this port under the famous Bering, bearing the names respectively of these saints.

Our explorers met American as well as other traders at this town of Peter and Paul, by all of whom they were treated very kindly, and the few days of their stay were pleasantly divided between social entertainments and delightful excursions. One morning they sallied out upon the narrow peninsula which separates the harbor from Avatchka Bay. The dense fog of the night had lifted, but hung low over the hill-tops and veiled from sight the distant volcanic mountains. Nature had spread even here in this country, so far away from tropical suns, her richest carpet of emerald green. Wild flowers in great profusion, among which were roses, the modest violet, and ostentatious tiger-lily, smiling in the sunlight and dripping with moisture. Whortleberries and blackberries were abundant, inviting the strangers to a generous and delicious repast. On one side of them was the quiet bay, above whose glassy surface the sea-birds flew and screamed in their wild freedom, and on the other was the harbor, seeming as safe and cozy as a far-away inland lake. The signs of God's loving smiles were every-where, but man had marred the landscape with his bloody footsteps. During the Crimean War the allies attacked the Russian fortress which crowned this hilly peninsula and defended the town. The assailants had

to climb the steep acclivity, and were easily hurled
back by its defenders. Again and again they renewed the attack, but succeeded only in exhibiting
a foolhardy valor. The allies retired ignomini-
ously from the contest, and their commander, in
the bitterness of his mortification at being repulsed
by a few Cossacks and peasants, committed suicide.
The shame belonged to the Government which
conceived and ordered the attack. As to the value
of the possible results, in their bearing upon the
issues of the war, they might as well have attacked
one of Kamchatka's volcanic mountains. Modest
moss flowers, set in their carpet of green, and nodding bluebells now strive to hide the furrows in
the ground made by the bloody conflict.

Another interesting excursion was made to a
small village nearly ten miles from the town, and
on the opposite shore of the bay. The ride was
made on the backs of the small, stout ponies of
the country. These ponies, like many other small
folks, are smart and frisky. As the legs of our
riders were long, and the ponies low, the stirrups
were made short to keep the feet from coming in
contact with the stumps. This brought the rider's
chin and knees into an unpleasant nearness, and
put him at great disadvantage in managing his
pony; this the knowing little beast understood,
and, being fond of a joke, especially when it could
be made at the expense of a *green* rider, he would
stop short in the midst of a brisk trot at the beginning of a sharp descent, so that the rider would
be precipitated over his head, and roll down to

the bottom. In such a case he would remain
standing quite still at the top, looking innocently
at his master as he picked himself up, as much as
o say, "Did it hurt you? I am sorry! You
should have kept your seat." On one such occasion, Bush's foot became entangled in the stirrup,
by which he hung when jerked from the saddle.
Pony was not satisfied to have the fun stop here.
She kicked furiously, disengaged the foot, and
sent its owner in the shortest possible time to the
foot of the hill. Fortunately no serious hurt was
done, but the pony was the only party which *enjoyed*
the incident.

The excursionists picked flowers as they swept
through the tall grass, listened to the songs of
numerous birds, raced their little horses, sung
American songs, shouted and hallooed, making the
hills echo to these expressions of their delight.
They were in just the frame of mind to enjoy a
romantic incident, but came near having a tragic
one. Bears and wolves abound in the vicinity,
and the cry was raised of "Wolf! wolf!" Pistols
were drawn, ready to give him a warm reception.
The eyes of several of the party were directed to
a stir in a thicket, which had caused the alarm,
and out of which suddenly sprung—one of the
party. Nobody fired, and so all could afford to
laugh.

A genuine bear adventure would have been a
godsend, supposing the bear was not over plucky.
But none came, and so we suppose the following
story, told by one of the residents of the town, an-

6

swered. A cow was at one time feeding just out
of the settlement, when a bear suddenly sprung
upon her back, with no good intention, as the cow
believed, so she ran into the town, arousing the
people by her bellowing. Guns were seized, and
vengeance was *attempted* on the bear, but he beat
a safe retreat. No doubt the cow thought the
hunters might, in the future, carry into the market
their own bears.

The excursionists returned in fine spirits, just
as the sun was setting.

Major Abasa was maturing his plans, during
these days of recreation on the part of his subor-
dinate officers, and the time of putting them into
execution was at hand. The programme decided
upon for the winter was this: Bush and Mahood
were to go in the "Olga" to the mouth of the
Amoor River, on the Chinese frontier, and, making
that place the base of supplies, were to explore the
rough, mountainous regions lying to the west of
the Ochotsk Sea, as far north as the Russian sea-
port of Ochotsk, a distance of five hundred and
fifty miles of an almost unknown country. The
major and Kennan were to travel north through
the peninsula of Kamchatka, with native team-
sters, and push on to a point near the extreme
northern waters which connect with the Sea of
Ochotsk; they would here be about five hundred
and fifty miles above the point at which Bush and
Mahood aimed; so Abasa would then go south-
west to meet them, while Kennan pushed on
northward. The whole plan will be plain as it

develops, if only this general outline be kept in mind.

As the party for the Amoor were soonest ready, they departed immediately. Kennan followed in a boat, the " Olga," to add a last good-bye. As he went over the side of the vessel in the final parting, the second mate, who filled also the office of cook, a kind-hearted sailor, said feelingly, in funny, broken English, "O, Mr. Kinney! who's a g'un to cook for ye? and ye can't get no potatuses!" His heart ached for his friend Kennan, in view of the privation he saw before him, the sum of which was the loss of the " Olga's " cook and "potatuses."

Leaving Bush and Mahood for a while, with our blessing upon their daring adventure, we will see how Kennan endured this extreme self-denial

CHAPTER VIII.

A NATIVE VILLAGE.

MAJOR ABASA and Captain Kennan pressed forward with vigor the completion of their preparation for the northern land journey. A young American by the name of Dodd, a fur-trader, who spoke Russian, and was well acquainted with the natives, was engaged to accompany them. A Russian, named Vushine, was to go as cook. The party were to depend upon each post or native town for the means of transportation to the next one. The emperor's indorsement of the enterprise in which they were engaged, an official copy of which the major carried in his pocket, was sufficient to assure this aid, for which, however, they purposed to pay. Under authority of this favor from head-quarters, horses were ordered for the start from all the adjacent villages, and a special courier was sent along the route which our party intended to follow to apprise the natives of their coming, and to direct them to remain at home, with all their horses, until the strangers should pass. So a dignity was to attend their coming which, as we shall see, insured comfort as well as safety.

The peninsula of Kamchatka, which they were about to travel, is, as the reader will see by refer-

ring to a map, an irregular piece of land east of
the Ochotsk Sea, measuring in extreme length
about seven hundred miles. It is divided lengthwise by a chain of volcanic mountains, some of
which are always emitting fire and smoke; well
toward the north of the peninsula these mountains break off abruptly into the Ochotsk Sea, leaving beyond a wide, level desert, which is the wandering ground of the wild Reindeer Koraks. The
inhabitants of the more southern portions consist
of Russians and Kamchadals, or settled natives.
The whole population, including the Koraks, has
been estimated at five thousand. The government, such as it is, is in the hands of the Russian
officer at Petropavlovsk. The climate, except in
the extreme north, is not severe, nor subject to intense extremes, and produces, as we have seen, a
fresh and luxuriant vegetation. The Kamchadals,
the most numerous of the population, are settled
in little log villages, scattered over the peninsula,
near the mouths of the small rivers. They are
occupied principally in fishing, fur-trapping, and
raising rye, turnips, cabbages, and potatoes.

Properly speaking, there is not a road in the
country, though we may call, if we please, the line
a party marks out as its course of travel *a road*.
Through this wild region, and over this chain of
mountains, the explorers proposed to travel. They
did not wish to be idle during the winter, which
was now at hand, and they could not sail north up
the Ochotsk Sea until spring.

Just on the eve of their start Dodd informed

Kennan that there was to be a wedding in the church, and assured him he would be interested in attending. Of course the reader will be interested, too, so we will stop and gratify our curiosity in seeing a Kamchadal-Russian wedding ceremony; it will be our only opportunity for such a sight.

A morning service being concluded, the marriage ceremony commenced in the body of the house. The man was a young Cossack, about twenty years of age; he was dressed in a dark frock coat trimmed with lace, and gathered, like a lady's dress, about the waist, the gathering being in fact only a few inches below the armpits. As a special adornment he had put on a great white standing collar, projecting above his ears. His cotton pants were out of humor with his shoes, and only extended within six inches of them.

The bride was a widow of forty. Her lover had never heard probably of the elder Weller's counsel to his son, who said, with a sigh, " Sammy, beware o' the vidders, beware o' the vidders ! " This unconscious " wictim" was walking to the altar, " and thinkin' in his 'art that it was all wery capital." The bride's dress was of that material known as " furniture prints," and was wholly without trimming. Her hair was bound tightly in a scarlet silk handkerchief, fastened in front with a small, gilt button.

As soon as the priest had finished the morning service he put on a black silk gown, but did not put off his heavy cowhide boots. The altar being removed to the middle of the floor, the priest took

his place beside it and summoned the couple before him. Placing in the hand of each three lighted
candles tied together with blue ribbon, he began to
read what was supposed to be the marriage service,
which he rattled off in a loud voice, regardless of
stops, but catching his breath in the midst of a
sentence, and hurrying on with increased rapidity.
The candidates for marriage were silent, but the
deacon, in the opposite side of the house, occasionally put in during the reading a dolorous response.
When the reading was finished all crossed themselves, devoutly but rapidly, many times. The
priest then asked the decisive question, which being answered satisfactorily, he gave a silver ring
and a teaspoonful of wine to each. More readings
succeeded, during which the bride and bridegroom crossed themselves and bowed continually.
The deacon closed his responses by repeating fifteen times, with wonderful rapidity, " Góspodi
Pomeelui "—" God have mercy upon us ! " He
then brought out two large gilt crowns, ornamented with medallions, and, blowing the dust from
them, placed them upon the heads of the bridegroom and bride.

The young man's crown was too large, slipping
down over his face and blinding him. The bride's
peculiar style of adjusting her hair prevented her
crown from staying on her head, and one of the
spectators was called to hold it on. The priest
now caused the couple to join hands. He then
seized the hand of the groom, and al commenced
a hurried march around the altar   The priest

dragged along the Cossack, who, blinded by his crown, trod continually on his leader's heels; the bride followed her spouse, and tried to prevent the crown from pulling her hair down while her attendant trod upon her dress as she followed to hold the crown in its place. Having gone around the altar three times, the happy pair removed their crowns, kissed them, and the ceremony was ended.

They walked leisurely around the church, bowing and crossing themselves before the pictures of saints, which hung against the wall, then turned to receive the congratulations of their friends.

There is one custom attending these Kamchadal weddings which has in part an Oriental appearance. When the company return to the house whence they come, children precede the married couple with lighted tapers and pictures of the saints.

Several of the American visitors speak of this priest as occasionally drunk during their stay, and as once "carried home on a shutter." We cannot write, as it would be pleasant to do, that his American friends set him an example of total abstinence.

Early in September our party commenced their perilous journey. Sending the larger part of their equipments on pack-horses to the little village of Okoota, on the Avatcha River, they took a whaleboat with Russian rowers, and passed over the bay to its mouth and up to the village where they would meet the horses and go forward by land.

But the rowers had partaken too freely of the wine
which had flowed freely in honor of the departure
of the strangers; they sung drunken songs, blessed
the Americans, and, occasionally, fell overboard.
Vushine pulled them on board by their hair, rapped
them on their heads with a paddle to restore so-
briety, jumped into the water himself to push the
boat from the sand bars upon which they rowed it,
and blustered round generally like a man of authority. But the sun went down, and they were
yet some distance below Okoota. So they ran the
boat ashore, beat down the high grass, pitched
their little cotton tent, spread a dry bear skin for
a carpet, made a table of an empty box, spread
over it a clean towel, built a fire, made tea, and
squatted down to a supper inviting of itself and
made royal by good appetites. After supper our
explorers sat by the dying embers of the fire talking until the twilight had faded into the deep
darkness of the night; they then rolled themselves
in blankets and lay down upon their bear skins to
sleep.

The little camp was astir early; Vushine was
prompt with his breakfast, after which the voyage
was immediately resumed. The scene was full of
a wild and romantic grandeur. The mountains
in the distance were sparkling in the morning sunlight; one of them, nearly eleven thousand feet
in height, and its summit covered with snow,
rested coldly against the sky; others, off in another direction, had thrown out their long banners of smoke which flashed near their broken

craters with flames. The wild ducks were on the
wing in great numbers, flying low on swift wings,
and uttering their hoarse quack as they passed;
and the mingled, unharmonious cries of geese,
swans, and sea-gulls filled the air, and awoke the
echoes of the hills. Now and then a noble eagle
launched from his solitary watch on some jutting
rock, and, spreading his broad wings, mounted upward in widening circuits, until lost in the depths
of the sky. The wild flowers, not yet nipped by
the frost, which had only slightly sent abroad his
chilling breath, beautified the banks on either side
in great numbers and rich varieties, and filled the
air with their perfume. We may well believe that
our voyagers were inspired by the sights and
sounds, and that the hours flew swiftly by.

About noon they made a turn in the river, and
came suddenly upon the village of Okoota. The
dogs announced their approach by vociferous
barking. The men who brought round the pack-
horses were here to welcome them.

As this Kamchadal village is, in its general character, like all others, we will tarry a moment and
take a special look at it. It is situated, as we notice on landing, on a slight elevation of land, as
these people do have some appreciation of pure
air and safety from the spring freshets. Scattered
clumps of poplars and yellow birch make about
all the means of shady retreats afforded them.
The houses, it may be plainly seen, are huddled
together near the beach. They are low, cheap
affairs, built of squared logs, notched at the end,

and the wide chinks filled with dried moss. The
roofs are covered with a thatch of long, coarse grass
or wide, overlapping strips of bark, and project at
the ends and sides into wide, overhanging eaves.
The window-panes are covered with fish-bladders,
sewed together and dried, through which the light
shines faintly as through glass. The doors are
square, and the chimneys are made of long poles
set in a circle and plastered with a thick clay.
We shall not fail to notice some curious-looking
buildings scattered here and there between the
houses. They are log tents, elevated upon four
posts. Kennan says they look like hay-stacks
running away on four legs. They are store-
houses for fish, where the dogs may not break in
and steal. Besides these there are other contriv-
ances in reference to the fish. We shall notice
high-square platforms made of horizontal poles,
on which they are dried. As fish are the chief
commodity of the people, and as the explorers
themselves are very glad to be served with them
on their travels, we must not mind the smell, even
if it comes on the breeze to us before we reach
the village. The native canoes, made of dug-out
logs, may be seen bottom up on the beach; seines
are spread over these canoes for convenient keeping. Long, narrow sledges stand against every
house, near which, fastened to long poles, are the
wolfish dogs, having the same general character
as those seen in other arctic regions, snappish,
voracious, yet able to fast a long time, rendering
to their masters a service of great value, but will-

ing at any time to kill and eat them if not prevented by their cowardly fear.

The last but not the least prominent feature of
the village is the Greek church, built of hewn
logs, and painted a brick red, covered with a
green sheet-iron roof, and surmounted with an
onion-shaped dome of tin, painted sky-blue, span-
gled with golden stars. The easy-going natives
have, as a general thing, given up their heathen religion for the forms of Christian faith introduced
by their Russian conquerors, and found no very
sharp transition in the change, and, we fear, no
very essential benefit. In cases of great distress,
as we shall have occasion to see, they fall back
upon the grossest heathen rites.

The physical appearance of these villagers is
peculiar, showing that they are not intimately
related to any other arctic people. They have
broad, flat faces, prominent cheek-bones, small
sunken eyes, long, coarse black hair, no beards,
small hands and feet, and slender limbs. They
possess no positive traits of character, and seem to
drift along from generation to generation toward
utter extinction as a people.

We have stated that this people make salmon a
principal article of food; but, of course, the immense number of wild fowls to which we have
alluded afford another staple means of support.
They have rather a cruel, though we must allow a
fair, means of killing them, as they are not well
supplied with guns. It is this: they take the advantage of the season when they are shedding

their feathers, and are, therefore, unable to fly. At such times the birds are swimming about in the rivers in immense numbers; the natives then turn out in a company of fifty or seventy-five canoes, drive them up a narrow stream where a great net is set for them into which they crowd; they are then killed with clubs, skinned, and salted.

The reindeer and black bear are less abundant game, but come in to help the supply.

CHAPTER IX.

A COMICAL MISTAKE.

THE stay of our explorers at Okoota was brief
After eating a hasty lunch, their ingeniously-
contrived packages, tents, furs, and camp conveniences were adjusted to the horses, the riders
mounted, and the "caravan," as Dodd called the
mounted company, started. Their way led along
the lower declivity of hills, back of which rose
volcanic mountains, whose snowy summits were
seen through the tree-tops. As the sun was going
down they rode into a little village, whose name
was so intensely Russian that Kennan failed to be
able to speak or write it, though the patient Dodd
repeated it, with ringing emphasis, sixteen times ;
so he called it Jerusalem. After our explanation
the reader will not suppose it has any historical
connection with the sacred Jerusalem of the Holy
Land. But this Jerusalem proved an acceptable
resting-place to the weary travelers. The courier
who had preceded them had so proclaimed the
dignity and importance of the coming strangers,
that the villagers saw the shadow at least of the
Czar himself in their persons. The rough plank
floors and walls of the rooms they were to occupy
had been scoured with water and sand to a creamy
whiteness. The furniture, in Kennan's room, con-

sisting of a bench, two chairs, and a table, was arranged conveniently on one side, and the clay oven
on the other side, and the windows were shaded
by flowery calico curtains.   The supper, which
was promptly served, was fit to set before a king.
It was made up of cold roast duck, broiled reindeer tongues, black bread and fresh butter, blueberries and cream, and wild rose-leaves crushed
with sugar into a delicious jam, accompanied with
such tea as American civilization does not provide.
The whole village had been laid under contribution for the necessary number of plates, knives,
and spoons, and china cups and saucers.   The
children, as well as the rooms, had been scoured,
to make the surroundings agreeable.

After this feast of dainties, our friends gathered
about them their fur robes, inflated their rubber
pillows, and lay down upon the clean floors, and
slept.

The major was astir early, much to the disgust
of some of the party.   But he was in a tempest of
excitement, and worse than wasted precious breath
in profane words on learning that all the horses
had taken a hasty leave during the night.   This
was annoying to a party fearing the closing up of
their way farther north by winter snows.   But the
detention proved one of only two hours, at the end
of which the truant horses were all returned, not
a minute sooner, though, for the profanity.

After another day's ride through enchanting
scenery our party encamped in a wild, mountain
gorge, into which fragments of volcanic rocks had

been hurled from above, and through which a cold stream ran, made by numerous cascades. Little plots of green grass, decked with odorous flowers, adorned here and there the sides of the stream. On one of these plots they pitched their tents. Camp-fires were soon burning brightly, tea served, and then followed the social chat and the refreshing sleep on carpets of bear skins. The hum of bees and the murmur of the stream over its rocky bed filled the air with a soothing music.

From this encampment there was but one night's halt before they entered the beautiful valley of Geneel, "the garden of Kamchatka." We must recollect that our party are pushing north near the eastern slope of the great range of mountains of which we have spoken, which, lying near the center, stretch far toward both north and south. The Geneel Valley lay in their route; it is thirty miles long, and of an average breadth of three miles. Through its whole length runs the tortuous Geneel River, bordered by occasional clumps of trees, and fringed by a rank grass. Rising on both sides are volcanic hills, having a great variety of form, but all presenting a wild beauty and grandeur. Midway from their snow-capped tops were belts of dark green pines; below these the ripened leaves of the mountain ash flamed in a crimson girdling; and yet nearer the valley the autumn golden yellow of the birches made another strongly-contrasted, horizontal line. Here and there the mountains opened into narrow, dark gorges, as if cleft by some mighty power!

The air was warm and fragrant, and, mounted on fresh horses, the travelers galloped over the plain with the freedom of a picnic party. Kennan and Dodd would urge forward their steeds until they were several miles in advance of the caravan, then dismount in some choice spot by the river's brink, tie their horses to their rider's feet, and feast upon the berries, with which the bushes were heavily laden, until their faces and clothes were deeply stained with the luscious juice.

The sun was yet an hour high when the village of Geneel appeared in the distance. The trail crossed the river, which they easily forded, kneeling upon their saddles to avoid getting wet. Soon they forded another bend of the river, but were immediately confronted with a third.

"Halloo there, Dodd!" shouted the major, "how many rivers do we have to cross in getting to that beastly village?"

"Only one," replied Dodd, dryly.

"Only one!" retorted the major. "Then how many times does this one river run past this one settlement?"

"Five times, sir. Why, you see, these poor Kamchadals have got but one river to fish in, and that isn't a very big one; so they made it run by their settlement five times, and by this ingenious contrivance they catch five times as many salmon as they would if it only passed once."

The major was surprised into silence, and fell into a deep study. Finally, he threw a withering glance at Dodd, and shouted in a voice of reproof:

7

"I say, Dodd, how many times must a given fish pass a given settlement, in order to supply the population with food, provided the fish is caught every time he goes past!"

Dodd burst into a loud laugh, dashed into the last bend of the stream, and led the way into the village.

They found good quarters with the head man of the place. Kennan and Dodd entertained themselves after supper by reading the latest information from the civilized world, from copies of the "London Illustrated News," with which the wall of their room was papered. American colored lithographs, hung here and there, showed the owner's appreciation of the fine arts.

The party were off early the next morning for a long ride to the next post. They had gradually changed their civilized costumes for those more suited to their rough life, until they began to look like a troop of banditti. Dodd's head was closely wrapped in a scarlet and yellow handkerchief. Vushine's hat was ornamented with a long streamer of crimson ribbon. Kennan wore a blue hunting-shirt, and a red cap without brim. Every man had a rifle slung across his back, and a revolver belted to his waist.

Thus fantastically dressed, and mounted on fresh, spirited horses, the major, Kennan, Dodd, and Vushine galloped ahead of the rest of the party. They vainly reckoned on frightening man or beast which might cross their path by their valorous, brigandish bearing. Just as they were

sweeping over the level plain at a spirited rate, a
large, black bear rose with silent dignity at the
feet of the major's horse. His horse plunged and
kicked furiously, and the whole party of travelers
were thrown into a terrific excitement.

"Don't shoot *me*," shouted the major, seeing
Kennan trying to level his gun at the bear. Vushine instantly gave the beast a broadside, of bird
shot, from his gun, which probably only "tickled"
him. Dodd would have done prodigies of bravery,
but his horse ran away with him. The bear only
was calm, surveying the situation with the eye of
one having command. He then trotted leisurely
away toward the woods. Our brave brigands followed him at a safe distance, shouting, "Stop that
bear! Stop that bear!" and peppering him well,
or endeavoring so to do, with pistol and bird
shot. It was not thought that the affair was of
any serious inconvenience to this dignified native
of the forest.

At the next stopping-place the explorers struck
the Kamchatka River, which flowed north-east-
erly. Here they exchanged the saddle for a raft,
which the couriers had in readiness. This raft
consisted of three large log canoes, placed parallel to each other about three feet apart, and joined
by poles laid across and lashed to them by seal-
skin cords. Over these was laid a platform about
twelve feet square, leaving a space in the bow and
stern of each canoe for the men with paddles. On
this platform, covered with fresh-cut grass, our
voyagers pitched their tent, spread in it a carpet

of furs, arranged their rubber pillows and blank-ets, and easily imagined it a state-room. Rifles and revolvers were hung up against the tent-poles, and heavy boots were displaced for fur slippers of native manufacture. The general baggage was shipped on another raft.

All being ready, the raft pushed into the stream, the villagers crowding to the shore, and waving them a good-bye.

The scenery of the country, so enchanting from the saddle, was even more so, as it passed in pan-oramic beauty while they glided down the river. Myriads of sea-fowl, and occasionally the great Kamchatkan eagle, enlivened the scene. The foliage of the forest was many colored, and of brilliant hues. The navigation was difficult, for sunken logs, sudden turns in the river, and fre-quent sand-bars, kept the men with the paddles on the alert. As the night drew on it was deemed unsafe to continue the voyage, and the rafts drew up to the shore. A semicircle was cut in the underbrush, and the blankets were spread upon the soft, yielding moss, upon which our explorers threw themselves, while Vushine started the camp-fire, and prepared the evening meal. This eaten, the party amused themselves in hurling fire-brands at salmon as they leaped from the water in their passage up the river, startling the ducks at the same time, which rose in dark clouds, screaming their dissatisfaction at the disturbance of their usual quiet by the intrusive and discourteous strangers. Tired of this boyish sport, our explorers lay down with their faces to the clear, tranquil sky, and fell asleep.

Our readers have learned that the romance of arctic traveling is subject to certain interruptions. Kennan's sleep was brought to a close a little after midnight by a pelting rain. He started up, rubbed his eyes, and surveyed the situation. His blanket was wet through, and his mossy bed was a mud-puddle. The major and Dodd had brought the tent ashore, crept under it, and were sleeping comfortably. Into this Kennan crawled, and had begun to sleep again, when all hands were ordered to the rafts. The moon was *supposed* to be risen, but it was dark, dismal, and rainy.

No tents could be pitched on the rafts in the gusty wind which brought at times deluging rain. So they rolled themselves in rubber blankets, lay down, not as during the day, in pleasant reveries, but in painful wakefulness.

The voyage was now dangerous, as well as uncomfortable. Sunken logs, tangled, overhanging tree limbs, and projecting points of land, around which the water rushed with great force, made an occasion of constant fear of upsetting, or a general wreck. But as the day dawned the rain ceased, the clouds cleared away, and the warm sun revived the cheerful aspect of nature. They soon came in sight of Milkova, the largest native village of the peninsula. A signal-gun brought the whole population to the shore. As they were landing a dozen rusty flint-lock guns continued the salute. The town had been apprised of their

coming by a courier from their last stopping-place
and so were ready to do them honor.   As the set
tlement was a short distance from the beach
horses were in readiness on which to mount the
explorers.   The saddles were high wooden frames,
with stirrups about six inches long.   Three or
four stout natives seized an explorer, and with
much more hearty good-will than gentleness lifted
him into a saddle.   Thus mounted, with chin and
knees in close connection, our friends started for
the village, with four or five of the "city fathers"
walking, with uncovered heads, as guards on each
side, while a long procession of men, women, and
children followed reverently in procession.   Those
nearest the horses punched them with sticks, to
inspire in them an activity suited to the greatness
of the occasion and the august personages which
they bore.   As they entered the town the spectators in the door-ways and on the streets bowed
with uncovered heads, and the simultaneous howl
of three hundred wolfish dogs added their assurance of respect.

The cavalcade stopped at the largest and best-
looking house, and, in spite of protestations of
surprise and indignation, the "fathers" laid hold
of and lifted the strangers from their saddles, and
helped them into a room, furnished and made
ready with the dainties of the season.   But, before eating, the major commanded the head man
—the mayor of the city—to come into his presence, and requested an explanation of these extraordinary, well-intended, but annoying atten-

tions. His honor came with uncovered head, low
bows, and trembling deference. A long conversation ensued, and, as little by little the truth un-
folded, the major's face relaxed its severity of
expression until humorous smiles were succeeded
by the most violent and uncontrolled laughter, at
which all laughed, though the occasion of it was
yet a mystery to his companions. When self-
possession was restored, the following statement
was made: The courier, sent by the governor of
their commercial sea-port, bore a letter to this
head man, in which the names and occupations
of our party were written. Now, when his honor,
who could read some, though not critically, read,
"Kennan, telegraphist and *operator*," his learning
was subjected to a severe strain. On the word
"telegraphist," he was "dead beat." But "operator," though not *imperator*—that is, emperor—had
an awfully august sound. If the coming stranger
was not the Czar himself, he must be the next
man to him. With this astounding news he elec-
trified all Milkova. Hence the town had been in
an agony of solicitude to show their loyalty, and
hence the salutes, the cavalcade and its honora-
ble escort, the procession, and the elaborate entertainment.

The revelation of the facts seems to have made
no change in the attentions of the people, for after
the feast our explorers re-embarked with the most
flattering attentions.

CHAPTER X.

UP A MOUNTAIN RAVINE.

WE have stated that the Kamchatka River, on which our voyagers were floating, ran nearly north for a long distance, near the foot of the great mountain range. At a point about midway of the length of the peninsula it turns east, and goes into Bering Sea. Just at this bend the Yolofka River, flowing from the west through a mountain pass of the same name, enters the Kamchatka. Not far from this junction the native town of Kloochay is situated. After a few days pleasant floating on the raft, through flowery and fertile meadows, and at other times passing under beautiful archways of overhanging trees, golden and scarlet with autumn foliage, always kindly entertained at the villages, and never for once attacked by ferocious bears, they landed at Kloochay on the fifteenth of September, just eleven days from Petropavlosk.

We must pause a moment here to view the magnificent scenery. Near us is a fertile plain, through which the river runs. From the plain rises several volcanic peaks, the highest of which, and the loftiest in all this northern region, is the Kloochefskoi. The explorers had seen its snowy summit when seventy-five miles at sea, and heard its rumbling, internal fires sixty miles away. A Russian officer estimates its height at sixteen thousand five hundred feet. For more than two centuries there have been, with but brief intervals, fire and smoke issuing from its crater. The winter snows of the vicinity are so covered with ashes that sledging is prevented for twenty miles around The natives speak of a terrific eruption which occurred in the memory of their fathers. One clear, dark, winter night the people were startled from their sleep by mighty thunderings. The earth shook, and the volcano uttered its voice. Far up the clear, cold winter sky lurid fires were blazing in heavy columns, surmounted by mingled smoke and flame. With loud rumblings, which reverberated from distant mountain-tops, the molten lava began to pour down the snow-covered sides of the volcano, its fiery streams illuminating the whole country for twenty-five miles around. On came this flood of flame until the upper half of the mountain glowed like a furnace. The simple natives, though awe-struck, were not frightened, and none thought of fleeing. They had heard neither of Herculaneum nor Pompeii, and they reasoned that where their fathers, for more than a hundred years had dwelt safely, they would not be destroyed. And their confidence was rewarded by their escape from injury. Yet to intimate what it could do but for the restraining Hand, the volcano, in the spiteful sputterings of its wrath, scattered its ashes, more than an inch thick, over the country for two hundred miles.

At the house at which the travelers were entertained in Kloochay were many pleasant prompters
to thoughts of their own far-away homes. Table-
cloths of American make covered the tables; pots
of flowers stood in the curtained windows; and
pictorial sketches of Virginian life embellished the
back of one of the doors.

The explorers now abandoned their rafts for
dug-outs—native canoes made of clumsily-exca-
vated logs, and not remarkable for either safety or
speed. In these they began the ascent of the
Yolofka River, the canoe men with long poles
setting them slowly against the stream. In this
way they ascended to the village of Yolofka, at
the head of canoe navigation. Here they found
in readiness ten horses which had been sent forward by land from Kloochay. Freight and men
being packed or mounted on these, they commenced climbing up the mountain pass. The
romance of Kamchatkan traveling began from this
point, to give place to intervals of rough matters
of fact. The trail was only a foot-path ten inches
wide, following the edge of the bed of a swollen
mountain torrent. It was, of course, winding,
rocky, slippery, here interrupted by fallen trees
and there by tangled thickets of trailing pines;
sometimes it ran along the narrow ledges of rocks
scarcely affording room for the cautious steps of
the horses. The pack-horses rolled down steep
banks, tore their loads off under limbs of trees,
and cut their legs among sharp, volcanic rocks.
Many times they crossed the stream, which was

occasionally done by desperate and dangerous leaps.

Kennan had a fearful adventure in attempting one of these feats of horsemanship. He was thrown violently from the saddle, his left foot being held firmly in the small iron stirrup. His horse landed in the stream, scrambled up the other side, and started in a frightened gallop up the ravine, dragging his master by one leg. He remembered trying to protect his head from the rocks by raising himself upon his elbows, and of receiving at the same time a blow in the side from the heels of his horse. When he next looked out upon his situation he was lying upon the ground, his foot in the iron of the broken stirrup, and his horse far up the ravine. But for the breaking of the stirrup his brains must have been dashed out. He was faint and badly bruised, but no bones were broken.

To add to the discomforts of this mountain journey, a cold misty rain wet and chilled horses and men.

Courageously braving all obstacles, the party, as the night was setting in, attended by a storm of half-frozen rain, reached the table-land of the summit. This was covered with a thick moss, eighteen inches deep, which held water like a sponge. Wading through this for several miles, they reached a poor dilapidated log-hut, whose sides and top had been banked with moss-covered earth No hospitable natives met them to bid them welcome to a warm fire and good tea. One

side of the hut had been torn down by storm
bound travelers, and in part burned; Vushine
commenced at once to make a rousing fire of what
remained, and soon had tea ready. Supper eaten,
and clothes warmed if not dried, put our weary
men in good spirits, and they spread their rubber
blankets on the muddy earth, rolled themselves
in fur, and lay down, and soon fell asleep. About
midnight they awoke. The fire was reduced to
a few smoking brands; the wind drove the rain
through the crevices which dripped in dirty
streams upon their beards and faces. They had
been literally sleeping in a mud puddle with
muddy water poured over them. They rose and
pitched their tent on the spongy moss outside,
preferring water to mud. They had only begun
to sleep in their new quarters when the tent blew
over. They repitched it, lay some heavy logs on
its lower edge from the old hut, then managed to
sleep until day-break.

They were a weary, forlorn-looking party as they
plodded on after breakfast over the table-land.
After awhile the clouds parted just long enough
for them to glance at the magnificent scenery of
their position. On the west was the Ochotsk Sea;
far away to the east was the Pacific Ocean nar-
rowing into the Bering Sea. Here and there were
lofty peaks of volcanic mountains, over which
hung dark fire-lighted clouds, and occasionally
they caught a glimpse through the mists of the
river which flowed through the mountain pass and
over the plains to the sea.

The descent from this table-land was at first rough and perilous, but they camped at night among berry bushes and beds of grass. The following noon they mounted fresh horses which had been sent to meet them by the head-man of the nearest village, who had been notified by a courier of their coming.

They now began to feel something of the pleasure with which they commenced the ascent on the other side of the mountain. They wound along a grassy plain, skirted by a forest, and were chatting freely, or leisurely admiring the scenery, when the suppressed shout of "A bear! a bear!" was passed along the line. Bruin was busy getting an honest meal of blueberries, and did not notice our party. Four men—the major, Kennan and two natives—were detailed to secure him for supper. Armed to the teeth with rifles, pistols, knives, and axes, they crept cautiously around through the timber until they were directly in front of their victim, and waited his approach. Nearer and nearer he came, as innocent of the danger hidden behind the logs and bushes as a child watched by a tiger. Choosing their time, the natives with their heavy guns at rest in the fork of a stick thrust into the ground for that purpose, devoutly crossed themselves, shut their eyes, and fired. At nearly the same moment the two American rifles cracked, and their balls whizzed. Poor, unsuspecting, innocent bear, to be thus assailed on his own soil by strangers whom he had never wronged! It seemed fair, then, that, instead of dropping down dead, or surrendering to be killed, skinned, and eaten, he should show his teeth and rush furiously at his assailants. This was to them an unexpected change of the programme, and the bear was for the moment master of the situation. But a pistol shot from the major at a very short range caused him to pause, and then to rush past them within ten feet of the muzzles of their empty guns, and disappear in the forest. A careful examination of his track and the bushes through which he hurried failed to reveal bloody marks. It was not likely, then, that if followed he would be found fainting or fallen in the way. Bear steak was not a pleasant topic of discussion that evening.

The next day they struck a village on the Tigel River which flowed to the sea, exchanged their horses for rafts, and floated the following night to Tigel, at its mouth.

Our explorers were now on the eastern shore of the Ochotsk Sea, at the second most important trading-post of Kamchatka.

CHAPTER XI.

A FEARFUL RIDE.

OUR travelers rested a few days at Tigel. They were aiming at Geezhega at the northern extremity of the Ochotsk Sea as the point from which they would make a new departure, they hoped, under favoring circumstances. They proposed to keep as near the shore as possible, but, as we shall see, they had proposed to themselves a journey beset with many difficulties. They, therefore, purchased and packed away in skin boxes a good supply of fur clothing; a large stock of provisions was secured; stores of trading goods, and such articles as experience had suggested to make the journey comfortable, were provided. Thus prepared they left Tigel, September twenty-seventh, accompanied by twelve men and fourteen horses obtained at that place. In six days, with the occurrence of no special incident, they arrived at Lesnoi, the last native village of Kamchatka. They were yet two hundred miles from Geezhega. Just before them the mountain range which they had crossed, turned into the sea. Over its volcanic ridges, broken into deep chasms, and overshadowed by lofty snow-capped peaks, they were obliged to climb before reaching the vast steppe—the arctic prairie—which lay beyond. They hoped to pass

the mountain with horses before the full force of
its winter storms should sweep over it, and to
travel *somehow* the steppe before it should be so
frozen as to require dog-sledging. The difficulty
of journeying on this great plain at this time will
be understood if the reader bears in mind that instead of being a hard soil, like our western prairies,
it is covered two feet deep with a rank growth of
soft, spongy, arctic moss, filled with water, with
here and there little hillocks of blueberry and
other bushes. During the summer and fall months
this moss yields to the feet of man and beast, and
makes traveling over it a continual wallowing,
horses going to their knees at every step. It
seemed, therefore, most fitting for the explorers
to wait at Lesnoi until the mountains and steppe
could be passed on dog-sledges. But the major
had reason to think that the party of which we
have spoken, to be sent up Bering Strait, and
landed on the eastern shore of Siberia to co-operate with him, might be waiting at the assigned
point of meeting. So he was determined to push
on at all risks.

The men of Lesnoi declared the journey over
the mountains just at this time impossible. The
snow, they said, had already began to fall on the
highest portions of the pass, and they were un-
willing to risk their horses, to say nothing of their
own lives. But the major was a man in authority,
and he made them very distinctly understand this
fact. He declared the journey could and should
be made, and they had nothing further to do in

the matter, except to get ready for an immediate start. Thus commanded, they began to talk the matter over aside among themselves, and the result of their earnest discussions was that the journey might possibly be made with lightly-laden horses, all the heavy baggage being left behind. Into this arrangement the major, after mature consideration, consented to enter. He had caused a whale-boat to be brought to Lesnoi from Tigel by native rowers, for an emergency. So he concluded to divide his small force into two parties. One party was to go over the mountains with unloaded horses, and the other around them in the whale-boat, which was to carry the heavy baggage. Just beyond the principal ridge a river called the Samanka entered the sea. At its mouth the two parties were to meet. As the mountain-pass was supposed to go near the shore, and as the whale-boat was thought to be able to keep near the land, signals were agreed upon by which they could communicate with each other.

Early in the morning of October fourth the major and Dodd embarked on board of the whale-boat, to which was attached a seal-skin canoe Kennan bid them good-bye at the beach, and started for the mountains, his command consisting of Vushine, a Cossack guide, and six natives. They took with them twenty unloaded horses, galloped briskly across the plain, up the pass, and were soon buried in the wilderness. The road, instead of running within sight of the sea, turned away from it, and into the dark recesses of alter-

8

nating crags and valleys. The party camped early, and Kennan climbed the nearest hill after supper to get a glimpse of the sea, but he could see only other peaks arise, some of which were covered with snow.

The camp-fire that night was dull, or seemed so to the captain, without his lively, story-telling companion, Dodd.

The next day they started early up a narrow, tortuous valley, overshadowed by volcanic peaks, and crossed now and then by deep, narrow creeks, which were succeeded by spongy swamps of moss. Just after a noonday lunch they started off in a rain-storm, the valley contracting to a deep, dark gorge, and the traveling becoming worse every moment. Through this gorge a mountain torrent poured its noisy waters in mimic Niagaras and magnificent cascades. The guide dismounted, and led the way along a trail so narrow and rocky that a goat could hardly keep his footing. Once a part of the ledge along which the party were cautiously moving gave way under the feet of Kennan's horse, and horse and rider descended with the sliding moss into the torrent. He had learned better than to have his feet in the stirrups, so he slipped off on the cliff side, and came down uppermost, though he had to "pick himself up" in a lively manner to get out of the way of the hoofs of his horse, as he struggled to regain his feet. The horse was bruised and cut, but not seriously hurt, and Kennan waded along the tor-rent, leading him back to the path, and with diffi-

Part of the Ledge gives Way.

culty mounted, with dripping clothes and somewhat shaken nerves.

As the night was setting in the party came to a
sudden halt. A mountain ran directly across
the valley, and seemed to forbid further advance
in that direction. Kennan cast an inquiring glance
at the guide, who pointed up the range and said
the road lay in that direction. The ascent was
covered, half-way up, with a forest of birch, succeeded by creeping evergreens, and then by black,
volcanic rocks high over all. Men and beasts
were too weary to attempt climbing that night, so
they camped at once. Vushine soon had a
cheerful fire and refreshing tea. Kennan then
crept into his bear-skin bag, feet first, and slept
well.

The morning opened with a fearful snow-storm,
which, before the party could start, covered the
ground several inches deep in the valley, and of
course must be much deeper on the mountain.
It seemed impossible to go on, but to return
might put in peril the object of the whole expedition : so the command was given to attempt the
ascent.

When fairly out of the shelter of the valley they
were assailed by a fierce storm of wind, bringing
clouds of snow which shut out every object except
those within a few feet. They dismounted and
waded through the soft, deep drifts, dragging
their horses after them. The sharp stones beneath the snow cut their seal-skin boots, yet they
dragged wearily upward, resting at times, and then

starting again, until they reached what seemed to
be the crest of the mountain, about two thousand
feet above the sea.

Here they were met by clouds of stinging snow-
flakes driven by a tornado of wind. Their wet
clothes froze into a crackling armor of ice, and
icicles hung from the visors of their caps. Half-
blinded, and shivering with cold, they descended
into a valley, then up over storm-beaten peaks
higher than before, and round craggy points, until
the points of the compass were lost and the whole
party was utterly bewildered. Kennan had observed for some time that the guide talked aside,
and anxiously, with the Kamchadals. At last he
came to the captain, and confessed in a desponding
tone that he was lost.

For two hours longer they stumbled blindly
about, getting more and more into the wilderness
of steep mountains and deep valleys. It was plain
something must be done. Kennan told the guide
he would lead, and, taking out his pocket-compass,
showed him the direction of the sea, bid him follow as the needle pointed, until they came out
somewhere. He looked in stupid wonder at the
little brass box, and exclaimed despairingly: "O,
sir, how does the compáss know any thing about
these mountains? The compáss has never been
over this road before. I have traveled here all
my life, and, God forgive me, I don't know where
the sea is!"

The guide was assured that the compáss was
wise in finding the sea in a storm. He refused to

follow its leadings, for surely a little box could not know better than an experienced guide.

The wind blew so fiercely that Kennan's horse refused to face it, and, dismounting, he led him, compass in hand, toward the sea. Vushine followed, and finally the guide and the rest of the company fell into line. Slowly, chilled, and wading knee-deep in snow, they pushed on, until in the middle of the afternoon they came suddenly out upon a storm-swept precipice. Down its rugged front, a hundred and fifty feet, the sea was thundering against its base with its mighty waves.

The guide looked up and down the coast for some familiar landmark, and when assured that he knew where he was, asked to see the "*compass.*" Kennan unscrewed the cover, and showed him the blue, quivering needle still pointing north. He examined it with curiosity and awe. He said it was truly "very wise," and asked if it always pointed to the sea? The captain tried to explain, but he walked away greatly puzzled with the question how a little brass box could find the sea in a country where it had never been before.

Our party pushed on toward the north during the afternoon, crossing ridges and plunging into valleys, until, just after dark, they brought up in a valley at the mouth of the Samanka River. Here there was no snow, but it was raining freely. There was no whale-boat party to be found, and no signs that any had been in the vicinity. They pitched their tent, made a great fire, eat supper, crept into bear-skin bags, and slept as only weary men can sleep. Their clothes had been wet or frozen forty-eight hours, and they had been in the saddle or wading afoot without warm food for fourteen hours.

The morning came—a Saturday morning—but it brought neither sight nor sound which afforded encouragement to our storm-bound adventurers The sea roared and the waves lifted up their voice as if deriding their condition. The whale-boat, if yet afloat, must surely go down in such a storm, or be dashed to pieces against the rocky shore. The rain yet descended in floods in the valley, and the snow clouds hung heavy over the mountains. The men kept closely as possible within their sheltering tents, hoping for some abatement of the storm, and some way of escape not now apparent. But their circumstances became suddenly more desperate. Vushine, the steward and cook, came to the captain with a rueful face, and announced that there was nothing in the camp to eat. He had confidently expected to find the whale-boat at the mouth of the river, and had taken only three days' provisions. He had not mentioned this until all hope of seeing the boat was given up. What could be done? Could a three days' return journey across the mountains, now covered with a deeper snow, be made without food for men or beast? This seemed the only resort, and orders were given for an early start in the morning.

When the morning came, and the desperate adventure was about to commence, the guide was

noticed to be in earnest consultation with his
comrades, and soon proposed to Kennan another
route of escape.   The beach, he said, ran along at
the foot of the cliff for thirty miles toward Lesnoi,
and then opened into a valley within a day's ride
of that place.   The cliff had a nearly perpendicular face toward the sea of from one to two hundred
feet, but the ebbing tide would leave a little strip
of the beach bare.   Now, said the guide, if we
can reach the ravine while the beach is bare, in a
little less than five hours' time, we shall avoid the
snowy mountains.

Kennan was not prepared for a proposal so bold
and dashing from the timid guide, and immediately accepted it.   The risk would be no greater
than in the mountain journey, and if it succeeded
would save a day's time to a starving party.   To
be sure, a thirty miles' gallop against the tide
would be a fearful one; but then their condition
was a desperate one any way.   If caught by the
sea, which was ten feet deep at the foot of the
cliff at high water, they might possibly escape by
abandoning the horses, and scrambling into some
crevice, or, if horses and men were swept away
like corks, it would be no worse than freezing or
starving in the mountain.

The tide had only begun to ebb, so there were
three hours before starting.   This time the natives
improved by sacrificing a dog to appease the an-
ger of the evil spirit in charge of this dreary region.   They cut the victim open with their knives,
threw his entrails to the four points of the com-

pass, and hung his lean body by the hind legs to a pole set in the ground. The storm, however, continued to rage.

At ten o'clock they mounted in hot haste, and started at a gallop. The beach was strewn with a drift of sea-weed, and obstructed in places by masses of rocks which had been throwns down from the cliff; yet they dashed forward, seldom drawing a rein on the best speed of the horses.

They thus made eighteen miles in good time, and without a special incident. Suddenly Vushine shouted, "A bear! a bear!" and reined in his horse so abruptly as to nearly throw the rider over his head. A quarter of a mile ahead what seemed to be two bears were slowly trudging along directly toward our party. Now, it was plain that if bears were to dispute the narrow pathway of the beach, it would occasion a fight, the time for which neither party could afford to spend, to say nothing of the chances of war, as the safety of all from being drowned depended upon flight. Kennan and Vushine put fresh balls into their guns, and reserved ones in their pockets, and crept cautiously near the cliff to secure a stealthy shot. They were nearly within range, and the balls in a moment more would have gone whizzing to their mark, when Vushine straightened up, and shouted, "They are no bears; they are people."

Immediately there came plainly in sight from a partial shelter of the rock two Kamchadals, dressed in fur, and gesticlating violently to Kennan not to shoot, waving at the same time something

white as a flag of truce. One of them, whom Kennan recognized as a native from Lesnoi, came forward, and handed him a wet, dirty piece of paper,
making as he did so a low bow. They were messengers from the major. The whale-boat party
were then safe. The note read as follows:

"Sea-shore, ten miles from Lesnoi, Octobeı 4.
Driven ashore by the storm. Hurry back as fast
as possible. ABASA."

These messengers left Lesnoi only a day later
than the Kennan party, but had been detained by
the storm. Finding it impossible to cross the
mountains, they had abandoned their horses, and
were attempting the rest of the journey on foot
by the beach. They did not expect to make it in
one tide, but purposed to find a hiding-place in
some crevice of the cliff above high-water mark
and wait for the ebb.

Our party could wait for no further explana-
tions. There were twelve miles to be made with
tired horses and saddle-weary men in a little over
an hour. "Ride! ride!" was the thrilling cry
which passed along the line, and the situation became more exciting every moment. At the end of
every projecting bluff the water was higher and
higher, and in many places it already touched the
cliff, with spray and foam. In twenty minutes
more the beach would be impassable. The horses
held out nobly, as if knowing that their own lives
as well as those of their masters depended upon

the success of the race.   Only one more project‑
ing bluff to pass !   Past this they galloped through
several feet of water.   In five minutes more they
reined up in the ravine.   The tide was beaten by
ten minutes !   The mountains had been " turned,"
and the way to Lesnoi was comparatively easy.
The messengers from the major returned with
them on two of their unloaded horses, but, as they
had exhausted their supply of food, the party were
yet fasting.

Though the danger from the tide was escaped,
traveling in the ravine was no pastime.   It was
obstructed by massive rocks, through which they
cautiously picked their way, and entangled by
trailing pines and dense thickets of alders, through
which they were obliged to cut their way with
axes.

They camped one more night, and rode without
food all the next day.   Just after dark they heard
the welcome howling of the Lesnoi dogs, and in
twenty minutes after Kennan dashed up to the
little log hut of its chief man, and burst in upon
the major and Dodd as they sat at supper.

CHAPTER XII.

AMONG THE REINDEER KORAKS.

MAJOR ABASA was immediately prostrated by a rheumatic fever. His anxiety and suffering in a five days' detention in camp on the storm-beaten shore was too much for him. Dodd and the Cossack Mereneff were sent to Tigel for a Russian physician, while Kennan and Vushine took care of their sick commander.

The passing of the mountains now before the season of dog-sledging was, of course, impossible. Not only were the men exhausted, but nearly every horse of the vicinity was for a time disabled. So the explorers had only to take a new lesson in waiting.

Kennan's duty as nurse, while Dodd was gone, required almost constant confinement, and the hours dragged heavily away. During the day he read much in the Bible by the dim light which struggled through a window of dried fish-skins. During the evenings he sat on a log in the little kitchen of the hut, which was lighted by a wick of moss in a tin cup filled with seal oil. Here he listened to the music of the natives, which was always plaintive, and sometimes drew tears in its expressions of deep sorrow. They have no war songs, like our Indians, and none expressing deeds of heroic daring. They, however, told stories, which deeply interested the strangers, of wild adventures in the mountains. Occasionally, when the weather was favorable, Kennan went out with his gun in search of game. He does not hint that he captured any bears; plainly, killing bears was not in the line of our explorers. He did, however, bring in a wild deer, shot on the mountains, and some wild fowls.

On the twentieth of October the physician arrived from Tigel, and at once bled, blistered, and steamed the major in the most thorough manner. He improved rapidly under this rough and unpromising treatment.

During all this stay at Lesnoi, nothing but the most unselfish kindness was received by the strangers at the hands of the natives. At one time the major chanced to express a desire for some milk. The chief man of the place replied that he would try to obtain some for him, but did not state the fact that there was not a cow in the place. A man was at once sent to the nearest settlement where a cow could be found, and the major had milk that night in his tea. From this time, while the explorers stayed, more than a month, they had a bottle of fresh milk every day, for which a man was sent twenty miles. No reward was asked nor seemed to be expected. The act was a characteristic kindness.

On the twenty-eighth Dodd and the Cossack had returned from Tigel with a fresh supply of provisions. Dogs and dog-sledges had been gath-

ered from all the immediate region. Great dil·
igence had been used at Lenoi in making bear-
skin sleeping bags, and in preparing fur garments
in general. The major declared himself "all
right," and orders were issued for an immediate
start for another effort to cross the mountains.

On the first of November a train of sixteen
sledges, eighteen men, two hundred dogs, and forty days' provisions, started for the great arctic
prairie beyond the mountains—the land of the
wild, wandering Koraks.

The snow was in good condition for sledging,
and so were the dogs. With a yelp and a bound
they whirled the travelers along through the valleys, over the mountains, and across the frozen
rivers, and, on the setting in of twilight of the
third day, our party looked from the top of the
last mountain ridge, down two thousand feet upon
a dreary expanse of snow, bounded only by the
distant horizon.

Resting awhile, they were able to feel more
deeply the wild sublimity of their situation. A
faint, pale light of the sun, already far out of sight,
lingered upon the highest peaks; a cold wind
from the sea swept over the encampment and
wailed through the pines; and the howling of two
hundred wolfish dogs echoed from the silent
depths of the mountains.

The moon was just lighting up the mountain
tops as the men roused the dogs, and the whole
train plunged into a dark ravine which led downward to the steppe. The light of the moon did

not penetrate into its depth, and masses of rocks
and clumps of trees were hidden along the path;
yet the dogs leaped recklessly down in spite of the
shouts of their masters to check them, and of the
stout, iron-pointed spears which they thrust into
the snow in front of the sledges between the runners. The spears, plowing through the hard crust,
raised a cloud of snow, which, as the rocks and
trees flew swiftly past, gave the train an appearance of being hurled with an avalanche into certain ruin below. But the practiced drivers were
masters of the situation. With steady nerves and
skillful hands they gradually checked the dogs
and the sledges, and in a marvelously short time
came out safely in the moonlight on the hard
snow of the broad plain.

Half an hour's travel brought the company to
a point where it was thought a Korak encampment would be found. But no signs of tents or
reindeer could be seen. While the guides were
deliberating, the leading dogs pricked up their
ears, snuffed the wind vigorously, and turned off
at right angles toward the dark outlines of a low
hill which had not before been noticed. With a
short yelp, and with intense excitement, they sped
over the snow like the wind. They defied all discipline, for a fresh scent of a herd of reindeer had
come on the breeze down from the hill. Up the
acclivity and down the steep they rushed, like the
swine of old when the devils were in them. From
the brow of the hill, in the clear moonlight, were
seen the conical tents of the Koraks, around

which were four thousand reindeer. In spite of
the Korak sentinels, and in spite of the threats
and fierce denunciations of their drivers, and in
spite, too, of the sledges which the spears caused
to drag heavily through the crusted snow, the
dogs dashed at the deer. The whole herd wav-
ered for a moment, and then broke into a wild
stampede, with the Korak drivers and sentinels
and two hundred fierce dogs at their heels. The
beat of thousands of hoofs upon the hard snow,
the clattering of antlers as they dashed together,
the hoarse bark of the frightened deer, the quick
penetrating yelp of the dogs, all mingling with the
vociferous shouts of the men, died away in the distance, and left the camp in comparative silence.

Kennan, who had not joined in the pursuit, improved the quiet by looking around. It was not
long, however, before the dogs of our party came
limping back, looking sullen and crest-fallen.
They had found that chasing reindeer, and drawing at the same time sledges which were made
into ice-plows by the stout spears thrust into the
frozen snow in front of them, was a little too much
for their strength, if not for their zeal. Besides,
the Koraks who joined in the pursuit, *lassoed* the
dogs as our Indians do their wild horses. So,
upon the whole, the dogs had the worst of it, and
the reindeer were soon brought back to their old
position.

The Koraks now crowded curiously about the
strangers, inquiring through their interpreter who
they were and what they wanted ; and at the same

time our party as curiously observed them. The Koraks did, indeed, make a very impressive group, as the clear moonlight shone upon their swarthy faces, high cheek bones, coarse and long black hair, bold and watchful eyes, and compact frames. If in some respects they resembled our American Indians, the likeness did not go far. Their mild disposition was placed beyond a doubt by the spirit with which they received the manner in which our explorers were introduced to them. Our Indians, on a like occasion, would have flourished their knives and tomahawks, and raised a terrific warwhoop. The Koraks treated it as a passing incident, as in fact it was, though causing them great trouble, and probably some loss.

The encampment consisted of four large cone-shaped tents, the frames of which were made of poles, over which reindeer skins were drawn. These were fastened firmly in their places by cords made of walrus hide. Dog-sledges of various sizes and patterns were scattered about on the snow, and several hundred pack-saddles for reindeer were piled in an orderly manner near the largest tent. While the strangers were going over the encampment to see the sights they were followed by fifteen or twenty of the Koraks as a sort of body-guard intent on observing their visitors. Both having, in part at least, satisfied their curiosity, a tall native stepped forward, and led the way to one of the tents, and, pointing to the dark hole, bid his guests enter.

Vushine, having on former occasions shown

himself expert in creeping through small holes,
made the first attempt to enter. It being rather
a tight squeeze, Dodd gave his feet as he entered a
vigorous push. Kennan followed, but both came
out much quicker than they entered, Vushine's
heels hastening Kennan's backward movement by
a rousing blow in his face.

"What's the matter, Vushine?" exclaimed
Dodd. "You back out as if the evil spirit was
after you!"

"Well," said Vushine, greatly excited, "you
don't suppose I am going to stay in that hole to
be eaten up by Korak dogs, do you? If I was
foolish enough to go in, I've got sense enough to
know when to come out. I don't believe the
hole leads anywhere, anyhow. Besides, it's full of
dogs."

The Korak guide seemed to enjoy the joke on
Vushine, but stooped down, drove out a pack of
savage-looking dogs, and lifted up an inner curtain, letting a red light stream through the dismal
passage. He then led the way on his hands and
knees, a distance of ten feet, and all entered the
large open circle of the interior of the tent.

A crackling fire of pine boughs threw a lurid
light over the blackened skins of the roof, and the
swarthy, tattooed faces of the women and children
who squatted around. A pot hung over the blaze
in which supper was cooking. Two bare-armed
women squatted near it, stirring the stew with a
big stick, and then with the same stick rapping
over the head a troop of snarling dogs which vent-

9

ured too near. The smoke from the fire hung in
a dense cloud only about five feet from the ground,
filling all the upper regions of the tent, and working its way slowly through the crevices at the top
into the open air. Sitting and lying down were
the only positions in which there was a tolerable
escape from it. Besides, the tent, or *yourt*, as the
natives call it, was seldom warmer than twenty
degrees below zero. So to escape smoke and cold
little rooms called *pologs* are built around the
inner circumference of the yourt. These are
nearly air-tight, eight feet square on the ground,
and four high. They are made of the heaviest
furs sewn together, and warmed and lighted by a
burning wick of moss floating in a dish of seal oil
The major hired the exclusive use of one of these,
and into it our explorers moved while Vushine
was preparing their supper. The crowd of natives
which had watched their every motion, not being
able to enter, poked their ugly looking, shaven
heads under the skin curtain and continued their
stare. Dodd suggested a vigorous smoking by all
hands. Lucifer matches were instantly struck to
light their pipes. Their sharp report and sudden
burst of flame caused every head to disappear,
and excited a burst of surprise outside, followed
by a confused jabbering. The heads soon returned, and the smoking was watched with great
glaring eyes. Dodd, who was never at loss for some
comical expedient, gave a sneeze as near like the
sudden puff of a steam-engine as possible. Every
head disappeared, and expressions of amazement

followed. But nothing could long keep the glaring eyes from under the curtain.

Tired of this fun, and hungry with a long and weary journey, the explorers were glad when Vushine announced supper. He had made a table of a little pine box which contained the telegraph instruments. On this he had placed some hard bread, slices of raw bacon, and tumblers of hot tea. These were the luxuries of civilization. Beside them, on the ground, in a wooden trough and a bowl of like material, were the luxuries of Korak hospitality. Good appetites and good manners both forbade slighting the unknown articles. Dodd tasted the contents of the trough daintily, pioneering for the company.

" What does it taste like ? " inquired Kennan.

" Like the mud pies of infancy," replied Dodd, with a grimace. " A little salt, pepper, and butter, and a good deal of meat and flour, with a few vegetables, would certainly improve it. It aint bad, though, as it is," he added, tasting it again.

The last remark induced a general tasting. A good appetite made it very passable. It proved to be "*manyalla,*" made of clotted blood, tallow, and half-digested moss taken from the stomach of the reindeer. These are boiled together, with a few handfuls of dried grass, and then the whole is molded into small loaves, and frozen for future use. It is the Korak bread.

After supper the weary explorers crept into their hired polog and slept.

CHAPTER XIII.

A CURIOUS MARRIAGE CEREMONY.

IN good season in the morning the major and his party were astir. Calling the Korak chief, which means with them the man who owns the greatest number of deer, he made arrangements for the journey to the next encampment, forty miles north.

Orders were at once given by the chief for the preparation of the sledges, and the capture of twenty tame reindeer. These tame reindeer differed from the wild ones only in having been taught to wear a single harness and draw a sledge. They are distinguished from the great herd with which they feed by having their ears slit and one antler chopped off; the latter cruel operation is performed so that when two are harnessed together there may be no clashing of horns.

The way the twenty tame animals, wanted for the journey, were separated from the thousands among which they were scattered, was quite ingenious. Twelve men, lassoes in hand, formed a narrow lane by standing six on a side, a few feet apart. Twenty other men took a seal-skin line two or three hundred yards long, and encircled a portion of the herd. With shouts and waving lassoes they drove them through the gauntlet. They reared and plunged, but dared not attempt to break through the line held firmly in the hands of the men, making thus a cord fence. When a reindeer with a slit ear passed through, a lasso uncoiled in air, and the noose fell upon his antler, and he was led away to the sledge.

The harness consists of a headstall, a collar to which a trace is attached, which passes between the fore-legs, and a rein adjusted to a stud in the headstall. They were harnessed to the sledges in pairs, and the caravan was soon ready. Our explorers bid their Lesnoi friends good-bye, seated themselves on the sledges, drew snugly about them their furs, and, at the word " go " from the chief, dashed away over the snowy desert.

We are not to imagine them gliding along behind a swift-footed animal, whose graceful motion and gentle spirit reminds them of reindeer and Laplander in the picture of the school-book of our boyhood. They found their reindeer spare, awkward, and heavy-footed. The frost accumulated in their nostrils, and they bowed their heads and panted, as if traveling was a burden.

At two o'clock they had made one half of their journey, so they stopped to lunch and let the deer feed. If the reindeer is not handsome nor very nimble, he is certainly one of the most useful animals. Our party had brought no grain for their teams. As soon as unharnessed they began to paw up the snow until they uncovered the moss which lay beneath. On this they made their meal, and then started refreshed.

The cold was intense. The moon arose and
lighted. up the seemingly boundless extent of
sparkling snow. The hours wore slowly away,
and so did the distance, as the travelers rode, or
walked, impatiently inquiring at short intervals if
they were not "almost there." About six in the
morning the tents of the second Korak encampment came in sight, and they were soon *squatting*
by the comfortable fire, and in the uncomfortable
smoke and filth of one of its interior circles.

Just as the strangers were sipping their hot tea
a startling form entered through the dark passage-
way, and stood suddenly before them. It was
that of a Korak in a flaming military coat of scarlet cloth, with blue facings and brass buttons.
Long festoons of gold cord hung across his breast.
At his side hung an elegant silver-hilted sword in
an embossed scabbard. From his ears hung long
strings of small colored beads. He was every
inch a repulsive savage except in his coat and
sword. To the major's questions concerning his
name, business, and place of abode he only made
a low bow. The Cossack interpreter was called,
and under his questioning the mystery was soon
explained. The Korak, when he understood the
inquiries, left the tent, and soon returned with a
paper carefully preserved between two thin boards
tied together by a seal-skin cord. This explained
all. It stated that the coat and sword were presented by the Russian Government to the present
owner's father for reindeer given to starving Russians. The son was, therefore, justly proud of

these mementoes of his father's good deeds, and, as soon as he had heard of the coming of the distinguished strangers, he had hastened to put them on, and to present himself in them. Having done this, his errand was done and he retired.

The next day our party rode over the "dead sea of snow" from early morning to four hours after dark, and reached the third encampment. They entered the largest tent, and found it crowded with men and women evidently in a state of pleasant excitement. They were about to seek a more retired and quiet tent, when their interpreter informed them that there was to be a wedding; so, though not bidden, and certainly without wedding garments, but torn and dirty from long and rough journeying, they concluded to stay.

The tent was very large, and its center about the fire was filled with men only, who were devouring reindeer meat, *manyalla*, and other luxuries of the wedding-feast, and warmly discussing, at the same time, some exciting topic. Around the inner circumference of the tent were twenty-six of the fur-skin-curtained rooms—pologs—of which we have spoken. About these the tattooed women crowded.

When the men seemed to have finished their feast, a drum began a slow but loud beat. Suddenly a tall, stern Korak entered with his arms full of willow sprouts and alder branches, and laid them in front of every polog.

"What is that for?" whispered Dodd.

"Wait and you will see," was the reply.

When the sticks were distributed the drum beat
a heavier tone, and the drummer commenced a wild
chant, in which all joined. At this moment the
front curtains of all the pologs were opened, and
the women in squads of two or three took their
stations in the door-ways each armed with one of
the willow or alder switches. The curtain of the
polog near the entrance to the tent now opened,
and a venerable man made his appearance, supposed to be the father of one of the parties, leading a fine-looking young Korak man and the dark-
faced bride. At their coming the drum beat
louder and faster, and the chant rose to a frenzied
wildness, the man in the center of the tent uttering at intervals a shrill cry of excitement. In the
midst of this uproar, at a signal by the native who
had led the couple out, the bride darted into the
first polog, and commenced a rapid flight around
the tent, lifting the curtains which separated the
pologs and passing under. The bridegroom instantly started after her in hot haste. If he caught
her before she had passed through the last—the
twenty-sixth one—she was then and there to be
pronounced his "lawful and wedded wife." If
he failed he must look elsewhere for a wife; or,
having already, as was the Korak law of custom,
served two years his would-be father-in-law for
this chance of catching his daughter, he might
serve him two more years for a second chance.

This being the way affairs stood between the
candidates for marriage, our explorers looked for
fair play in the chance, and no interfering. But,

to their surprise and indignation, though it was, to
be sure, none of their business, the women at the
doors of the pologs hindered the bridegroom in
every possible way. They switched him lustily
with the alder branches and willow sprouts.
They held down the curtain under which he attempted to creep. When he rose to his feet, and
attempted to run, they put out theirs to trip him
up. In the meantime the drum beat, and the
spectators shouted encouragement or derision according to their humor. Of course, before he was
half way around, the fleeing woman had entered
the polog near the tent door.

The game seemed lost, but the ambitious lover,
nothing daunted, persevered, and, though switched,
blindfolded by the curtains which the women skill-
fully threw over his eyes, and tripped up, he at
last reached the last polog, the music ceased, and
the company began to disperse. The ceremony
was over.

"Were they married?" inquired our explorers
of their Cossack interpreter, who had watched the
proceedings with the evident satisfaction of one
who understood the case.

"Why, yes, your honors," was the prompt reply.

"But he did not catch her!"

"O," said the Cossack, with a grin of surprise
at the greenness of the strangers, "she waited for
him in the last polog! If he caught her there, it
was enough." This absurd heathen ceremony
seems to have been invented to give the woman
a chance to break any distasteful arrangement of

selfish parents, or to enable her to escape from
her own pledge.   How far it all is from a sacred
Christian marriage !

When the explorers came out of the tent to take
up their quarters in a smaller, more retired one,
they were surprised to see several Koraks shouting and reeling about in a state of decided intoxication.   They knew that not a drop of intoxicating drink could be found in this part of Kamchatka.
Yet these men were drunk.   There certainly had
been nothing which intoxicates at the wedding
feast.   On inquiring it was ascertained that they
were drunk on toad-stools !   A peculiar kind of
this article, growing in the timbered lands of
Siberia, has long been known to the tribes as producing when eaten an alcoholic effect.   Taken in
large quantities it is a deadly poison.   Taken in
any quantity habitually it soon shatters both mind
and body.   Its sale to the natives has been wisely
prohibited by the Russian Government, yet the
toad-stool dealers in heathendom, like their kindred in sin, the liquor-dealers in Christian lands,
break the law for guilty gain, and drive quite a
large business.   A poor Korak, made desperate
by his fiery appetite, has been known to give twenty dollars' worth of furs for one toad-stool.   At all
times it is an expensive article in its first cost, as
well as final effects, to its poor victims.

The traders, during their encampments, learned
other important facts in reference to these wanderers of the snowy desert.   They had, like all the
arctic tribes we have met, their priests, or *shamans*,

and used the wild, exciting ceremonies such as we have in other chapters described, to learn the mind of the Evil Spirit, the only spiritual being of whom they have any idea. There is one fact told of them in reference to their priests which is not true we think of others having such priests. If at any time they suspect the priest of cheating them, they whip him soundly. If he winces and appears to suffer under the lash like other mortals, he loses his credit and office. No doubt, if they discovered *all* the fraud of these men, the profession would be wiped out of existence.

Besides incantation their false religion has but one other rite. They offer dog sacrifices to appease the wrath of the Evil Spirit. Sometimes twenty dogs are killed and hung up by their hind legs to secure a good catch of fish. To their credit, perhaps, they offer in these sacrifices their best dogs, though one of the explorers at one time suggested that the poorest would do just as well. They caught at the idea, and thought they would try it sometime.

These Koraks have one peculiar superstition. They will never sell a *live* reindeer. You may buy a hundred or a thousand carcases, but never the living animal at any price. The only reason given for this is the exclamation: "Sell living reindeer! that bad—*very* bad!"

With the custom of these northern tribes of killing the sick and aged we shall become acquainted.

CHAPTER XIV.

YANKEE DOG-SLEDGING.

THE explorers arrived at the mouth ot a river
which emptied into an arm of the Ochotsk
Sea near its extreme northern end. They entered
the native village cold, weary, and hungry. The
people of the town, if a small squalid settlement
could be so called, were a dirty, savage looking
set of men and women, more haughty in their
bearing and much less kindly disposed toward the
strangers than any they had yet met. Their
houses were unlike all others. They looked like
huge hour-glasses, large at the bottom and top,
and drawn in at the center. Our friends mounted
to the top on a ladder, and slid down on a pole
through the smoke-hole into the interior. There
was no other door, and no window.

These huts of the settled Koraks are built of
logs of drift-wood picked up on the sea-shore. A
human habitation more uncomfortable could hardly be conceived. Its interior was black with the
smoke with which it is almost always filled. The
fire is made under the hole in the center, upon
flat stones. A great brass kettle is kept hanging
over it, in which they stew their deer meat and
boil their fish. Of course, those sliding down the
pole, being dressed, as all are, in fur, shed a shower

of hairs into the cooking food. This is nothing, however, for this people, and all who sojourn with them learn to regard hairs as a necessary ingredient of all dishes. Occasionally the stew or boil is flavored with dog. For instance, when the snow drifts about the hut so that the pack of hungry dogs climb to the top, and quarrel for the best place at the hole to snuff the savory stew below, one will tumble down into the kettle. In such a case the cook takes him by the back of his neck and throws him out through the hole into a snow-bank to cool, and complacently proceeds to finish cooking, and to serve to the family the improved dish.

Around the interior, on three sides, a platform is constructed, a foot from the ground and six feet wide. On this square fur pologs are made, as in the tents of the wandering Koraks, and in these the inmates try to hide away from the cold and smoke, for rest and sleep.

Our party had never been in so disagreeable a situation. Brutal-looking men, wearing spotted deer-skin clothes, strings of beads from their ears, and heavy knives, two feet long, in sheaths hanging from their belts, crowded the hut they occupied, squatted about them, and stared, with great, wicked eyes, into their faces.

Such was the situation of our explorers when a fine-looking Cossack slid down the pole and presented himself to the major with a low bow, and at the same time handing him a letter. He was a messenger from the Governor of Geez

hega at the head of the gulf. The courier, which
every-where heralded their coming, had arrived at
Geezhega ten days before, so its commandant had
sent his representative to aid their advance. The
Cossack soon cleared the tent of the savages, giving orders to them to get ready their dogs and
sledges to carry the strangers forward on their
journey. Thus relieved of disagreeable spies on
their every movement, they spent the evening and
night in comparative comfort.

A new experience in traveling now awaited them.
In the morning their old drivers were paid off in
tobacco, showy calico prints, and beads, and the
baggage and provisions were transferred, under the
orders of the Cossack Kerillof, from the deer-
sledges of the wandering Koraks to the dog-
sledges of their settled relatives. It was nearly
noon before all was ready. The major, Kennan,
and Dodd had each a sledge—consisting of a cof-
fin-shaped box, into which the feet were thrust,
while the rider sat up in the end, with something
like an old-fashioned chaise-top over his head.
There was a curtain to draw over the front of this
top to protect the face from the cutting wind and
stinging snow. Kennan says: "Imagine an eight-
foot coffin mounted on runners, and a man sitting
up in it with a bushel basket over his head; and you
will have a very correct idea of a Siberian '*povoska*,'
or dog-sledge." The drivers were thoroughly ugly.
They sat on the covered end of the box, driving
each fourteen savage dogs, while the rider, wedged
into the other end, unable to move, was entirely in

his power. When the rider intimated that he
wanted to stop, the team was put at its highest
speed; if he wanted to hasten on, it was just then
that the savage wanted to stop and smoke ; if there
was a steep ravine, down which the explorer would
go with some caution, he was launched to the bottom like a snow-ball. It was a small matter to the
driver that his sledge turned bottom up and its
passenger *rode* face downward underneath. When
the driver wanted to rub the runners of his sledge
with a wet deer skin, so that the water freezing
might form an ice-shoe, he stood the sledge on its
rear end, with the passenger head downward, and
took his time for the operation.

Kennan, having endured this rough treatment
until endurance seemed to cease to be a virtue,
succeeded in freeing himself from the sledge, and,
putting a pistol to his driver's head, berated him
soundly. But the savage knew but little about the
pistol, and nothing of the words of the threat, so
he looked complacently at his novel gesticulations.
Finally the major succeeded in getting the drivers together, and, through the Cossack, made them
understand that unless they behaved better they
would be turned over to the Russian governor at
Geezhega for punishment. They paid some attention to this. They seemed to know what punishment from that source meant.

These settled Koraks once owned herds of reindeer and were *wanderers* on the arctic prairie, but
losing, by some extraordinary disease among the
animals, this means of support, they settled near

the sea, and live mostly on fish. They are the most degraded of all the Kamchadals. The reasons for their special depravity are plain. From the Russian traders they have received the arts of lying, cheating, and stealing, and from the American whalers they have obtained rum and habits of licentiousness. To perfect them in wickedness and to assure their speedy extinction as a people, they eat in large quantities the narcotic toadstool.

Once during the long drives over the snow-covered desert, it occurred to Kennan that he might, to the advantage of his independence and comfort, drive his own dog-sledge. He had been watching the way it was done, and learning the dog language. It looked easy enough. Besides, it was, of course, quite certain that an American of education and large knowledge of men and things could do what an ignorant, stupid Korak could. So, choosing what seemed a favoring condition of the weather and prairie, he assumed the front seat and the spiked stick. The Korak, in yielding his official position, silently turned up his nose at his successor. But Kennan attributed this to the well-known envious feelings of retiring office-holders toward incoming ones. He gave the word of command to the leading dog—a genuine savage—to quicken his pace. Instead of doing this, the brute slackened his speed, looked over his shoulder at the new commander, and turned up his nose. This, Kennan felt, meant mischief. Such contempt of authority could not be allowed, so he hurled the spiked stick

at him, which native drivers do with terrifying effect. But the dog dodged it and turned his nose
up still higher. Kennan attempted to recover the
weapon as the sledge slid past it, but Yankee culture failed where Korak ignorance would have succeeded. Just at this moment several wild reindeer darted out from behind a slight rising of the
ground several hundred yards ahead, and bounded
over the steppe. Instantly the dogs uttered a
fierce howl and rushed after them, without the
fear of their new master before their eyes. The
sledge bounced over the snowy ridges, often on
one runner. The Korak slipped off behind in good
time to be out of harm's way, and Kennan was
without an iron-pointed stick to thrust into the
snow between the runners in front of the sledge to
check the dogs. The deer darted down a ravine
and the dogs rushed to its brink. Kennan could
not tell how sharp its descent might be nor how
great its depth, but there was no help for him, so
he shut his eyes and held on for the plunge. But
the leading dog, on reaching the brink, turned off
at a right angle, bringing the whole train round
like a whip lash, snapped Kennan from the sledge,
and sent him down the ravine eighteen feet, head-
foremost into a snowbank. The object of the
leading dog seemed to be to get rid of him, that
the deer chase might be less incumbered, and this
he certainly accomplished; but the sledge slid
over the declivity and became entangled in a
clump of bushes, and brought the whole team to a
stand-still. The dogs howled their dissatisfaction

10

at this sudden and unexpected restraint, while the reindeer made good their escape.

While Kennan was floundering about waist deep in snow, the native driver made his appearance on the edge of the ravine. With a mischievous grin he shouted, " American dog-driver no good." Kennan didn't feel much like entering into an argument on that point, so the Korak mounted the driver's seat, the spiked stick assumed its terror, the leading dog's nose dropped into its proper place, and the cultivated American took his place under his skin canopy, as to dog-driving a less conceited if not a dryer man.

A few more haltings at dirty, smoky, hour-glass yourts, and our explorers, with their train of fifteen sledges, dashed into Geezhega, saluted by the howl of many hundred dogs, to which their own dogs made fitting response. Under the Cossack's lead they halted before a large, comfortable-looking house, with double glass windows, where arrangements had been made for their reception. They entered a neatly swept Christian-looking room, threw off their well-worn and dirty traveling garments, and were but just seated when the door opened and the Russian governor entered. He was neatly dressed and bowed most graciously. His blue coat and pants of broadcloth, spotless linen shirt, seal finger-rings, and dainty little cane, caused our friends to feel awkward in their attire of "wandering Koraks in reduced circumstances." But the governor, with the address of a true gentleman, made them feel at home. He was all nervous excitement while he walked the floor and plied the major with questions concerning his own Russian capital, from which he had not heard for a year. The death of Lincoln, the end of our Civil War, news six months old, was fresh to him.

Having learned something of the outside world, and also a little of the plans of the explorers, his excellency left them to wash, rest, and resume the clothing of civilization, but before he retired left a cordial invitation for them to come to his house and dine. The travelers had passed suddenly from the wildest life of the desert to almost the voluptu-ous hospitality of an Eastern court.

CHAPTER XV.

THE ARCTIC NIGHT.

TEN days were spent in Geezhega by our ex·
plorers. During this time the major was gathering information on which to determine his immediate line of exploration. His party had come
up, as we have seen, the east coast of the Ochotsk
Sea. Down the west coast from where they now
were to the sea-port of Ochotsk was a distance of
five hundred and fifty miles * of mountainous tim-
berland. From that point to the mouth of the
Amoor River was about the same distance. This
last line of country Bush and Mahood, with whom
we parted at Petropovlovsk, were already surveying. The major concluded, after much discussion,
that he and Vushine, with a party of Cossacks and
dog-sledges, would start immediately and survey
the upper portion of this route and meet them at
Ochotsk. He hoped to make the trip in a month.

From Geezhega north-east to the mouth of the
Anadyr River, on Bering Sea, was still another five
hundred and fifty miles, of an almost treeless
country, made up largely of *steppe*, or grassy plain-
land, like that over which our party had just passed.

* Our explorers differ in their estimate of the distance of the
three great sections of their telegraph route from Bering Sea
to the Amoor. We give that of Kennan.

Kennan and Dodd, with native and Russian help-
ers, were ordered to commence at once this part
of the route. Thus the whole plan included a
survey from the Bering Sea, through eastern Siberia, down, as we have stated, the western shore
of the Ochotsk to the Amoor, a distance of about
eighteen hundred miles. The line of the telegraphic wire was to be laid out, and natives set at
work cutting poles. Here was work for an Arctic
winter.

Kennan and his party appeared to have the most
difficult part of the enterprise. The natives reported that there were only two villages of any importance, Penjina and Anadyr, between Geezhega
and the Anadyr. The first was in the midst of the
great plain, and the second on the Anadyr River,
more than two hundred miles from its mouth.
The Kennan party did not propose to go further
than Anadyr the first trip, and hoped to reach it
in twenty-five days.

Kennan was off December 15, 1865; the major
went his way soon after, and both were to return
to Geezhega in April.

The morning of Kennan's start was clear and
cold. His company consisted of ten men on eight
sledges, drawn by nearly a hundred dogs. The
employés presented a novel appearance in their
gayly trimmed fur coats, red sashes, and yellow
fox-skin hoods. They started in a cloud of flying
snow, which stung their faces like sparks of fire.
The cold was intense, and although it was noonday the sun, low down in the heavens, glowed like

a red ball of fire, and although he had been above the horizon only one hour and a half, he had completed half his daily journey. Our party traveled until the twilight deepened into darkness, and then stopped for the night at the house of a Russian peasant. They had made ten miles. While the explorers were drinking tea a messenger from Geezhega came in, bringing two frozen blue-berry pies as a parting token of good will from the major. Dodd expressed a fear that they would not keep, and, as a precautionary measure, ate one. Kennan deemed it quite necessary to follow his example in order to receive the intended benefit from the major's present, and he dispatched the other.

The next day they reached a log-hut in a small forest of tamarack-trees. The hut sufficed only for Kennan, Dodd, and their cook, and the rest camped by a huge fire outside. Though the cold was thirty-five degrees below zero, the outside campers drank their tea and ate their supper with a relish, told stories, joked and laughed uproariously, and sung merrily until a late hour at night. It seemed only just cold enough to make than spirited.

Leaving the tree-sheltered hut in the early morning, the train galloped out into the cold, silent, snowy desert, as boundless to the eye as mid-ocean, and relieved by no tree or shrub or sign of living thing. The weird enchanter, Aurora, whom we met when on our "North-Pole Voyages," came forth in the northern horizon, to beguile the lonely travelers, and amaze them

with his wonder-working power. He touched the
snowy sahara, and it became a blue tropical lake,
on whose shores rose the walls, domes, and minarets of a beautiful oriental city; luxuriant foliage
overhung the clear blue water, and were reflected
in its depth.   It was a seeming summer in winter,
and a feigned life in frozen barrenness.   The ap-
parition faded, glowed, and faded again, and
glided into two colossal pillars sculptured from
rose quartz; these, uniting their capitals, formed a
stupendous arch, glowing with resplendent light.

But not with celestial things only did the enchanter play.   He touched the terrestrial objects
not far from the eye with a curious enchantment.
Bare hillocks and dark objects on the snow assumed marvelous forms, and crows became wolves
and black foxes, so perfect in appearance that
more than once the cheated explorers started
after them with their guns.

Night came on, and the cold grew more intense.
Only by running beside their sledges could the
men keep warm.   No sheltering trees appeared,
and they dare not camp on the snow-drifted plain.
Five hours by starlight they rushed on, longing
for a covert of trees, as a sailor in a storm longs
for a sheltering harbor.   At length the foremost
driver announced with a shout the distant looming
up darkly of trees against the eastern sky.   The
dogs caught the inspiration of the sight, and quick-
ened their speed.   They soon reached a small
stream in the very midst of the desert.   The unharnessed dogs were fed their one fish each, mak-

ing their entire daily allowance, in receiving which
they snarled and snapped at each other; but,
having eaten, they lay down on the snow, curling
themselves up in a hundred frost-covered balls,
and slept.

The driver, at once made three sides of a square
with the sledges, banked up the outside with
snow thrown out of the middle, and built a huge
fire of trailing pines on the open side. The floor
of this fort-like inclosure was strewn with twigs of
willow and alder, a shaggy bear-skin thrown over
them, and the weary explorers, having removed
their fur stockings, moist with perspiration, lay
down with their feet to the fire, awaiting supper.
Yagor was not long in getting ready the hot tea
and dried fish. Creeping into their fur bags, they
chatted, told stories in entire comfort, until they
fell asleep. The drivers piled high the pine
branches, and sung their wild, mournful songs far
into the night.

Just after midnight Kennan awoke and peered
out of his fur sleeping-bag. The fire had burned
down to a red heap of embers which threw a
ghastly light over the dark outlines of sledges, men
and dogs. Beyond stretched the undulating snow-
covered desert until it was lost in the distance
and darkness. The constellations sparkled out
of the silent, solemn depth of the sky. The whole
scene was oppressively grand and awful. The
soul seemed alone with God.

Suddenly the silence was broken by a long
faint, wailing cry, rising upon the still night-air

like that of one in mortal agony. Gradually it
deepened and swelled into a volume of mournful
sound, and then died away into a despairing moan.
It was the signal cry of the Siberian dog, so wild
and startling, that it sent a shudder through the
lonely listener. In a moment the mournful cry
was taken up on a higher key by another dog;
then two, three, ten, forty, seventy, a hundred
dogs howled together the dismal shouts of the
arctic night; then, one after another, they dropped
off, closing with the prolonged wail of the leader
with which they commenced. This howl in the
night seemed a fit expression of the moral and
physical desolation of the country.

Succeeding the wail of the dogs were the flashes
of the aurora, varying in beauty of color and form,
and at times setting the whole heavens aglow.
May not this symbolize the moral light that shall
yet break upon this cheerless desert?

The next night the explorers spent in an hour-
glass hut of a small native village. From this the
Geezhega drivers returned, and our explorers
waited two days for the sledges from Penjina,
which the governor of Geezhega had ordered by a
courier to be sent.

Two exciting surprises met our party here. One
morning a messenger all the way from Petropavlovsk slipped down the pole into their midst. He
brought dispatches for the major, being directed
by the natives to our party. He only knew that
they contained orders from the telegraph company's ship, which had just touched at that port

when he started. Kennan, without opening the letters, sent the messenger off immediately to overtake the major. What news did they contain? He wished he had opened them. While in this perplexed frame of mind the sledges arrived from Penjina. One of the drivers talked with Dodd about a story that was told by the wandering Koraks of a party of white men who were left by a ship in the fall at the mouth of Anadyr River. If so, it must be the Macrae party, which had expected to receive the co-operation of our party before now. They were then separated from the nearest trading-post, Anadyr, by a long stretch of desolate, treeless country, over which the foot of civilized man had never ventured. They would perish there! What could be done!

Kennan and Dodd talked long and anxiously, and finally resolved that on their arrival at Anadyr they would organize a large party of natives, and make a desperate venture for their relief.

Our party, under the guidance of the Penjina men, pushed over the steppe for two days without special incident. On the third day a fearful storm arose. The men cowered down in a hastily made camp, but the fires were extinguished, the dogs and sledges were covered with snow, and there was nothing that could be done but to creep into the fur-bags and wait. Two days were thus spent dismally. The storm then broke. The dog-food was spent, and they must travel the next twenty-four hours without eating. At the end of this time the drivers said Penjina would be reached if they traveled night and day. This was done, except that just before midnight of the following morning the drivers stopped and let the dogs sleep. They said that if the dogs went to sleep when it was dark and woke up in an hour and found it day-light, they imagined that they had slept all night, and were satisfied. This was a way they had of cheating them.

The short day of a few hours passed, and night was upon them, yet they had not come in sight of Penjina. In the darkness the sledges became sep-arated, and both divisions groped about at a venture. Finally, Kennan and Dodd, and a sledge which remained with them, struck Penjina River below the village. As they were going up stream on the ice they saw a party of sledges whom they took to be strangers, coming down. The parties hailed each other with a " Hallo!"

" Where are you going? " asked Kennan.

" To Penjina, to be sure; aint it *down* the riv-er?" was the reply.

It proved to be the other division of our men, who had lost entirely the points of the compass. The up-stream party were right, and all soon dashed into Penjina, waking the inhabitants with a shout which was answered by the fearful howl-ings of the village dogs.

CHAPTER XVI.

A RUSSO-GREEK CHRISTMAS.

THE Penjina people, mostly Russian peasants, were very kind to our travelers, and entered with interest into their telegraph project. They, of course, had never heard of a telegraph, but sixteen of the ablest of their men were engaged to cut telegraph poles, twenty-one feet long and five inches in diameter at the top. Faithful to their engagement they entered at once upon their work, but as they cut discussed among themselves the precise purpose for which the Americans intended to use them. Some argued that they intended to build a wooden road from the Ochotsk Sea to the Anadyr River, so they could travel back and forth in the summer. Others contended that two men could not make so long a road, and that the poles were to be used to construct an enormous house. But all agreed that poles only five inches in diameter at the top were not big enough for any conceivable purpose, so they cut down trees of a goodly size, five hundred in all, and piled them along the desired route as so many poles, none of which were less than a foot through at the small end.

On the return of our surveyors they were all condemned as of no use, and they probably still remain where they were piled, monuments of the evils of independent thought.

On the thirty-first of December our party left Penjina for the long run of about two hundred miles to Anadyr, across the bleak steppe. The journey was not attended by any special circumstance except the intense cold; that was truly arctic. New-year's-eve found them in camp, sitting before a fire of trailing pines, covered with their heaviest furs, and yet making a desperate fight with the frost king. The mercury was fifty-three degrees below zero. Their soup, as it came boiling from the fire, was eaten in a hurry, that it might not freeze to the plate; their eyelids froze together while they drank their hot tea. Tin plates, knives, and spoons burned the bare hands when touched, almost as if they were red hot; water spilled on a piece of board only fourteen inches from the fire froze solid in two minutes; the warm bodies of the dogs gave off clouds of steam, and even the bare hands of the men, wiped dry, exhaled a thin vapor when exposed to the air. Yet, eating plentifully of their oily food, and creeping into their fur bags, the cold was defied. It was only when a high wind attended such intense cold that men and beasts dared not venture abroad.

After twenty-three days of rough traveling the explorers entered Anadyr. The sledges drew up before the house of the Russian priest. The dogs of the town had howled their welcome, and a curious crowd surrounded the house, conspicuous among which was the tall priest, with long, flowing hair and beard, dressed in an ample black robe, and holding in his hand above his head a long tallow candle which flared wildly in the night air. The crowd bowed their respects to the strangers as their pastor courteously introduced them to his house. It was, indeed, a *home*, delightfully contrasting with their out-door camps on the storm-beaten desert over which they had traveled. The floor was carpeted with soft deer skins, which yielded to their footsteps, and a blazing fire in a neat fire-place flooded the room with a cheerful light. Tiny tapers burned before gilt shrines, and a few illustrated papers lay on a stand in one corner, and every thing was arranged with taste, and bore that air of comfort which suddenly transported our friends to the far-away land of their loved ones. Nor was this arctic home wanting, as its cheerful aspect assured them, of a wife— "a pale, slender lady, with light hair and dark eyes"—and three pretty children.

After an excellent supper of soup, fried cutlets, white bread and butter, with delicious tea, made cheerful to Dodd at least by a free talk in Russian, the tired travelers retired to a Christian bed.

Four little villages grouped together, having in all about two hundred inhabitants, compose the settlement called Anadyr, or, as it is generally spelled, Anadyrsk. It is on the River Anadyr, a little south of the Arctic Circle, and is almost as much shut out from the world as if it were in the midst of the Polar Sea. Its people had never seen an American before. Indeed, they had never

before been visited by any foreigner, except in a
single instance when a Swedish officer of the
Russian service made them a call in 1860. Its
people are Russians, and a few natives live among
them, adopting their customs and religion. A
small Greek church, and rudely-built log-huts half
under ground, whose somber light, if they ever
get any from without, struggles through blocks of
ice cut from the river, compose about all there is
in Anadyr to sustain its claims as a town. Its
trade appears to consist mainly in exchanging tobacco for furs. Its chief customers are a fierce,
warlike native tribe called Chukchees, who were
long the bitter enemies of the intruding Russians,
and had nearly driven them from the region, when
a love of this vile weed caused them to cease their
hostility. It was many years before a genuine
peace existed between the parties. The Chukchees for awhile presented their furs on the point
of a spear held in a strong hand. If the Russians
chose they might take them off, and hang in their
place an equal value of tobacco ; otherwise there
was no trade. The sharpness of the polished
blade of the spear and the strong hand at one end
seem to have determined the honesty of the bargain. This method was not favorable to a brisk
business, nor to the development of good feeling,
and in time was discontinued.

Thursday, January sixth, our time, was the Russian Christmas. The Americans were up four
hours before day to attend an early service. The
stars shone brightly through a clear atmosphere,

and a brilliant aurora streamed up over the tree tops. The whole population was astir, and in every house gilded tapers were lighted before the holy shrines and pictures, and fragrant incense filled the air. The little log church, even at this early hour, was crowded with devout worshipers. The sides of the room were adorned with pictures of Russian saints, before which were burning long wax candles. Clouds of incense rolled up toward the roof from swinging censers. The gorgeously-attired priest gabbled, in a deep-toned voice, rapid prayers in a language nobody understood, swinging at the same time his censer, and continually bowing, crossing himself, and kissing a huge Bible.

The ceremonies attending the administration of the Lord's Supper were deeply impressive; but the most effective part of the whole service was the singing by the choir, our explorers standing for hours enduring the mixed-up jabber of the priest to listen to the accompanying chanted prayers and hymns, rendered in rude but deeply emotional strains. In the welcome pauses of the priest's rehearsals the choir interspersed a beautifully modulated " Gospodi pameelui "—God have mercy!— again they sang " Padai Gospodin "—Grant, O Lord!—while the stillness of the audience seemed almost painful.

During the whole service the Cossacks and natives were apparently absorbed in devotion. They crossed themselves and bowed reverently in response to the words of the priest, and at times prostrated themselves, pressing their foreheads and lips to the floor. It was deeply impressive to see these fur-clad people at one moment standing in a devoutly listening attitude, and then suddenly dropping upon the floor, like ripened grain before the mower's scythe, leaving only the strangers standing in the midst of a hundred prostrate forms.

At the close of the morning service the choir sang a joyful hymn to express the rapture of the angels over the Saviour's birth, and the unharmonious chime of bells in the little low tower of the church rung out as best they could their notes of gladness.

Kennan and Dodd returned home, and had just finished their breakfast when six sober-looking men filed into their room, paused before a sacred picture, crossed themselves, and began to sing a charming melody beginning with the words, "Christ is born." Having finished the song they turned to Kennan and Dodd, shook hands, and wished them a merry Christmas. Dodd, who understood the specific point in the visit, gave them a few coppers and they retired, repeating wishes of long life and many blessings on the Americans. One band after another came in the same way, with songs and good wishes, and extended palms for coppers, until nearly all the male population of the village had come. A troop of boys, more zealous for gifts than devout, cut short their song with "Christ is born, gim'me some money."

At sunrise the tapers in the houses were extinguished, and the holiday merriment began. Dog-

11

sledges, loaded with young women, rushed down
the hills and dashed through the streets, occasion·
ally capsizing into snow drifts, while merry shouts
and the sound of the jangling bells filled all the
air. The women made friendly calls from house
to house in gay calico gowns and crimson head-
dresses, and the men played foot-ball on the frozen
snow.

On Sunday evening following Christmas the
festivities of the sacred week closed with a grand
ball given by the priest at his house. The ball
itself was probably quite as decent as the average
of such assemblies in our land. The time chosen
for it, as well as the occasion itself, was a sad ex·
pression of the low spiritual character of these
Russo-Greek missionaries.

CHAPTER XVII.

RESCUED COMRADES.

SOON after New-Year's, according to the Russian reckoning, Kennan began to discuss in earnest the project at which we have hinted, of a journey down the Anadyr to Bering Sea in search of the party of white men, whoever they might be, who were, as stated in the report of the wandering Koraks, encamped somewhere near its mouth. So far the reports were rather vague. That there were civilized men there was made certain by the statement in the report that the snow-buried hut of the strangers had a curious iron tube running out of the top, from which came smoke and sparks. No Siberians could invent such a description of a stove-pipe. But it was difficult for Kennan to believe that the co-operating party promised by Col. Buckley, the chief engineer of the telegraph company, would leave in this wild country a party late in the season many hundred miles from any station of civilized men. Besides, Kennan's superior, Major Abasa, had decided to leave the Anadyr unexplored until spring. But the query that arose in Kennan's mind was, did not the letter which passed through his hands just after he left Geezhega for the major, speak of these very men, and would he not on opening it send a courier order-

ing him to go to their relief? In view, then, of the
possibility of the strangers being of the telegraph
party, and of such an order to go to their relief,
Kennan decided to start as soon as possible. He
called for volunteers from among the natives to
accompany him, but with one consent they began
to make excuse. No man, they said, ever went
down the Anadyr in the winter; the cold near the
coast was awful and the storms terrific; there was
no fuel of any kind in that region, so that no fires
could be made; and, in fact, men and dogs would be
sure to perish. Such was the view of the people of
Anadyr, but Gregorie, Kennan's Cossack guide, an
experienced old man, talked differently of the enterprise. He had been, he said, a hundred and
fifty miles down the river in winter; the trailing pine so far was plenty for fuel, and it was not
a worse country to travel than much of that over
which they had come. He was willing to go with
all his dogs and sledges. The priest also spoke
encouragingly, and declared his willingness to go
if necessary.

On the credit of these statements Kennan told the
natives that he should go, and showed them the
written authority given him by the governor of
Geezhega to demand of them men and sledges for
all kinds of service.

Under this pressure eleven men agreed to go,
and preparations were commenced with vigor.
Yet the difficulties were appalling. The exact position of Anadyr in the arctic region had never been
recorded, and Kennan had no instruments to de-

termine it. It might be two hundred miles from the mouth of the river, and it might be five, though they hoped and believed it was not more than two. But the question of distance entered largely into the question of the amount of food to be carried for the men and dogs, for none could be obtained on the way. Besides, they had no means of knowing whether the encampment they sought was near the mouth of the river or fifty miles from it.

While thus perplexed, and yet getting ready to start, a Cossack, an acquaintance of the priest, came into Anadyr, fresh from a camp of the wandering Koraks; he had their latest news concerning the exiles near the coast. This news ran thus: There were five men living in a hut made of bushes and boards; the hut was covered with snow; they had plenty of provisions; they made a fire in a very curious manner by putting black stones into an iron box, while all the smoke came out through a crooked iron tube, the top of which turned round when the wind blew; they had also an enormous tame black bear which they allowed to run loose around the hut, and which chased away the visitors.

When Kennan heard this very clear statement he hurrahed in exultation. He was sure the hut was occupied by his comrades of San Francisco, whom he left waiting to be ordered to the mouth of the Anadyr. The "black stones and iron box" told that they had a coal fire, and the "tame bear" was "Robinson's Newfoundland dog," a great pet among the explorers, and whose photograph Ken-

nan had brought with him. The statement further
said the hut was on the Anadyr River, about a
day's journey from its mouth ; so their enterprise
for the rescue of its inmates assumed a more definite form.

The party were now ready for a start, consisting
of Kennan, Dodd, their guide Gregorie, and the
eleven Anadyr men, eleven sledges and a hundred
and twenty fierce, shaggy, wolfish dogs. The
train drew up before the priest's house and received
his hearty " God go with you ! " The whole village came to see them off. Some who had relations with the adventurers indulged sad forebod-
ings that they should never see them again. The
drivers went into the priest's house, prayed and
crossed themselves before the picture of the Saviour. The dogs were then let loose and they
dashed away with frantic speed in a cloud of
snow.

The party sped on from day to day, sometimes
on the frozen river, and then across snow-covered
plains, camping out in all kinds of weather, and
braving the intensest cold. The trees along the
river bank grew more and more dwarfed each day,
until on their tenth day out, they disappeared altogether, and the Anadyr, which had extended its
banks a mile apart, ran through a plain, white,
dreary, and shrubless as the sandy desert, and
bounded only by the horizon. They had traveled,
they thought, about two hundred and fifty miles
since leaving Anadyr, but how near they were to
the sea-shore they could not tell.

They dug in the snow for wood to boil their water for tea, but found only cranberry bushes which
would not burn. The thermometer went down
to thirty-five degrees below zero, and a storm was
in the sky which might shut them up in a dreary,
fireless, almost shelterless camp for ten days. It
was under such circumstances that Kennan and
Dodd threw themselves, tired and burdened by
the prospect before them, upon their furs to rest.
With much coaxing a few green bushes had been
made to burn and tea was made. Dodd sipped a
little and put the cup down with a puzzled look;
he tasted again and pondered, and then shouted
with a joyful voice, "Tide-water! the tea is salt!"
Kennan sent men to the river for ice, and it was
carefully melted. It was certainly salt. They
had reached the tide-water and the mouth of the
river could not be far away. They must now keep
a sharp lookout for the stove pipe and the "tame
bear."

They slept only six hours and started at midnight.
The clouds had passed away and the moon shone
brilliantly. They rode through the night, and
next day until the long twilight had set in. They
felt assured that they must now be near where the
Chukchees, as they reported, had seen their snow-
buried companions. The rosy flush of day faded
slowly and the darkness set in, while the mercury
went down, down to minus fifty degrees. Nature,
silent and gloomy, frowned upon the intruding
strangers, while they seemed to be traveling upon
a boundless frozen ocean. The banners of auroral

light waved in the north, asserting the dominion of
the stern Arctic Spirit.   After awhile the moon
arose, preceded by mock moons which refraction
had sent to dance in fantastic forms.   The blood-
red face of the moon added a wild and almost fearful strangeness to the scene.   The whole train was
awed into silence; the shouting and hallooing of
the drivers ceased, and the hours wore slowly and
wearily away.   Twenty miles had been passed
since they had arrived at what they supposed to
be the region of the stove-pipe, yet only a vast expanse of steppe appeared.   The train had traveled
twenty-four hours without a pause, except a few moments before sunrise, to cheat the dogs into a little
rest.   No warm food had been taken, and hunger
and weariness were telling upon the suffering men.
The feet of the dogs were swollen and cracked
and left the snow stained with their blood.   The
drivers drew their furs more closely about them,
and were sullen and silent as if indifferent to a
near and certain death.   If the train stopped to
camp, there was no wood for a fire, and the nearest trees or shrubbery were fifty miles in the rear.
The company had been extended as widely as it
was safe to do and not endanger a separation, and
every little dark spot had been examined along the
line until hope, long deferred, seemed about to
die.   Dodd, who had for some time trudged mood-
ily beside his sledge, finally gave his driving stick
to a native, drew himself into his furs, and lay
down on the sledge to sleep.   No commands nor
entreaties could make any impression upon him.

It was the fearful stupor which precedes freezing. Only Gregorie and an old Chukchee seemed to have sufficient life to continue the search, which they did, walking ahead and digging into the snow for wood, going along the banks of the river and examining every object, and at times making short runs into the snowy plains to the north.

The burden of mind, at this crisis, of the responsible officer, Captain Kennan, was almost crushing. Should he abandon the search when he might at any minute find the stove-pipe and rescue his friends, who might otherwise die a miserable death? On the other hand, should he by persevering imperil the lives of his present command, while *possibly* those whom he sought may have broken up their hut and gone off two months before with the wandering Chukchees, for the very last news from them was now full two months old. Thus perplexed, the dangerous condition of Dodd led him to give orders to halt, break up one of the sledges, and prepare hot tea and a warm supper, hoping to revive him.

It was plainly now just such an exigency as those in which the great Deliverer had so often come, and in which man seemed powerless. The order to halt had just passed the commander's lips, and had not reached beyond those nearest him, when a faint halloo reached his ear. He threw back his fur hood, and listened, while the blood rushed violently to his heart. "Again, a faint, long-drawn cry came back through the still atmosphere from the sledges in advance." The dogs pricked up their ears, listened, and rushed to the front. Here the foremost drivers were gathered about the American whale-boat, turned bottom side up. The hut must be near. Just then a shout came from Gregorie and the old Chukchee. They had found the stove-pipe!

Kennan dropped his dog-whip, left the dogs to go where they pleased, and rushed to the spot. Half bewildered, on arriving at the long-looked-for spot, he walked back and forth in front of the snow drift from which the funnel issued, saying softly to himself, " Thank God! thank God! "

Dodd, who had been aroused from his half-frozen state by the excitement caused by the discovery, proposed that they try to find the door. No sound came from within, and its inmates, if any remained, were evidently asleep. In the meantime Kennan mounted the snow-drift, and shouted down the stove-pipe in a loud voice, " Halloo the house! "

A tremulous voice from within replied, "Who's that? "

"Come out and see! Where's the door? " replied Kennan.

The voice from within did not succeed in making him understand where the door was, and he began to tramp round the funnel to find it. While doing so he suddenly fell into a tunnel made by an excavation in the snow from the door-way, and covered over with sticks and skins. Through this tunnel thirty feet long, the inmates went in and out. As Kennan broke through its roof he landed

at the feet of one of the men who was just coming
out in his shirt and drawers; holding his lighted
candle high over his head, and peering with glaring eyes into the darkness, the man demanded who
was there. Kennan tore off his fur hoods and
mask, and spoke in good English. He was at
once recognized and embraced. Three of his old
companions, Harder, Robinson, and Smith, attended by Cook, the Newfoundland dog, were the
inmates, and the whole rescue party were soon
in the cabin, huddled together, sipping hot tea.
Dodd and Kennan nearly fainted on entering,
from hunger, exhaustion, and anxiety, as well as
from the sudden change from fifty degrees below
zero to sixty above.

The rescuers having eaten and slept were soon
recruited. They then listened to the story of the
hut party. They were landed at the mouth of the
Anadyr by one of the company's vessels in September. They were five in number, and having a
good whale-boat and plenty of provisions, the en-
engineer-in-chief, Col. Buckley, entertained no
doubt but they would easily ascend the river to
some trading-post before it froze, and thus connect with the Abasa party. But the unusually
early, severe cold sealed up the waters almost immediately. Having no dogs nor sledges they
could only go into camp and wait for spring, or,
as they faintly hoped, the coming of some of
Abasa's men. Their hut was made of drift-wood,
a few boards left by the vessel, and bushes, all well
banked up with snow. It was drear and damp.

Here by lamp-light they had lived for five months They were visited by the wandering Chukchees, who sold them fresh meat, and blubber for their lamp. But on no conditions would they sell a live reindeer, on account of a superstitious notion that to do so would bring great disaster upon them. We have seen the same notion among the Koraks. So they could not get away on reindeer sledges.

Three weeks before the Kennan party arrived, two of them, Macrae, the commander, and Arnold, went off with a company of Chukchees, hoping to find a civilized people, and possibly their old companions of the exploration. They had not been heard from, and Kennan hoped to find them at Anadyr on his return.

After three days of rest and refitting, the whole party, rescuers and rescued, started for Anadyr. The winds pelted them with fine, frozen snow, the cold was intense, and the way rough. But they had plenty of food and furs, the inspiration which success in a good cause always gives, and a resting-place in view, and they sped swiftly on and arrived there all well and in good time.

The whole settlement, notified of their coming by the howling of the dogs, came out to meet them. But Macrae and Arnold had not been heard from. Several more weeks of anxious waiting and they came not.

CHAPTER XVIII.

THINGS HUMOROUS AND SUBLIME.

WHILE our party were waiting at Anadyr they had a fine opportunity to study the native character. The natives seen here are of three classes: the wanderers composed of Koraks and Chukchees; the Chinese natives, that is, those having plainly a Chinese origin, including several tribes; and those of the Turkish origin, called Yakoots.

The wanderers are the great reindeer men. They are essentially our American Indians—like them in their physical appearance, but less like the fierce savage. We met their kindred in Alaska.

The Chinese natives own fewer reindeer, but make a more varied and better use of them, are mild and inoffensive, have submitted without gainsaying to Russian rule, and have accepted, so far as they have any religion, that form of Christianity brought into the country by the Russians. They are the great squirrel hunters for the markets of the world.

The Turko-Yakoots are the "iron men," who love to hover about the Polar Sea. They take to the cold as lizards do to the sunshine. The mercury at their principal settlement *averages* thirty-seven degrees below zero during the three winter months, and is regarded by them as the peculiarly comfortable season. They may be seen in the streets when the cold is minus forty degrees, clad in a shirt and loose sheep-skin coat, laughing and looking as if it were only a refreshingly balmy air. They are the " working men " of the north. The Siberians say that you may take a Yakoot, strip him naked, and set him in the midst of a desolate steppe, and return in a year to that spot and find him living in a comfortable house connected with barns and hay-stacks, and owning herds, and enjoying himself like a patriarch. They use the Russian ax with great strength and skill, felling with it the forest trees, and constructing with only this tool a good house, even to the making of a paneled door. If the North-Pole voyagers succeed in reaching the land they dream of, and discover a continent where the mercury freezes solid in midsummer, and want to colonize it, these Turko-Yakoots are their men.

The wanderers of the Indian stamp were the most frequent comers to Anadyr, and their lively, inquisitive turn of mind afforded our explorers some amusement. One clear, cold day Kennan had been using his field-glass out of doors, and a crowd of them gathered round him to see what he was doing. He allowed one of them to look through it at another native who was standing out on the plain at a distance of about two hundred yards. He looked at him through the glass, and then again with his unaided eyes. This he did several times, his face bearing more and more a

mingled expression of surprise and incredulity
which was irresistibly comical. He had no idea
that the man's change of position was such merely
in appearance. It was, he seemed to think, a
mere trick of the strangers who had some way of
cheating him, or else the wonderful instrument
actually drew the man two hundred yards to the
end of the glass when the observer looked into it,
and put him back when he took his eye off. But he
was not to be cheated. He held the glass to his
eye with one hand, and tried to catch the man
with the other. Finding this did not succeed, he
brought the instrument to his face very slowly,
watching the man at the same time to see if he
started; and when it was quite near his eye he
looked through it suddenly. But he had to give
it up. There was the man, one moment afar on
the plain, and in an instant at arm's-length.

He laid down the glass and began to explain its
wonderful powers to his companions who had been
looking on with amazement at his unaccountable
actions. But they indignantly denied that the
man on the plain had moved at all, while he of the
glass stoutly maintained the instantaneous-move-
ment theory, and turned to Kennan for his decision of the question But Kennan only laughed
convulsively while the puzzled observer ran to the
man on the plain for *his* testimony in the case.
Of course the *observed* testified that according to
his best knowledge and belief he had not been
made to skip back and forth in a twinkle two hundred yards, and the innocent, confounded observer

came under the suspicions of his comrades as to the soundness of his mind.

The reader must regard the case as an instruct-ive lesson in the interest of charitable judging.

Soon after this a party of these same natives were with Kennan at a camp out on the steppe. Dodd, who was away in another direction, sent him a note which reached him as he sat by the camp-fire. He read it, and frequently burst into a loud laugh at some of Dodd's strokes of humor. The natives stared at him, and touched each other with their elbows significantly, as much as to say, "Just see the crazy fellow!" Finally an old, grave man ventured to ask Kennan what he was laughing at.

"Why," said Kennan, holding up the paper, "I am laughing at this."

The old man looked serious and turned to his companions, and they all discussed the cause of his laughing. After duly weighing the matter each offered his theory of solution, but none was entire-ly satisfactory. At this important crisis when de-bate was warming into a wrangle, the old man went to the fire, took up a smoking, half-burned stick and, holding it up before Kennan, asked, "Now what would you think of me if I should look at that stick for a moment and then laugh?"

"Why," said Kennan, candidly, "I should think you were a fool."

"Well," replied the old man, "that is just what I think of you."

All the natives agreed to this view, and were de-lighted to think the American had entrapped himself in the argument, for to their mind looking at a piece of paper and laughing was all the same as looking at a burnt stick and laughing. Another lesson of charity in matters of difference of opinion.

During this waiting there was another and a more instructive turn given to the thoughts of our explorers. The aurora brought out its displays in the wildest and grandest manner. One clear, dark, cold night, as our party were about to retire, Dodd happened to step out to look after the dogs. Instantly he rushed back, as if amazed, shouting, "Kennan! Robinson! Come out quick!" All sprang to their feet and ran out. The heavens seemed on fire! A broad arch spanned the whole heavens—an immense rainbow of prismatic light! Crimson and yellow banners floated from its upper edge far into the depths above. The arch continually quivered with its ever-changing colors. while the streamers from its edge flashed back and forth like the sword of some mighty angel who came to announce the judgments of God on guilty man. At intervals of one or two seconds vast breakers of phosphorescent light rolled out of the north, from the limitless ocean of space, and swept steadily and swiftly across the heavens and disappeared in the depths beyond.

While the observers looked with wonder, the auroral bow, with its waving streamers, began to move upward, enlarging its span and increasing its grandeur. At the same time another arch of equal brilliancy formed directly under it, shooting up-

12

ward slender, rainbow-colored lances toward the
North Star. At this point the exhibition assumed
an appearance of awful grandeur. The streamers
hurried back and forth from the horizon to the
zenith. Luminous bands, like great wheels, re-
volved swiftly across the heavens. Then came an
immense wave of crimson, surging up from the
north, which deluged the whole sky, and threw its
rosy reflection upon the snow-covered earth.

Scarcely had expressions of amazement and
fright formed upon the lips of the gazers, when a
vivid flash of orange filled the whole heavens, even
to the southern horizon. The spectators involun-
tarily listened to hear a thunder crash follow this
sudden glare of light. But only the subdued
prayer of "God, have mercy upon us!" of the af-
frighted natives broke the solemn stillness. Nature
was hushed into silence before the solemn revealings of its God.

Suddenly, while the heavens seemed turned to
blood by another wave of crimson, both arches
were shivered to fragments. But the thousands of
pieces assumed the form of parallel perpendicular
bars, each displaying all the colors of the rainbow.
Amid the suppressed cries of " God, have mercy ! "
the whole heavens became a molten sea of color
and fire, and then gradually the scene changed
into the calm, quiet glow of the stars.

February wore away and March came, but no
news from Macrae and Arnold. Had they perished
on the desolate arctic desert of cold and hunger,
or been murdered by the Chukchees? Perhaps they

still dragged out a miserable life far away from Christian homes and sympathy. At any rate, their case was one of serious concern.

Kennan was dissatisfied with the route through which he had come to Anadyr from Ochotsk. As we have seen, it was destitute of timber and every way unfavorable for the proposed telegraph line. He therefore started out with Robinson, on the fourth of March, to find a better one, and succeeded in finding a line of travel almost connected by the streams running into the Anadyr on the one side of a ridge of hills, and those running into the Penjina River, and so into the Ochotsk Sea on the other, wooded and just the route desired.

While out he was met by a messenger from the major, who had received letters from Col. Buckley concerning the men left at the mouth of the Anadyr. The letter contained a command from the major to Kennan to go at once to their rescue at all risks. This, as we have seen, he had done. So he hastened back to Anadyr, where, on his arrival, he found Macrae and Arnold safe and well. They had suffered much, and at times almost despaired of ever seeing again any but savage faces. But from every danger they had been saved.

All now in good spirits prepared to hasten to Geezhega and surprise the major. In the mean time we will go and follow the fortunes of Bush and Mahood, from whom we parted at Petro-pavlovsk.

CHAPTER XIX.

PERILS IN THE WATERS.

BUSH and Mahood stepped aboard the "Olga" August 26. The farewells were full of hope, but had a tinge of sadness in them. Great perils, both on the land and the rivers, from savage beasts, and scarcely less savage men, awaited both parties.

The day was beautiful—a flood of warm sunshine, making glad all nature. The snow-capped volcanoes sparkled in its beams, and the tiny moss-flowers and clusters of green foliage on the sloping hill-sides, still dripping in the morning dew, glittered in its rays. Birds of rich and varied plumage, and the usually shy seals, with their large, soft eyes, all seemed to presume upon the gladness of the hour, and ventured quite near the vessel, as if to express a farewell blessing. God whispered to the explorers in all about them, saying, Trust *me*, and be not afraid.

Sailing awhile south, well away from the rocky shore, the voyagers turned west, to enter the Ochotsk Sea, but were confronted by a long line of compact islands, which separate it from the Bering Sea. Great caution, favoring winds, and propitious currents, are necessary to secure a safe passage through these barriers. The Fog, a fickle

lounger, with clouded brow, must be inquired of
for permission to pass these islands. Though it
was high noon when our vessel neared the reef, his
gloomy mantle covered it.

"There she blows!" exclaimed the captain,
pointing to a jet of water just ahead of the ship.
All rushed forward to see the supposed whale.
Just then the lookout shouted, "Breakers ahead!"
In another moment the vessel was beset on three
sides by breakers, whose angry waves shot clouds
of spray thirty feet into the air. A heavy swell
was rolling in from the seaward, as if to forbid escape. Instantly all was excitement and activity.
The prompt orders from the quarter-deck were as
promptly obeyed. The ship came round like a
well-trained steed, and gave her stern to the surf-
beaten rocks. A fair and fresh breeze carried her
several miles away. The voyagers began to be
merry over their recent peril, and to jest at the romance of a shipwreck, and life on these volcanic
islands, with its Robinson Crusoe experience, and
amused themselves at the thought of the sensation
their story would make in the papers when they returned home. But they soon thought that an entirely different kind of mention of their escape was
due their great Captain. The wind suddenly
subsided to a painful calm. The sails flapped angrily against the masts as the ship rolled helpless-
ly in the shoreward rushing billows. The fog, as
if to mock them with a sight of their danger, lifted
its veil, and showed, at no great distance, the surf-
covered rocks toward which they were drifting in

the strong current.   The deep sea lead was thrown,
but down, down it went, reporting no anchorage.
The rough sailor thrust his hands into his pocket,
surveyed the situation with his experienced eye,
and whistled solemnly.   No breeze came to the
rescue, and the distance between the vessel and
the wave-beaten rocks where she must be ground
to fragments lessened every minute.   Bush and
Mahood waited on deck until they heard the orders
to the mate to clear the tackle for lowering the
long-boat, and then went below and packed in
their seal-skin bags such articles as they deemed
indispensable.   Their rifles and a good supply of
ammunition were placed beside them.   The romance of a shipwreck seemed inevitable, and possibly there was before them the novelty of a Crusoe life on a barren island, but whether they would
get home to put their story in the papers was not
so certain.

Having completed their preparations, the explorers returned to the deck.   There was no breeze,
and the fatal rocks were within rifle-shot.   The
lead was once more dropped, but no bottom.
Nearer and nearer the vessel drifted, while the
mate waited, tackle in hand, for the captain to
shout, " Let go the long-boat; all hands tumble
in ! "   At that moment a sailor shouted, "There's a
puff! "   Puff after puff came, each one growing
stronger, until the ship paused, then came round,
and, slowly struggling with the inward current,
sailed into the open ocean.   Who will say that
God, who holdeth the winds in his fist, did not

send this timely " puff," which was the breath of
life to the imperiled voyagers?

Sailing further south, they passed by daylight
into the Ochotsk Sea, crossed it, and entered by
the southern end of the great island of Saghalin
into the gulf of Tartary. Into the northern portion of these waters the Amoor River empties, but
the gulf narrows as it extends in that direction,
and for a hundred and fifty miles is full of rocks
and shallows. So the " Olga " turned into a little
port of the mainland, called Castries, to engage a
steamer to tow her up. Not finding a steamer in
waiting, our explorers concluded to take an inland
route to the mouth of the Amoor. This route is
of peculiar interest, and will open up to us a new
country and people.

The Amoor, coming from the south and west, is
at the village of Marinsk, only fifty miles due west
of Castries. The river then runs nearly parallel
with the gulf, northward, for a hundred and fifty
miles, and then turns east, and empties, as we
have stated, into the upper waters of the Gulf of
Tartary. Over two thirds of the distance between
Castries and Marinsk, the placid waters of the
lake Kidzi are extended, the lake seeming really
but an expansion of the Amoor itself. Over the
remaining sixteen miles the Russian government
has built a road of logs. The steam-engine will go
screaming through its excavated hills before long,
no doubt.

Our party found kind entertainment in Castries,
at the house of a German merchant. They were

waited upon by the Russian officers with all court-
esy, their government having ordered that the explorers should receive every possible assistance.
As they were to start for the lake on the morrow,
the officers sent men through the vicinity to pro-
cure horses for the journey. In the meantime
provisions, blankets, and the other necessities of
the ride were packed into as snug parcels as possible. But only two saddles could be found in the
place, and but three horses. As the captain of the
"Olga" had decided to go, and a man was quite a
sufficient load for a horse in such a country, the
supplies and baggage were unprovided for. To
meet this necessity the commandant of the post
detailed three soldiers to serve as pack-horses.

Our party was astir early in the morning, nothing daunted by dark, threatening rain-clouds
which overcast the sky. The soldiers pushed on
ahead. The captain mounted the horse without
a saddle, but was promised a turn in the stirrups.
The clouds soon did as they promised, poured
down a copious rain. The corduroy road was ex-
ecrable, the logs being displaced, wet, and slippery. The soil, where the logs were displaced,
was a heavy, sticky, yellow clay, admitting the foot
of man or beast, but resisting its removal. The
poor water-soaked soldiers were soon passed. The
horses stumbled and rolled about like ships in a
heavy sea. The captain declared he didn't like a
"deck passage," by land or sea, especially where
there was nothing to prevent him from falling
"overboard." He was in danger, he said, of be-

ing "shipwrecked" before he could "make a
port." It was as well to be merry, though the body
if not the heart ached. Six long weary hours expired
before the lake was reached. "The station" at
which they were to embark consisted of one small,
dilapidated hut. The weary travelers knocked
and were answered by the angry bark of a dog.
They shouted, but none responded. Wet, tired,
and hungry, they were about to take possession of
the premises, under the law of necessity, when
two men were seen approaching on the lake in a
box-shaped boat, and two other persons came in
sight on the beach. The boatmen proved to be
Russian soldiers and keepers of the station. The
others were natives of the soil. The soldiers
spoke German, with which the captain was familiar, so a good understanding was soon secured between the parties. The weary horses were led to
a shelter near by, and the travelers were introduced into a smoke-blackened room, lighted by a
piece of fish-skin, thrust into the aperture of the
log wall. A large brick stove occupied three
fourths of the stone floor. In two of the corners
were narrow, filthy-looking beds, and in another
corner a small table and two stools. The host offered the voyagers some food, but it was so black
and repulsive that, though they were hungry
enough, they declined it on the plea that their
supplies would soon arrive.

The rain poured down in torrents, causing much
solicitude about the poor, plodding, well-laden
soldiers, which, added to the filthiness of their

quarters, made the hours move slowly to the hungry, waiting men. Finally, by much persuading,
the host brought out from an out-of-the-way crevice, his small supply of tea. A full bowl of this put
our party in better spirits.

While yet waiting we may study the two specimens of the natives of the country who were before them. They were man and wife. Their
dresses consisted of the shreds of greasy seal-skins,
the feet and legs being bare. Their long, coarse,
black hair had once been braided, the man's into
one, his wife's into two cues; but it was now terribly tangled and was becoming more so every
moment by their long, dirty fingers, which they
thrust into it to resent the attack of innumerable
little creatures whose home and employment they
thus disturbed. As they were first seen on the
beach there was nothing to distinguish the man
from the woman, except that the man was smoking a long-stemmed pipe, with an amber mouth-
piece and brass bowl, while the woman carried
their catch of fine salmon. So it is among the
heathen, the wife is known as the heavy burden
bearer. The color of this couple was a cross between that of the American Indian and the Chinese.
Their eyes were almond-shaped, their noses flat,
and their cheek-bones exceedingly prominent.
They were plainly of the Tartar race, of a tribe
called Gilaks, and related to the Tungusians, whom
we have met elsewhere. These Gilaks were in
possession of the lower Amoor when the whites
first visited that region, and seem to have been

there for an indefinite period. They number about eight thousand. With their customs and character we shall become more acquainted.

The lady of the hut in which our friends were just now unwillingly waiting thought to do them honor by a more becoming attire. She neither washed her face nor combed her hair, but mounted one of the beds in the corner, and put off, rather immodestly, her ragged, filthy seal skin for one a little less so. But a change of garments plainly enough did not rid her of the persistent little enemies of her person.

It was late in the afternoon when the soldiers arrived. They were wet and weary, but a bowl of tea, a full supper, a warm fire, and especially a generous pay in Russian rubles completely revived them. Our explorers, having eaten of their own stores and been refreshed, resolved to embark and reach the next station, six miles distant, hoping to find better quarters for the night. The station keeper made ready his boat, a kind of Mississippi River flat-boat on a small scale. Our party, with one of their soldiers as an interpreter, and the boatman and baggage, loaded it down nearly to the water's edge. But the lake was as calm as a city park pond, and they pushed boldly out into its midwaters. They had not gone far before the rain descended and the wind blew. The waves were not long in raising their white crests, and in keeping all hands busy in baling out the boat. But the situation became perilous, and they were glad to make at once the nearest shore. It was

plain that somebody must take to the land. This,
Bush, the captain, and the interpreter consented
to do, while Mahood and the boatman pushed on
with the baggage and boat.

The land party had a sorry time of it. The distance to be walked by the shore line was ten miles,
the way was intercepted by half-sunken logs, between which the coarse grass reached to their
shoulders, and hummocks were thrown in here and
there to increase the obstructions. The rain fell in
torrents and they were drenched to the skin. Yet
the first hour they made good progress, skirting
the bays and rounding point after point. Half
the distance had been accomplished when their
strength began to fail. The rain increased and
the darkness had become so dense that they could
not see each other at arm's length. Utter blind-
ness was about as good as sight in such a situation. They held each other by the hand for mutual assistance when stumbling or falling. At last
the grass was so thick, high, and tangled that they
could not press through it, so they took to the
lake, and plodded on, often waist-deep in mud
and water. Through another hour they persevered,
rounding many more points, hoping each one
would be the last. Finally, the clouds parted a
little, and they saw a black cape a mile ahead.
" That *must* be the last," they said, "and when we
reach it we shall see the light of the station." Thus
cheered they made a desperate push. The point
was reached, but all beyond was dark—a silent
and unbroken sheet of darkness. They could go

no farther, and so sank down on the wet grass. They had no matches, and there was no dry wood with which to make a fire. Here now they were, wet, tired, and hungry, with wet grass and mud beneath them, and darkness every-where, to all of which was added the fact, pleasantly communicated by their interpreter, that the region was a famous place for bears. Just at this moment Bush thought of his revolver, which he had carefully kept dry for an emergency. It was the God-inspired thought which we have so often noted as coming to the explorers in an extreme necessity. Three shots were fired in rapid succession. Scarcely had the last flash vanished in the darkness when there came, to inspire their drooping spirits, three answering pistol shots. In half an hour after they heard the cheerful dip of oars and Mahood's cheering shout. They were rescued.

CHAPTER XX.

DOWN THE AMOOR.

THE station was a commodious log building. It contained four rooms, heated by large oven stoves, and seemed to the escaped men a very palace. While their wet clothes were giving way to dry ones from their satchels, the host was preparing tea. The table was set, a huge loaf of brown bread was served in a large china dish, accompanied by a plate of butter, in which the bodies of numerous cockroaches were preserved, all of which was soon followed by hot tea. Our men proved to all observers that hungry persons are not afraid of dead cockroaches. They ate, drank, lay down on beds of dry hay and slept, and awoke in good spirits to renew their voyage.

Before leaving they breakfasted on fried trout and *brick* tea. Brick tea is the staple article of tea of the humble people. It is a compound of the coarse leaves and stems of the tea-plant, dried, pulverized, and mixed with bullocks' blood until a thick paste is formed. This paste is then made into brick-like cakes, which are baked hard. It is shaved off in powder when used, and to hungry and weary men is tolerably palatable.

For the next trip the explorers took a larger boat and a new boatman. They had become prej-

udiced against foot journeys by the lake shore,
notwithstanding their romantic character and the
sensation they might excite when printed in the
home papers. Their old soldier boatman grumbled
at the compensation he received for his night's
row, though it equaled a ten months' pay from the
government.

The morning was beautiful and warm, the lake
placid, and the boat ample and well handled.
Glittering fish here and there shot from the water,
attracting the eyes of the hawks, which swooped
suddenly down upon their prey. White storks and
swans waded among the reeds and rushes in the
swampy shore, and occasionally large flocks of
geese started up at the approach of the boat, swept
round in a graceful circuit overhead, and settled
again on the lake. The whole scene was calcu-
lated to cheat one into the belief that no night of
murky darkness ever settled on these quiet waters,
and no pelting rains nor troubled waves ever drove
belated voyagers to journey afoot in the quagmires
and hummocks of the shore. But *our* explorers
could not be so cheated by appearances.

The next station contained a large log-house
and fifty soldiers. The only boat for farther progress was a large barge, the use of which was kindly
offered to our party by the officer in command,
with nine men to row it. The rowers were merry
as school children, and the explorers in a contented frame of mind, so the time and the miles slipped
swiftly away, and they arrived at Marinsk on the
Amoor at five o'clock. The strangers found hos-

pitable quarters with a merchant, the commandant, unlike his countrymen generally, giving them the cold shoulder.   There are no inns in this country for strangers.

The town extended along the river for miles, and consisted of scattered log-houses.   A few of them had gardens and ornamental grounds in front, and a gayly-painted Greek church, with domes and minarets, showed that the *priest*, if not the school-master, was broad.   Would that these priests were *teachers*, as they do not seem to be, of the saving truth they profess to represent.

The mighty Amoor may well kindle our enthusiasm as we look upon it through the eyes of our explorers.   It was first made known to the general world through its discovery by the Russians, in 1843.   But it has been stated that the Chinese sailed on its waters before the days of Solomon. It is twenty-four hundred miles long, and navigable for steamers fifteen hundred miles.   Its banks afford all varieties of climate and soil, and, following its valley from their extreme homes, the strange fact is said to occur of the animals of the arctic regions becoming neighbors to those of the torrid zone.   Here the Bengal tiger springs from his covert upon the reindeer, and the wild boar hunts in the same forest with the polar hare.

The explorers started down the river the next morning in a barge kindly furnished by their merchant friend, rowed by five soldiers reluctantly detailed by the governor of the station.   Steamers for the mouth of the river would start in a few weeks, for which they chose not to wait. The whole town came to the beach to see them off. The men loitered about with folded arms and long-stemmed pipes, which seemed a part of them-selves, they were in such constant adjustment to their mouths. The women, with their heavy bur-dens of wood and water, paused to look at the strangers.

It was ten o'clock in the morning before our men were fairly off. Their barge had a clumsy sail, upon which, however, they did not much de-pend. The current alone bore them onward four miles an hour. Their part of the boat was fur-nished with clean, soft hay, over which their robes were thrown. Reclining on these, with a soft spring-like air, they were prepared to enjoy the enchanting scenery which rapidly passed before them like a grand panorama, as it was, by the hand of the divine Artist. The river at first spread out over the meadows on either side, a mile in width, reaching to the base of a range of blue hills. There were wooded islands occasion-ally, and rising uplands with rich vegetation, with here and there a spur of the hills coming down to the river on which nestled the humble but pict-ure-like homes of the Galiks. These people were busily engaged in catching salmon, the very finest specimens of which abounded in the river. These were thrown from their seines upon the shore in great numbers, their silver scales flashing in the sunlight, a sight provoking to the appetite of the daintiest epicure.

13

It was four o'clock in the afternoon before the voyagers landed for dinner. Their boat had turned by the steersman into a cut-off of the river which curved round for a considerable distance through a meadow of tall grass, until suddenly the government station came in view. It consisted of one ample log-house, and the many out-buildings of a well-to-do farmer. It was owned by a Pole whom the government employed to render assistance to the travelers on the river. The horses, cows, dogs, and domestic fowl thronged the premises in great numbers, and were thrown into a seemingly pleasant sensation at the coming of the strangers. The owner and his smiling wife received them cordially. A short time only intervened between the intimation of hunger and a well-prepared dinner of fresh milk, new eggs, and a recently-caught salmon. All these the voyagers complimented by disposing of a quantity which surprised themselves, and evidently excited the wonder of their host. The other members of the boat party were in the meantime having a merry time over their abundant provisions cooked by a fire on the beach.

Having eaten, our friends enjoyed a few moments of observation of the premises, and of chat with the kind host. Captain Bush complimented his fine situation. The old man shook his head, and went into a dismal story of the disaster he had suffered two years before in the overflowing of the Amoor. The whole vicinity had been inundated, his hay was all swept away, his cattle

died of starvation the following winter, and he was
reduced to poverty. Though he had recovered
nearly all in only two years, he wept in reciting
his great calamity. Bush hinted that it would be
well to remove his hay to an upland not likely to
be reached by the flood, a precaution which the
old man had never adopted, but the hint seemed
lost.

Among the curious things about the premises
was a plow made of the natural bends of the limbs
of trees, lashed strongly together with thongs;
there was not a particle of metal about it. It was
the plow of the olden time, for the genuine Yankee
had not been that way, though, perhaps, he is planning by this time to go.

When the voyagers again took to their boat the
evening was setting in. They were accompanied
by a little son of their host, who desired a night's
sail. The rubber sails were spread to the gentle
breeze, the sailor-soldiers struck up their melodious boat songs, and the explorers threw themselves
musingly upon their blanket-covered hay bed to
enjoy the scenery and the enchanting influence
which the surroundings inspired. Occasionally
the songs called forth responses from some Galik
village as they passed, but the melody of both
boatmen and villagers was often drowned in the
fearful howlings of numerous dogs, whose night-
dreams the strangers had disturbed.

There was one sailor who did not sing, but
when not taking his turn at rowing or other duty
of the boat, was cuddled down beside the boy

passenger.   Bush urged him to sing, but his whole
attention was absorbed by his interest in the boy.

"Don't urge him," whispered the helmsman.
"The boy has a pretty sister."

Love puts on the same airs and has the same
methods in all lands!

The spell of this enchanting boat ride was soon
broken.   Dark clouds obscured the sky, and the
boat drifted on in the dense darkness, the shore
line on either side seeming an ebony wall.   Suddenly out of the blackness came vivid flashes of
lightning.   Hurriedly the voyagers rolled up their
blankets, and covered themselves and baggage
with their large rubber spreads.   Scarcely was
this done when down came a torrent of rain, as if
some water-spout had broken over them.   In a
few moments the lightning and rain had ceased,
but the darkness remained.   For two hours more
they drifted on at the will of the current.   At
length the men seized the oars, and landed the
boat at a venture.   The best shelter that they
dared to hope was some rock or tree, where, building a fire, they might wait for daylight.   But the
sound of their voices brought the welcome barking of dogs.   Soon men with torches appeared.
They had landed near an encampment of Russian
soldiers who were engaged during the day in
catching salmon.   The torchmen led Bush, Mahood, and their companion, the Dutch captain, to
their hut.   This was nothing more than a small
shelter made by tacking birch-bark to a slight
frame of poles.   Rows of bunks, comfortably wide

enough for one person only, lined each side, and
contained two men apiece. The chance for an
hour or two of sleep did not look promising, but
two of the soldiers immediately vacated their
bunk, saying, with emphatic good-will, that they
would go with the boatmen and little boy to another encampment not far off. Three men in a
narrow bunk! Well, they must make the best of
it. The two younger generously perched themselves as best they could upon the outer edges,
and gave the captain the middle, and the blanket
was drawn over the three. Bush's place was
against the side of the tent, where the rain, which
was now falling freely, kept him well sprinkled.
Mahood clung to his edge to prevent being precipitated into the middle of the hut, and both
slept as a man does clinging for his life to the
top of a mast. The captain the while first indicated that *he* intended to sleep, then turned over a
few times to show a wise adjustment of himself for
that purpose. In this last operation he rolled the
entire blanket about him as tightly as the wrap-
per about an Egyptian mummy. When the day
dawned Bush and Mahood were glad to escape
from their position of torture. The captain lay
upon his back sweetly sleeping on. When at
length he slowly opened his eyes, he stretched
himself and yawned. "Well!" he said, looking
complacently around, "these accommodations are
not so bad after all. I don't know when I have
slept better."

That's often the way in the world. The favored

do not inquire how much pain their comforts may
have cost others.

The next day was pleasant, and the sailing delightful. Many Galik villages were passed, and
the natives were seen busy with their silvery-scaled
salmon, which they were catching for winter use.
Their curious-shaped hats were a pretty sight, especially when a large number of people wearing
them were grouped together. They are ingenious-
ly made of thin, flexible birch-bark, in the shape
of an open umbrella of a small pattern. They
keep off the sun, and shed the rain, and must be
very light and easy to the head. About all other
styles of hats for ladies' wear in our own country
have been in fashion ; we suggest that they try the
Galik hat. The scenery of the remaining voyage
down the Amoor was varied, and the incidents interesting. At one time they passed between high
rocky bluffs, reminding them of the Highlands of
the Hudson ; at the foot of these bluffs, on the
shelving shore, the Galiks were engaged in catching salmon, some of them using their light, fancy
canoes.

While drifting at night between these high banks,
it was intensely dark. Out of this darkness came
occasional flashes of lightning, and in one instance
a violent storm. To vary the monotony of this
night voyaging, the steersman and rowers would
fall asleep grasping their oars, and let the boat's
masts get entangled in the overhanging willows,
and the boat itself go thumping, stern foremost,
against the shore.

As they approached the mouth of the Amoor the shore spread into broad meadows, which were covered with stacks of hay; beyond these, on the right, was a range of hills, at the foot of which ran the telegraph wires back to Castries Bay.

With pleasant memories of their ride on the Amoor, our party arrived safely at Nicholas at its mouth.

CHAPTER XXI.

A NOVEL TOWN.

THE fur-trading town at the mouth of the Amoor, to which our adventurers had come, had been settled only about fifteen years. It contained five thousand people. It is situated on slightly-elevated level land, on the north bank of the river, which is at this place a mile and a quarter wide, and very shallow, especially in front of the town. It is guarded by four forts in the river, giving it a military air.

As the strangers drew near the wharf numerous little water craft hovered round their boat, among which were the Galik canoes, laden with salmon for sale. The camp-fires along the beach, and the groups of men, women, and children huddled near them under their frail skin tents, made a novel and pretty scene. Following the road our company came to the town above, whose low, cheap log-houses reminded them of its recent origin. Its main street, extending two miles along the bank of the river, had plank sidewalks, and opened on the upper side into a square, on which was the Greek church and public buildings.

Gray-coated soldiers and gayly-dressed officers were promenading here, enjoying the evening air, ind chatting merrily as in any home town. Teams trundled along the street, drawn by hardy little horses, which seemed happily deaf, or at least indifferent to the bitter words hurled at them by their drivers.

Situated on the church square was an American-looking house, which was occupied by the United States commercial agent, Mr. Chase. Here the explorers found kind and homelike entertainment.

This town was named after the Czar Nicholas, and, as its Russian rendering is spelled in as many different ways as we have seen books which contain it, and none of them spell any thing to the English reader, we have chosen to translate it into plain *Nicholas.* Nicholas has many foreign commercial houses, among which are several representing the United States. The community is divided into many grades, the lines being drawn sharply by the weight of one's purse. The merchants are the upper class, a fixed and definite sum being named as a condition of being so ranked. To this class is committed the local government of the place, the mayor being chosen from it. It is not stated whether there is any difficulty in enforcing the law which requires a merchant to serve in this office when elected. It may seem to republican minds quite unfair to give "the people" at large no voice in the government; but such will be somewhat relieved to know that the merchants are *required* to pay all the taxes.

The business is chiefly that of trade for fur with

liquor, sugar, tea, flour, and salt, but mainly with liquors. There are in the unfortunate town seventy five places where it is sold, each one of which, no doubt, is mightier for evil than the church on the square is for good. This explains why the merchants are required to pay the taxes, for, as they are the liquor dealers, it is not presumed that any others have any money after paying for their daily dram. If this same upper class were made accountable for all the crime their alcohol instigates, out of their number, we are sure, most of the jail convicts and subjects for the gallows would come.

On the main street, along the river bank, a public park has been laid out. A school for young ladies has been established, and one for the children of the soldiers.

We remarked, in noticing the plow made of the roots of trees, which the explorers saw on the Amoor, that the Yankee had not arrived in that far up-river country. But he has reached Nicholas. Machine-shops, a foundry, and a saw-mill are in full operation, under the management of some American gentlemen. Now, with a church, schools, a public park, a lively trade, and manufacturing establishments, Nicholas has a good future before it, clouded only by the seventy-five liquor shops.

We might have added, in speaking of the drawback on the town's future prospect, that the women are a small minority of the population; we cannot say whether the thrift of the liquor trade has kept the women away, or whether its thrift comes from their absence.

Our visitors attended a banqueting occasion in honor of an incoming governor who had just arrived. It seems to have been an enjoyable occasion, only that not a woman was present. At an evening ball given soon after, the ladies were out, "jeweled, and elegantly attired;" "but," says our American observer, "I could not fail to notice the almost total absence of beauty among the fairer sex." At a pause in the dance these ladies suddenly all disappeared. In answer to an inquiry as to the occasion of this, he was led to a side room, the door of which stood ajar. Our inquisitive friend was invited to look in, and there, "with knees crossed," and ranged round the room, each with a cigar in her mouth, and enveloped in smoke, were the missing ladies. Their almost total lack of beauty was, we think, accounted for.

The stay of thirty-five days of our explorers at Nicholas was improved in making diligent inquiry concerning their route to Ochotsk, where they were to meet Major Abasa, a distance of five hundred and fifty miles. A small portion of this was known to a few persons; but the greater part had never been trod, so far as known, by the foot of man It was wild and mountainous, and at the mention of it the natives shook their heads, and remarked seriously, "If you go far into that region you will die there."

The point in the route which was a little known was Tugur, on Tugur Bay, some twelve days' jour-

ney up the coast. For this station, by the help of
the governor of Nicholas, they secured a fair outfit of furs and provisions, and reindeer for riding
and for the packs. A Pole by the name of Swartz,
who had been at Tugur, was most fortunately secured as interpreter. A Cossack by the name of
Yakov was appointed to travel with them for about
a month. Eighteen deer were with difficulty secured, four of which were to carry Bush, Mahood,
Swartz, and Yakov, and fourteen to carry the provisions, a small canvas tent, the cooking apparatus, and scientific instruments, with a very limit-
ed supply of furs. In fact they depended upon re-
newing their outfit of food and furs at Tugur. Two
Tungusians—fur-clad, wild-looking natives—were
secured as deer drivers and guides to Tugur, they
riding their own animals.

On the twenty-first of October Bush, Mahood,
and Swartz took a little Government steamer kindly put at their disposal, and started for Lake Orell,
sixty miles north, while Yakov and the two natives proceeded with the deer by land to the same
point.

To reach the lake they first steamed up the
Amoor; into this river the waters from the lake
poured through many sluices and channel-ways.
These were in places narrow, often shallow, and
wound through the prairie in ever varying curves.
Into one of these the little craft soon entered, and
sailed with great caution, and for awhile quite
pleasantly. They drew up at a little village, hoping to learn something concerning Yakov and his

company; but failing in their inquiries, Mahood and Swartz were sent off in a native canoe to hunt them up; but they returned at night cold, wet, hungry, and desponding, for they had seen nothing of the deer train.

They started again, but sailing became increasingly difficult. When within twenty miles of the lake, ice began to form and increase alarmingly. Through this the brave little steamer cut its way, its paddle-wheels shivering the glassy surface into myriads of particles. The ice grew thicker and thicker and the progress slower and slower, when suddenly a snow-storm burst upon them, shutting out the shore so that the boat could be steered only by guess. Running in this way awhile, it suddenly grounded. Backing off they steamed a little farther and grounded again. The pilots confessed that they knew nothing of their whereabouts, and the officer of the boat reported the fuel nearly spent. Here was a sad condition of things—in an unknown, snow-covered land, in a crippled boat, with a small stock of provisions. It looked, to our adventurers, like defeat to start with, and their hearts for the moment grew faint. There was nothing to do but to try the backward track.

Rounding about they had sailed an hour and a half when they came upon thirty soldiers fishing for a winter's supply. Bush and his men went ashore, were well received, and their spirit revived; they at once determined to lay in a good supply of fuel by the help of the soldiers, and renew the effort to reach the lake. They tried to secure the help of some of the soldiers as guides, but they flatly refused. They would, they said, be frozen in and starved.

Just in time two Yakoot canoe men came paddling up the river. These were the "iron men," such as we met with Kennan. They were ready to do and dare any thing. Besides it began to rain and the mercury fell below the freezing point.

With a good supply of fuel the steamer turned round and renewed her fight with the ice. Under the guidance of the Yakoots there was no more running aground, and they soon entered the lake, plowed their way with a hard strain on the frail boat for a mile or two, and entered clear water. The open lake, about thirty miles long by twenty wide, was reached.

Sailing on they saw the smoke rising from a little clump of trees. Landing they found a camp of Galiks. Here the steamer left the exploring party and returned. Nothing could be learned of the deer train under Yakov. The tent was pitched by the Yakoot pilots, who had remained with them, and Mahood and Swartz borrowed a canoe of the Galiks and went in search of the missing party. But they soon returned unsuccessful, though they had heard hallooing.

After eating a good supper of fresh salmon and tea, prepared by the Yakoots, the searching party went out again. While they were gone Bush attempted to make himself comfortable in his new canvas tent, but a rain set in and it leaked so badly that he found it better to move about outside. A fire was tried, but it only smoked. In this strait he entered and made himself at home in the tent of his neighbors, the Galiks, into which we will peer.

CHAPTER XXII.

REINDEER RIDING.

THE tent was made by drawing strips of birch-bark, sewed together over poles sloping to the ground and forming a shed-like shelter, open at each end and on one side. The open side fronted a steep bank above the beach, which sheltered it from the wind.

As Bush and Swartz approached, a woman was boiling, in a pot over the fire, some fresh salmon, and steeping tea which the explorers had given them for their fish. In the tent, at one end, was a baby strapped into a box-like cradle, open at the foot, beyond which its little feet extended; the box being hung to the top of the tent by strips of deer skin the baby's toes just touched the ground and enabled it to dance up and down, and to swing round. It was a Galik baby-jumper in which the little one laughed and crowed like any other baby.

Near the jumper sat two haggard, wild-looking women making garments from a filthy deer skin. They took little notice of the baby, but glanced sharply at the cook to whom they gave frequent orders, and scolded angrily two naked little boys who were contending with an old toothless, hungry-looking dog for the possession of a deer-skin bed.

Other dogs lay around as if equal owners with the humans of the place. But the chief figure was a hag-like woman, with shriveled skin drawn over her bony frame, sunken eyes, and long hair dangling over her face. She was catching certain little creatures from the head of a dirty-faced girl, and *not* throwing them away when caught. The whole scene of dogs, women, and children was a sad picture of a heathen home.

At five o'clock Mahood returned, cold, wet, hungry, and desponding, for he had seen nothing of the deer-train.

After another weary day of waiting the explorers, as they sat in their tent, heard the welcome cry from a native of "Alane!" They had learned that this meant deer. Rushing from the tent they caught a glimpse, a half a mile distant, of the deer party under Yakov's command picking their way along the beach. The Tungusians were leading the deer, while Yakov made his way slowly along the shore in a boat. They had been detained tour days by the ice.

The two Yakoot sailors were now dismissed with pay, which excited their admiration for the strangers. With tears in their eyes they bid them good-bye, crossing themselves and invoking many blessings.

The next day was devoted to repacking their stores. We have seen the reindeer as used by Kennan's party on the great snowy desert. There they were harnessed to sledges, and though we did not find them beautiful-looking nor swift-footed,

14

they were very useful. Now we are to see them used very differently. Our party and their goods are to be *carried* by them, not drawn.

First, the pack-saddles are to be arranged. These are two small satchels or pads made of buckskin, lined with moss or hair, and connected at the tops by natural bows made of pieces of deer horns selected with their natural curves. These are filled with stores and placed, not on the deer's back, but on his fore-shoulders, a space being left between the buckskin pads for the shoulders to work easily. Not more than one hundred pounds are put upon one pack-deer. The ridden deer carry a man weighing much more, as he is not such dead weight. The saddles for the rider are like the pack-saddles, only broader, and made to stand out further from the animal's shoulders.

All being ready, the whole company were astir early on Thursday morning, October twenty-sixth. It consisted, as we have seen, of Bush and Mahood, our explorers, Swartz the Swede, Yakov the deer-driver, and his two aids, the natives Constantine and Mikhaeloff, whom we shall know as "Mik." The fourteen pack-deer were divided into three trains, each train fastened one after the other by their halters, and led by Yakov and his aids.

Every man being at his assigned place in the train, the word was given to mount and move off. The reader will remember that the saddle was on the high shoulders of the deer, fastened by only a

single girth which passed around his body, and
that there were no stirrups or any kind of support
for the feet. The *reins* were only an ordinary halter. Of course, to mount and ride safely required
much practice, and this Bush and Mahood had
not had. Mahood made a bold spring, just missed
gaining his seat, and came to the ground. Bush
made several attempts, but failed, and was compelled to call upon one of the men to lift him on.
The Galik children were much amused at the
awkwardness of the strangers, and laughed heartily, as any children would have done.

When on, it was no easy matter to stay in the
saddle, as the skin on the deer's shoulders is very
loose, and the saddle slips at every step, first this
way and then that, keeping the rider rolling about
like a sailor on his sea-legs. Our explorers were
quite proud of the fact that they did not fall off
more than once in a mile.

A little less than five miles over a rough,
swampy trail, proved far enough for the first day,
and all were glad to camp. The natives cut long
poles, thrust the large ends into the ground in a
circle, and brought the tops together. Over this
frame skins were drawn. Branches of trees and
twigs were strewn over the ground inside on which
to make the beds, a space being left in the middle
for the fire. A good supper, and sound sleep soon
followed.

For many days the train plodded slowly on,
wading through marshes, where the deer wallowed knee-deep in mud and water, and the riders

had to walk, fording streams and pushing aside
the bushes of their banks, the way made doubly
disagreeable by an almost constant rain.   Short
journeys and frequent camping had to be the rule.
To pass the time away in camp, as well as to secure fresh meat, short hunting excursions were
made, the natives taking their best-trained deer.
A good stock of a large, tender-fleshed bird
was the general result of their hunts.   Once,
while waiting in camp, Bush, to pass away the
time, took Mik's picture.   The fellow had never
seen a mirror, and so had never looked into his
own face.   He was terribly mortified and vexed
at the sight.   But Constantine enjoyed Mik's dis-
comfiture, jeering and laughing, as much as to
say, "It *is* ugly looking, but it looks just like
you;" and, we suppose, to show poor Mik how
a handsome man's face looks in a picture, he
begged Bush to take his.   When this was done,
Mik laughed and jeered, and Constantine looked
heartily ashamed and humbled.   How it does
take the conceit out of people, whether in heathen
or Christian lands, when they see their *own*
faces !

Soon after both of these men, having borrowed
a pair of scissors, trimmed up their dangling
locks, washed their faces, and combed their hair,
and came to Bush begging him to take their pictures again.

The traveling as well as camping needed some
relieving incident, so Bush and Mahood proposed
a race of the deer they rode.   There were no

spurs nor riding-whips with which to urge their animals, but each engaged one of the natives to poke them in the rear, while all the hands shouted them on. The result was a trifling quickening of their *walk*, but not for a moment a run. They finished the race in company.

On the fourth of November several inches of snow covered the ground, at which the explorers rejoiced, as it promised another mode of traveling. The next day they ascended a ridge of land which gave them a view of the many bays of the sea-shore. Down this ridge to the barren plain they slowly plodded, then crossing the rivers as best they could, often only after a circuitous search for a ford, they made their way toward Tugur, the point from which they hoped to take a new departure, refreshed, refitted, and more fully instructed concerning that part of their way which lay beyond. Tugur is an old whaling station, on Tugur Bay, employing about sixty men, who go out from the shore, take whale and grampus, and bring them to the beach, where their oil is taken out. It will be recollected that our explorers had met at Nicholas Mr. Lindholm, one of its principal men, who had assured them that here they might find friends and supplies. What, then, was their disappointment in finding the place forsaken! Not a living being could be seen in the whole immediate vicinity. A note was tacked to the door of the commander's house, addressed to Lindholm, telling him that for want of supplies all hands had gone to Manga, another whaling station, nearly a

hundred miles farther up the coast. It was to
Tugur that Constantine and Mik had engaged to
come, and by no consideration could they be induced to go another mile. Here, then, our party
were at a stand-still.

CHAPTER XXIII.

OVER THE MOUNTAINS.

AFTER some careful search through the deserted place, Bush found in an out-of-the-way hut an old, blind Tungusian woman, bending over a few embers which smoked in a rude fireplace. She was the picture of loneliness and destitution. She gladly welcomed the strangers, shaking hands all round, and singing plaintively her salutation. From her they learned that there lived about five miles up the coast an *employé* of the company who remained in charge of a few cows.

Leaving Constantine and Mik to bring up the deer, the rest of the party pushed on for the hut, which they readily found. It was small and mean, but afforded the hungry, weary, and desponding men a most refreshing hospitality. Plenty of fresh venison steak and new milk were set before them. Good news was added to good eating by the statement of their host that there was a settlement of Yakoots—the " iron-men "—only a few miles off, and that, as usual, they were rich in meat, fur-clothing, and bedding. Still more in the line of good news was the fact that the Tungusian "head-man" of all the district lived at the same village. Furnished with official indorsement from the governor at Nicholas, our party were sure of the head-man's good offices. So after supper, the whole train having come up, they started for the village. The disappointment at Tugur was almost forgotten, the trail was a good one, and the deer even were inspired with fresh courage, and actually trotted—the first trot of the whole journey.

On arriving at the village, about fifty persons, men, women, and children, rushed out of the huts to meet them. They were well dressed and intelligent-looking, and spoke the Russian language readily; so our party, through Swartz, were at once in easy communication with them. In fact, the interpreter found among them some former friends. The hospitality of one of the largest and best houses was proffered and accepted. The Russian tea urn was brought on, and refreshments served, but the host could not be persuaded to partake until the guests had finished.

In the roomful of dark-skinned, curious lookers-on was a little girl of very fair complexion, having long sunny hair, and light blue eyes. She seemed perfectly at home in the midst of her dark companions, and none of them appeared to notice that she was not in all respects of them. The visitors learned that her parents were Russians, and having died these people had kindly adopted the lonely orphan as their own.

Captain Bush succeeded in purchasing of the head-man a deer train, and in securing the services of two native drivers, as Constantine and Mik were to return at once. A full stock of provisions and furs were obtained of the Yakoots. The new drivers, Vassilly and Eoff, were young and active, and entered with spirit into the enterprise. The first had a lady love at the terminus of this stage of the journey, whom he had purchased for eighty reindeer. This was a great price, as his people consider one rich who owns a dozen of these animals; but his lady was a chief's daughter, and, in his estimation at least, not to be valued by the vulgar standard. There is, however, another phase to this matter of wife-purchase. The father, who sets the price, is expected to endow the bride with a herd of deer equal in number to that paid by her suitor. So it was after all only a shrewd way the old folks had of stimulating their would-be son to secure at marriage a good start in life.

The party left the friendly settlement in good spirits. The fresh deer were much more lively than those they had just dismissed. The one Bush rode considered it a good joke to slip him off into the snow, now quite deep. The route lay along the coast awhile, and then more inland, across streams, through bushes, and, finally, up a mountain range. The guide, Yakov, led the way through a gorge which brought them unexpectedly upon a beautiful table-land. The whole country traversed the last three days was full in sight. Far above them was the mountain ridge to which they must climb. Eoff had gone ahead with the pack-deer, and was already creeping along at a dizzy height. As the rest pushed on they found the snow on the mountain side frozen in a measure which lessened the wading, while it required great caution, for to lose a foothold and slip back might send rider and deer, like an avalanche, among the bowlders below. So slippery was the ascent that the men threw themselves several times upon the snow and laid hold of its inequalities with their hands. The weather was fine and the wind calm, or their progress would have been impossible. Had they been, while thus climbing, overtaken with one of the fiercer snow-storms which so often occur in these mountains, they would have been precipitated into the depths below, scattered and left to perish miserably. But all arrived safely at the top. Here the view was grand. The Tugur River and bay were in full sight. The intervening country, which they had found in traveling so rough and uneven, seemed level as a floor, its snowy covering of dazzling white relieved only by the dark shadings of occasional forests. On every hand, nearer to them, bold volcanic peaks towered far into the upper sky. No wing of bird nor voice of living thing broke the painful silence which reigned around, or relieved the universal desolation.

The musing on this bleak summit was brief. As the men had walked up, they decided to ride down, though we presume the deer were not consulted in this arrangement. But the question was how to mount, as, standing in the deep snow, there was no footing from which to spring into the saddles

It must be remembered they had no stirrups, and that the rider's seat was a movable one on the deer's shoulders. Finally the drivers lifted our men bodily into their saddles, and, from long practice, easily vaulted into their own.

Captain Bush's deer was a short-legged, spirited little fellow. He brought up the rear, but could not step far enough to walk in the tracks of those going before, which caused him to flounder about generally, now in the deep footholds, and then body deep in the untrodden snow. Of course his rider was pitched off. How to get on again was a question which concerned Bush, but did not trouble the deer. After walking awhile they came to a small sapling, by climbing which Bush again mounted. By this time the train was far ahead, which fretted terribly the ambitious little beast; to regain his companions he made a desperate effort to hurry and sent his rider again into a snowbank. Another long walk followed. Three more trees were climbed in succession, and as many falls endured before the train was overtaken.

All reached the foot of the hill in safety and camped. The snow was much deeper and softer than they expected, so that the weary reindeer could not paw up as usual from underneath it their supper of moss. Some boughs of trees were thrown to them from the moss of which they picked a scanty meal. No wonder that they resented this, and that the camp was alarmed at midnight by the shout that the deer had all taken a sudden leave and returned over the mountain

Eoff, tired as he was, started on snow-shoes to
bring them back.   His Yakoot endurance and integrity were put to a severe test, but he proved
equal to the occasion, and returned with them in
the morning.

Our fur-clad men now followed the course of the
streams which started in the hills over which they
had come and flowed toward the sea.   Their camp
at night was varied by amusing or stirring incidents.   At one time Bush and Mahood opened a
box of mustard to be used at their meal—a home
relish in which they had not before indulged.
The Cossack, Yakov, watched the preparation and
use of it with great curiosity.   He had heretofore
found that the occasional variations in the meals
of the Americans were attended by something
especially nice.   So when they had turned from
the repast he and the Yakoots bolted down each a
generous mouthful.   It was too quickly swallowed
to be fully tasted, but in their throats and stomachs
it was as a live coal.   Bush and Mahood were
suddenly startled by a dismal howl.   They sprang
out of the tent to the camp-fire, near which Yakov
lay prostrate, his face in the snow and his mouth
covered by both hands.   He was blowing as if a
flame from a furnace had gone down his throat.
The natives were thrashing round like mad men.
No serious injury came of the incident, and the
sufferers from this time held at least some American luxuries at a discount.

The Arla River, whose course they were following, widened and deepened every hour, and they

soon struck the trail of natives who were fishing
through the ice. Their camp was at one time by
a camp of these fishermen. Their method of taking
the fish seems to be just that which we have described as witnessed by Dall on the rivers of
Alaska. A brush fence is thrown across the river
beneath the ice. Narrow passages are left in a few
places, through which the fish swim. At these
passages a long, funnel-shaped trap, made of willow
work, is placed, into which the fish find it easy to
enter, but difficult to get out. The fish thus taken
are of several varieties and all of delicious flavor.
Not far from the fishermen our travelers came upon
the cattle-farm of a Yakoot cattle merchant, of
whose locality and reputation they had been informed at Nicholas. His Russian name was Sol-
avaoff. His numerous hay-stacks, jutting from the
snow, and the large herds of cattle, showed the well-
to-do proprietor.

Here our weary explorers for awhile rested.

CHAPTER XXIV.

A THRILLING STORY.

ENTERING with our men the hut of the chief man, we shall want to look round upon it and its internal arrangements, as it is in some respects unlike any thing we have seen. It is built of small, split logs, standing on end, instead of resting upon each other lengthwise. These logs are made to slope inward, making the sides of the house somewhat like our French roofs. The roof also is made of split logs, resting on heavy posts. The whole is banked over with clay, making the house look on the outside like a mound of earth. Two small openings are left in the side for air and light; over these, fish skins, sewed together, are drawn, in place of glass. Sometimes blocks of clear, thick ice, answer this purpose, and will last for months.

The room into which we are introduced is about twenty feet square, having against three sides raised benches, answering for bunks in the night and seats during the day. But the marked feature of the room is the fire-place; the chimney and fire-place are one, constructed of poles, standing endwise, and bound together with withes and plastered over with clay, one layer being put on and dried, and then another, until the whole is very thick and solid. This holds the heat a long time and throws from its surface a bright illumination over the room.

The influence of the Greek Church is apparent in the presence of holy images and pictures. The Russian tea urn, with its inviting contents, soon appeared, with a good supply of fresh milk. These did not surprise our visitors, but when plates of genuine griddle-cakes were set before them, smoking hot, an unexpected association with home life attended their disappearing appetites.

The following day our travelers started off with fine weather and in good spirits. They crossed first a plain, and then the Tela Hills. From the top of these they obtained an extended view of the western coast of the Ochotsk Sea, with the Yuggur mountain range, which followed it far northward, looking even in the distance as if they frowned upon the daring explorers. Along the summit of this range they were to extend their surveys.

Descending the hills they followed the Uda River toward the coast. The wolves in great numbers howled around their camp-fires at night, but with coward fear kept out of the range of the guns. They cannot often be shot, but as their skins are valuable, the natives poison great numbers of them with a drug obtained of the Russians.

They have, though, a cunning way of taking them alive. They build two circular pens, one within the other, having walls ten feet high, separated by a passage-way so narrow that a wolf can

just squeeze through it, but cannot turn round
in it.   There is no entrance to the *inner* pen except over the top of the wall.   In this a carcass of
a deer is suspended.   In the first wall there is a
door opening into the narrow passage-way between the walls.   Through this the wolf, as he
smells the deer meat, squeezes the door open
against the inner wall; he goes round until he
comas back to the door again, and, as he cannot
turn, he pushes past it, and shuts himself in.   The
natives, climbing to the top of the wall, spear or
shoot him at their leisure.

The next resting and recruiting place was Algasee, a trading town near the mouth of the river,
having its importance from a trade with the whalers, which, in times past, have made this part of
the bay an anchoring place.   They were quite disappointed when about twenty people rushed out
to meet them, to learn that these composed the
population.   The dogs, however, were much more
numerous, and gave the strangers a howling welcome.

They entered a hut and enjoyed a good meal of
deer flesh, washed down with tea.   Just after the
appetite was satisfied, and they were chatting together, they were startled by the musical tones of
a Tungusian boy, eight years old, who was singing
"John Brown."   It brought a sudden rush of
thoughts of native land and home, which were almost overpowering.   The little fellow had caught
the air from the whalemen.   If the whalemen had
carried into these cold and desolate regions for

the children a Sunday-school melody, it would have sounded still more thrilling.

A few miles below Algasee, where they were now stopping, and nearer where the whale ships anchored, was a little village to which the natives resorted for trade.

Swartz, the Swede, had, in connection with this whale-ship trading village, an exciting story to tell. He was, three years before, while in the employ of the Russian-American Company, making a journey along the coast with some Tungusians and a reindeer train. Coming to a place where a narrow arm of the sea made far up into the land, they attempted to cross on the ice, which seemed thick and strong, and extended far out to sea. When the train came near the opposite shore they discovered that a channel of open water lay between them and the beach. It was too deep and wide to ford, so they turned up the bay and traveled along the channel to find an ice-bridge to the land. But to their dismay they soon learned that the channel was widening, and the whole floe drifting out to sea. A fresh breeze sprang up from the shore, increasing the speed of the great ice-field, and tossed the sea into white-capped waves. The ice on which they stood proved to be neither thick nor strong; it bent and quivered under the shocks of the rolling sea which threatened its utter dissolution. To lessen the weight upon it, the deer and men were distributed over the ice. Further and further they drifted until the land was left in the dim distance. To increase

15

their terror a sudden and loud report announced the breaking up of their ice-field. Report followed report, like the successive explosions of a battery, and a large crack in the ice ran within a few rods of where they were standing. A few moments later the sea was crowded with cakes of ice, large and small, grinding against each other and filling the air with those terrifying noises which so alarmed the early voyagers in the arctic seas. Still, their own raft remained large enough to bear its involuntary passengers.

Night came on, dark and bitterly cold. There was nothing of which to make a fire, and no shelter. The men lay down in their furs and attempted to sleep. The deer shivered behind a hummock, huddling together for mutual warmth. When they attempted to lie down their fur froze to the ice. Cold, weary, and almost desperate with thirst, the deer finally came where the men were lying, and attempted to lie down upon them, which was prevented with difficulty; one of them, in an effort to quench his thirst with the snow on the chin of Swartz as he lay asleep, actually ate off a part of his beard.

This drifting lasted four days, during which the men subsisted on dried fish, without water, while the poor beasts had nothing. The ice-raft had worn away to a size so small that the breaking off of a few more fragments would drop the wretched party in the sea to perish. Any slight unfavorable change in the wind or waves would bring on this crisis suddenly. When, on the fifth day, hope had

nearly expired, the wind changed and blew toward
the land, and their ice-raft struck for a few moments a projecting point ; they had scarcely made
their hurried retreat when it swung off, took a
seaward current, and was soon out of sight.

Four of the deer died immediately. The party
were now sixty miles from the mouth of the Urdu,
and were four weary days in reaching its trading
village.

CHAPTER XXV.

THINGS GRAVE AND GAY.

OUR explorers were glad to learn soon after coming to Algasee that there was, about fifty miles farther up the Urdu River, a trading village of more importance, called Oudskoi, containing two hundred people, a head-man, and a priest and church. To this they determined to go, and were delighted to learn that their journey could be made with dog-sledges. They had never tried this mode of conveyance, and promised themselves a pleasant change from the *shoulders* of the deer to the sledges of the dogs.

Early one morning the little village was astir. The sledges had been packed, and the morning meal was soon eaten. Thirty dogs out of the many in the village had been selected to draw the three sledges; these were harnessed and tied to trees to await the moment of starting. They had eaten their one good-sized fish apiece, the only meal for twenty-four hours, and were as eager for a start as a hunter's dogs. They howled and snapped at each other in their own pleasant, amiable way. Several of those not chosen for the journey came round, inviting themselves to be of the party. One little fellow, from the commencement of the preparations, jumped as high and barked as loud as the oldest and biggest of the pack, and when the harnessed dogs were loosened and attached to the sledges, he wheeled into line, saying in good plain dog language, " Let *me* go too ! " and when he was ordered off, his head and tail fell, and he moved away in disappointment and grief.

As dog-sledging was new to our men, and the contrast in fleetness to deer-riding was very great, they were thrilled with delight; but as it is not new to our readers, we need notice only an incident or two, just to keep them fresh in the romance of the thing.

The dogs of the different teams, though old friends at home, had a decided *team* ambition and jealousy. At one time, as a team which had traveled in the rear was evidently succeeding in the attempt to pass another one, the dogs of the beaten team snapped at their successful rivals. Of course the others snapped back, for what else would *dogs* do ? and of course, having snapped all round, the two teams were stopped, and, in spite of the shouts and lusty blows from the driving sticks of their masters, a general fight ensued. The harnesses were sadly tangled, limbs were maimed, blood was shed, and in the end it was very plain, even to the dogs, that the fight was causeless and profitless—like most all fights.

At another time a fox, for the fun of it, darted from the woods upon the ice, and scampered up the river just ahead of the teams. The dogs put forth their best speed. But fox had no sledge to draw, and he was fresh in the race. The result was that those who rode made most excellent time, and the game, when tired, slipped into the woods over the bank and escaped.

At one time they had just come out of a piece of woods on the bank of the river; along its edge the dogs bounded for awhile, and then, in a moment, all disappeared. The riders hardly knew what had happened until they picked themselves up in a very light snow drift on the river, ten feet perpendicular from the point of the disappearance of the dogs. The team was soon all right, and gliding along the smooth ice.

An hour and a half after the night had set in, the train made a turn in the river, and came suddenly upon the cheerful lights of six or eight low log buildings. It was the neighborhood of Oudskoi.

On entering the head-man's house they were surprised at being greeted in the home style and in good English. The salutation came from Captain Hutchinson, an American whaler, an old friend of Swartz, but whose presence here was unexpected.

The host scarcely waited for the guests to remove their furs before he brought on his bottles of strong drink. Though a young man, his face bore evidence that he tarried long at the wine—or something stronger. He drank with his guests, and repeated the glasses so often that they thought it prudent to decline further solicitations. Nothing discouraged in the bad business, he drank alone for awhile, when the priest, who lived farther up the river, coming in, they both continued tc drink until they were wild with the intoxication The robed debauchee finally sprang into the floor with a three-stringed Russian instrument, struck up a quickstep, and commenced singing and skipping about the room, his long, coarse hair whisking wildly back and forth.

Supper being announced, the strangers were ushered into an adjoining room, and seated at a small table. On the table there was only a large dish of hashed meat and potatoes, a decanter of liquor, and six forks. The Americans naturally waited for plates to be brought on. but Swartz seized a fork and thrust it into a smoking potato and commenced eating. " We are all expected in this locality," he remarked, "to eat out of the same dish. ' To hungry men food is more than ceremony, so they all thrust in their forks, and made a good dinner.

After the repast the drunken priest, Father Ivan, entertained them, through Swartz as interpreter, with what he called a good joke played off upon the head-man. They were in the habit, it seems, of gambling together. One night, at the beginning of the game, the pious father drew a frightful picture of Satan on the piece of paper used to record the game. The picture was on the lower edge of the paper, and this edge he placed nearest the governor with the superstitious notion that it would cause him ill luck. But the robed villain lost constantly. Thinking the sa-

tanic picture was the cause, he hit upon the following shocking expedient to turn his luck, and
laughed while he told of it, more as if he were a fallen spirit from the lower world than God's minister. He slyly slipped the paper aside, made three
crosses upon the forehead of the picture, and,
having blessed it after the manner of the priestly
blessing of his Church, christened it the Almighty.
He then turned it next himself, and claimed that
at that time he began to win. The game was continued all night, the priest coming out ahead.

How sad that the heathen themselves should be
polluted by such a teacher of sacred things.

The next day was the Sabbath, and our explorers attended church. It was a small log-house
with a low tower and dome, and situated on a
bluff exposed to the rudest blasts of the wind
which easily penetrated its cracks. It contained
no place for a fire, nor a single seat of any kind
for the worshipers. As our friends entered the
simple-minded audience were all kneeling, and
they continued either to stand or kneel. Opposite the entrance, back of the altar, through a latticed door leading into the "holy place," could
be seen our drunken priest of the last evening.
He was dressed in a beautiful robe, on which were
wrought elegant scroll-work figures. He was bowing and chanting before a crucifix, while "a deacon" with two young Cossacks were responding
from an alcove at the right of the altar. On each
side of the latticed door hung chandeliers, containing lighted candles, and all about the room

hung pictures of saints, before each of which were clusters of wax candles. The worshipers seemed devout, and even the face of the hypocritical priest assumed a sanctimonious expression which one not knowing him might have mistaken for the look of a true saint. After the service some of his companions in dissipation tarried to receive his blessing, showing how utterly wanting are his flock of any ideas of a spiritual life. When the service was over the explorers by invitation accompanied the priest to his house, and were introduced to his amiable-looking wife, and two interesting young sons. But the three attracted the attention of the visitors by their frightened and broken-spirited expressions in the presence of the head of the family. This, they afterward learned, was owning to his brutal treatment, the wife and children being frequently beaten. What better could be expected of a drunkard and gambler. He invited our explorers to occupy a vacant room in his house during their stay, which they did thankfully, as no other accommodation was so good. In his house was a Russian bath, such as we have seen in our journeys with Mr. Dall in Alaska. Captain Bush and his companion were "put through" this process of cleansing in the most approved style.

In the room where Bush and Mahood lodged, and in which they made their home, were two pictures of saints. These, of course, were held in great reverence by all the Cossacks and natives who might have occasion to visit the room. Be-

hind these the explorers deposited their funds.
They had been told that stealing was the besetting
sin of these people. But, knowing their reverence
for the images of saints, our friends inferred· that
if they should discover the money they would regard it as under the peculiar care of him whose
face was before it. As a matter of fact their funds
were not stolen.

From the time the strangers came to Oudskoi
the governor had been trying to convince them of
the peculiar merits of horse flesh as an article for
an epicurean dinner, and intimated that he had
some flesh of that sort, "tender and good," and
that whenever it was agreeable to them he would
have it prepared for them as a special token of his
regard. So kind was this offer that they in court-
esy expressed their pleasure in accepting his invitation to dinner. On entering the house there
was a smell, not "of the field which God had
blessed," but of the stable. They sat down at a
small table as on a previous occasion, the only
dish being that containing the meat, around which
were arranged some forks. The meat was cut into
thin slices, and rolled around bunches of fat—or
so it *seemed* to them. The inevitable strong drink
was at hand, of which the head-man took a generous sip, and then took a piece of the meat on his
fork, ate it, and smacked his lips, as much as to say,
"Gentlemen, help yourselves; it's most excellent.
Having good appetites, and stomachs which had
lost some of their delicacy by their experience in
the country, and hoping, too, that the dish con-

tained the least objectionable part of the horse
they did eat, though the meat was as tough as
leather and as nauseous as a drug. The dish was
soon cleared, his excellency eating three fourths
of the whole. They soon after learned that they
had eaten the *entrails!* They concluded that
horse steak might be good.

The sacrament of baptism was administered,
while our friends were at Oudskoi, to the infant
child of the governor. The details of the ceremony are too disgusting for our pages. The solemn rite in the hands of the ignorant, wicked priest
became a solemn mockery; besides, it was plainly
a matter of gain, as fees were expected from all
concerned in the ceremony.

It would be pleasant to think that the priest of
Oudskoi was, as an unworthy minister of sacred
things, an exceptional man, and that the priests
of the Greek Church in Siberia were generally
truly holy men. But the Siberians have a saying
which expresses their estimate of their general
character. They say, when they wish to express a
man's utter worthlessness: "He is so great a ras-
cal they will not even make a priest of him."

The Greek Church has its schismatics in Siberia. The priest gave our travelers the following
facts : The sect is called the Starobradets. Their
points of dissent from the parent Church are profound—we mean that they are as much so as those
of many other distinct parties in the Christian
family. The first is a negative one; they deny
that since the year 1616 any new genuine saint has

been discovered. The priest declared that they had been caught by a special, divine communication in an attempt to blow up with gunpowder the image of one of the modern, and, as they say, sham saints. Their second and only other point of dissent concerns the manner of holding the fingers in making the sign of the cross. The orthodox party, in crossing themselves, extend the thumb and the first and second fingers, pinching the ends together, and closing the third and fourth fingers. To this arrangement of the fingers the dissentients stoutly object; their reason is that in so doing in making the sign of the cross, one appears to be holding a pinch of snuff! and all tobacco they hold to be unclean. They extend the first, second, and fourth fingers, closing the thumb and third finger.

The priest did not give the statistics of this sect, that we might judge of their progress in their reformatory movement. As to the point which they make against tobacco we are with the dissenters.

CHAPTER XXVI.

ON SNOW-SHOES.

THE explorers remained at Oudskoi, waiting to secure a deer-train from the Tungusians of the vicinity. This time was in part improved in learning to walk with snow-shoes, as much of the next stage of their route must be made afoot. These shoes are made of a white birch frame, covered— or *soled* we might say—with skin taken from the legs of elk, deer, or horse, the hair running toward the heel so that they slip easily forward, but not back. They are six feet long and ten inches wide, and a pair weighs eight pounds. The Siberian boys of this region use them for sliding down hill, in the place of coasting-sleds. Captain Bush and his comrades went out to a hill-side by the church every day to practice this kind of coasting. As one must *stand* on the snow-shoe sled a long staff is used by beginners to aid in keeping the balance. The first time Bush attempted to coast without one the priest made the sign of the cross over him as he was about to start. He made the descent without a fall, and, no doubt, the priest felt that the sacred sign was connected with the success. We shall see that this snow-shoe practice was of great service to our party.

On the nineteenth of December sixteen deer had

been secured and a fresh outfit obtained of provisions. ˉUkov gave place to another Cossack
whose name was Ivan. With much difficulty two
Tungusian deer-drivers were induced to go, as they
had heard the almost universal prophecy of the natives and Russians, both here and at Nicholas, that
our explorers would perish on the terrible mountain paths through which they proposed to go. The
next halting place at which they aimed was Ajan,
far away north, on the coast of the Ochotsk Sea.
The Juggur range of mountains ran near the coast,
over which and far inland ran the trail to Ajan
usually taken by the deer-trains. But the explorers wished to survey a route for the telegraph wire
nearer the sea, and so in easy connection with supplies, therefore they determined to keep as near
the shore as possible.

The Oudskoi farewell was quite ceremonious
and *effecting*, at least to the priest and head man,
for they *drank* their regrets at parting in a fearful
number of glasses of strong drink. According to
custom their neighbors and families, old and young,
handsome and ugly, male and female, kissed the
strangers good-bye. The Cossack soldiers in a
line at the door, with muskets, and a long procession of citizens, honored by their presence their
departure. As they mounted the sledges, and the
dogs received the word to start, a volley from the
muskets gave the last adieu.

The deer-train with an outfit had gone ahead to
Algasee under Ivan. They found the train all
right on their arrival, the deer having been turned

Christmas-eve.

out to feed; but on the morning as they were about to start northward the Cossack brought the vexatious news that the wolves had eaten two of the pack-deer. The outfit had, therefore, to be reduced by just the amount these two would have carried.

The route lay along the sea-shore to the very edge of which the cliffs of the Juggur hills at times came, so that for several days the train stumbled along, the men walking on snow-shoes, and now and then lifting the deer, packs and all, over steep and rough places.

On the twenty-fourth of December they traveled over a more level country, crossed a stream, ascended a wooded hill and encamped. It was Christmas-eve; and as they made note of the occasion it will be interesting to look into their camp. A strip of deer-skin drawn over a half circle of poles forms the tent. Twigs of trees are thrown down on which fur robes are spread, and on these Mahood and Swartz are reclining in pleasant chat. Against the open side of the tent an immense camp-fire crackles and blazes, the flames and sparks rising among the thick, overhanging branches of the fir-tree under which they have camped. The native drivers are flying about bareheaded, bringing wood for the fire and ice from a stream for the tea-kettle. The saddles and packs are strewn about beyond the tree-trunks, reflecting the light of the fire and looking like specters in the darkness. The deer are industriously pawing up their supper from under the snow, and occasion-

ally they pause and look up to stare at their masters.
Bush, clothed in furs from head to foot, sits cross-
legged by the fire with his leather-covered docu-
ment-box by his side. He is journalizing under
difficulties. He dips his pen into a thick glass
inkstand, writes a little, and the ink freezes on the
point of his pen. He then thrusts it into the blaze
of a candle which stands on the box, and renews
his scribbling. A pencil wont do, as the lines become by the wear too faint. In a marvelously
short time Ivan has hot tea, and sets before them
a good supper. There is a romance at least in
this place for a Christmas-eve celebration, but the
thoughts of the explorers wander far away to the
cheerful homes in Christian lands, and the warm
hearts which beat with love for them.

The route on the following day led them along
the bank of the Goram River, which flowed down
the gorge in the mountain. They could no longer
travel north, for a steep cliff extended to the sea.
So up the mountain, westward, along this river they
toiled, the men walking and pushing or dragging
the deer. Higher and higher they climbed, while
narrower and narrower became the river, until
they could easily jump across it. The cold became intense, defying the protection of furs and
the warmth of the camp-fires. Swartz froze his
nose and one of the drivers froze his toes and chin.
Captain Bush sprained his ankle, which swelled
and pained him intensely. The exertions of the
party caused a profuse perspiration, the steam of
which covered with a fleecy ice their beards, eye-

brows, eyelashes, and furs, giving them the appearance of a troop of patriarchs. The mercury had
fallen to thirty-five degrees below zero. Swartz
easily took the frost out of his nose by the appli-
cation of ice, but the poor driver suffered an agony
of pain with his swollen feet and legs. They
were now on the summit of the Juggur mountains.
They halted and dug a place in the snow with
their snow-shoes large enough for the tent. Small
branches of trees were then thrown down, and over
them their robes for beds. The natives cut poles
and put up the tent at short notice. Ivan soon
had a blazing fire, and a few moments after shouted: "Chi gotova"—Tea is ready. A supper of
boiled deer meat and "black bread," with "six
cups of tea," relished all the better from the win-
try air of the mountain-top.

When bed-time came, the explorers, even under
these circumstances, put off the furs worn during
the day, turned them, hung them by the fire to
dry, put on sleeping dresses, and so were better
prepared for sleep at night and the endurance of
cold by day.

The view in the morning was wild and grand.
Far below were the dark woods, becoming more
and more indistinct, through which the river, up
whose banks they had ascended, wound its way,
and around them bald peaks stood with solemn
dignity as guardians of this domain of deathlike
silence.

The descent was steep and dangerous. The
snow was hard, and only by great caution did the

16

train avoid sliding with fearful velocity on to the next terrace of the ridge, or being dashed against obstructing rocks and trees. The pack-deer fared the hardest. Their packs slipped, came down upon their necks, causing long delays in their re-adjustment. Only by breaking through the crust could they keep from slipping, and in breaking through they wallowed in the snow. The men were obliged to walk ahead and break a path for them, and at times to lift them over the ridges one by one.

Reaching the foot of the ridge they traveled a few miles in a narrow wooded basin, and camped, men and beasts being entirely exhausted. They had crossed the mountain range which separates the sources of rivers which empty into the Ochotsk Sea on the east from those which pour into the Arctic Sea on the north, two thousand miles apart.

During the next day they were made glad by striking the trail of a Tungusian train which was plainly not far in advance of them. Before night they came upon their camp. Eight persons, men, women, and children, rushed from the tent to wel-come them; but their deer, which were feeding a short distance off, rushed upon those of our train and a fight ensued, noisy by clashing of antlers, but innocent of harm to either party. This was certainly a most discourteous salutation to give to the strangers, but the contending parties were soon pleasantly feeding together.

Our train had lost their way, and had blundered upon these hunters. One of them, whose name was Alexai, informed them that they need not have crossed the summit of the mountains, but should have left the valley of the Goram, through a little tributary to the north, and they would then have struck an old trail leading back again to the sea. He further told them that they must return and take this trail, it being, even now, their shortest and best route.

The explorers took at this camp a needed rest of two days. The first of these was New-Year's day of 1866. Like their Christmas-day, it had a Siberian character. They made a New-Year's call at the tent of the hunters. They found the ten inmates of the one not large tent very busy. The men were making snow-shoes, and the women sewing skin garments. The children were getting all the amusement possible out of their small means. They were happy in their way, and rollicking like other children. A fire burned in the center of the tent, the smoke of which took its own slow time in finding its way out of the top, through a small hole. Our callers were soon smoked out and retired.

Going outside, nature provided a better entertainment. The atmosphere was filled with fine frozen particles, like mist, but the heavens were without a cloud. The brilliancy of the sun was so toned down by the crystallized particles that it could be looked in the face by the naked eye. A luminous band encircled it, faintly tinted with rainbow colors. In this band, directly above the sun, was a mock sun, and two others at equal distances from the first were further down in the.luminous circle. From these mock suns, in opposite directions from the true sun, a trail of light extended, while parts of three other brilliant bands, one over the other, gave a finishing touch to the heavenly picture. It was a sight worthy of its divine Artist, and was kept on free exhibition for two hours. What would New York or any of our great cities give for such a New-Year's entertainment! Yet he reserved this for his less-favored children of the Siberian tents.

Among their provision boxes the explorers found one marked "turkey." This they had served up for a New-Year's dinner. It was not as savory as the home article of the same name, but with the help of a good appetite, and some imagination, they were enjoying it well, and had well-nigh cleared the platter, when Swartz held up up a bone between his fingers, at arms' length, and exclaimed, with a rueful face, "Cat! it's cat, man, and I've been trying to swallow one of the tail joints!" And, cat or turkey, the meat was eaten. But a more careful examination of the bones led the feasters to conclude that they had eaten neither turkey nor cat, but a wild bird of an un-known name.

CHAPTER XXVII.

INCIDENTS BY THE WAY.

THE fresh start of our company was under favorable circumstances. Alexai, one of the
hunters, had agreed to accompany them as a
guide, providing his own deer and provisions.
The drivers had exchanged their deer for fresh
ones, and new snow-shoes were purchased.

The Juggur range was recrossed further south,
and without difficulty, and soon the train was
again on the Goram River. On the third day's
travel they turned up the Econda River, and began to ascend northward. Had they been guided
by a hunter of the region they would have taken
this stream on their upward journey, and saved
about a week's time and much toil. They encamped, at the end of the second day's ascent,
on table land covered with trailing pine. They
had learned to value the sight of these knotty
shrubs, not only because they made splendid
camp-fires, but because good deer feed was always found near them. But the deer were not
dependent upon the sight of the trailing pine to
tell where the moss on which they fed could be
found. Though the snow which covered it was
five feet deep, they scented it by putting their
noses in the snow. By this God-given means of

knowing where their food is, they never dig in the snow in vain.

We have seen during all our arctic rambles what wonderful eaters all its cold-enduring people are. The natives of this region were not exceptions. While in camp on this route Captain Bush witnessed an illustration of this. Alexia and one of the drivers, soon after the fire was made, sat down to a gallon kettle of hot tea, every drop of which they drank in a few moments. They then cooked a four-quart pailful of boiled fish and soup, which they soon devoured. At this moment the other driver, who had lagged behind, came up cold and hungry. The same pail was twice emptied by the three of hot boiled beef, and they even cracked the bones for the marrow. Then, after rinsing the pail, they cooked it full of mush, and ate that. After this they commenced on cold, dried fish, the quantity devoured not being estimated. At Bush's hour of retiring, not much later, they had built a fire of their own, and the last noise he heard before falling asleep was the cracking of bones. It was presumed they had boiled and eaten another pailful of beef, and were finishing off with more marrow.

Like the Esquimo, the people of this region will at times consume a week's provisions in one night, and eat nothing the other six days. They seem to have the capability of doing many days' eating at one meal. Swartz told the story of six Yakoots, who, two years before, were sent from Ajan to an inland town with a number of horses. On the way one

of the horses broke its leg and could not travel
They bound it down strongly with cords—their
customary way when they wish to kill a horse—
cut open the beast with a knife, and one of them
thrust his hand into the cavity and extinguished
its life by compressing its heart with his hand.
They believe that this cruel method makes the
meat better flavored. At night the six natives sat
down to the carcass, and in the morning all had
been eaten except the skin and bones.

On the seventh of January the train had reached
the summit of the range which had impeded their
northern route along the sea-shore. The wind
was high and directly in their faces, bringing a
blinding snow which shut out the sight of every
object a short distance off. They trod closely
upon each other's heels so as not to get scattered
and lost. Their noses and faces froze and were
thawed out as usual with snow. They descended
rapidly and safely, and soon struck a river running
to the sea. After nearly two days of rough traveling they were made glad by the barking of dogs,
and they immediately came upon a tent occupied
by a girl of seventeen and a brother of about ten.
They were children of a hunter known as Old
Ephraim, who was out tending his fox-traps. The
children were not in the least daunted by the presence of the strangers, but continued playing with
some native toys. These were various animals cut
with scissors from birch bark. Bush expressed his
surprise at the correct proportions and artistic
beauty of these toy animals, and asked the girl

who made them. She smiled and said she made
them herself. The strangers perhaps expressed a
doubt of this in their faces, and she at once took
her scissors and birch-bark, and, without first
marking an outline, produced two or three very
pretty animals, which she gave to Captain Bush.
God's gifts are not all given to the favored children
of civilized lands.

Old Ephraim returned about dark with three
squirrels, with fur of great softness and beauty.
Their backs were gray, bellies white, and their
heads, bushy tails, and ears of tufted hair, a glossy
black. The ladies of almost every country are
proud to own a skin of one of these beautiful little
creatures.

The hunter expressed no surprise at the presence of the strangers. He sold them deer meat
for present use, and a young live deer to be killed
on their journey as they should need it. When
they were about to depart in the morning, thinking to please both father and daughter, Mahood
opened his box of trinkets, which were brought
along for trading, and put a necklace of beads
around the fat neck of the girl. Instead of expressing gratitude or pleasure, she made some very
ugly faces and stretched her neck this way and
that, making at the same time vigorous efforts to
swallow, as if she was afraid of choking. Mahood
then removed it from her neck and tied it about
her waist, but still she regarded it with cool indif-
ference.

After leaving Old Ephraim's tent they came

suddenly upon a party of Tungusians just preparing to camp. They were at the moment unloading from one of the deer two little boys. They had each been thrust into a fur bag, the bags tied together and thrown over the pack-saddle while traveling, one balancing the other like any bags of freight. On another deer was a baby, balanced by a large kettle. Each of the children were sewed up in a single piece of fur, which answered for jacket, pants, hat, and boots, and in this plight thrust into the bags, and nothing was visible but their small, shining, black eyes. The boys seemed regardless of the cold in these wrappers which God had made for the wild animals, and when they were stuck down in the deep snow, while the men pitched the tent and made the camp-fire, they laughed and shouted in childish merriment.

Our party soon struck the post-road from Ajan by the sea to the central points inward. Following this they were soon at Ajan. This was one of the refitting halting places put down in their programme of travel when they left the Amoor River. It is situated on a peninsula, making one side of a bay. It is sheltered by a grove, and commands an extensive view of the sea-coast. Here at one time, on the deep waters of the bay, scores of American whalers could be seen at anchor, their men busy in procuring the oil from the whales caught in the Ochotsk Sea. Here the Russian American Fur Company had one of its largest stations. But too many harpoons had driven the finy monsters

from the Ochotsk, the fur trade had diminished, or
its furs gone to other stations, and our men were
sadly disappointed in finding it a small, poor village, with no means of furnishing them with fresh
deer, men, and provisions. Their case would have
been embarrassing indeed, and they, perhaps, compelled to return, but for the aid given them by the
kind Russian official in charge of the station. He
first took them to his own home, and then set them
to house-keeping in one of the very commodious
houses used formerly by a high official. He sent
men far into the interior after a deer-train and
supplies. In the mean time they were entertained
by feasts, music, and dancing. We hear nothing
of the priest's hospitality or drunkenness, and so
we conclude there was none in the place. Pleasant day excursions were made to interesting points
in the vicinity. At one time they climbed a steep,
barren peak of the peninsula. From its top they
looked far out upon the stormy Ochotsk, and over
a distant range of the ice-bound shore, north and
south, and saw in the west the rugged, snow-capped
tops of the Juggur Mountains. A chilling dreari-
ness pervaded the whole scene and gave no pleas-
ing promise of the remaining portion of their exploration, a part of which led over the mountains.
Their kind host declared that the mountain route
was full of danger, and that, in fact, only the most
daring hunters had ever passed over it. He ad-
vised the usual, far inland, circuitous trail. But
our men wished their telegraph line to keep near
the sea-shore, and this mountain route lay in their

way, and they determined to brave its difficulties.
They hoped and believed that the perils would
not be greater than those already encountered.
So they returned from this glimpse of the way they
were to go with an unfaltering courage.

The agents of the governor, sent inland for deer,
succeeded in finding a Tungusian head-man who,
finally, after our men had been delayed nineteen
days, was ready with his deer-train to carry them
about half way to the sea-port of Ochotsk, at which
point they were assured they would find a rich old
native who would carry them the rest of the way.
The reader will remember that Major Abasa and
party were now plodding their way from the north
to meet Bush at that place, the half-way town of
the whole western shore of the Ochotsk Sea. This
long delay gave our men much uneasiness, fearing,
that the major might already have arrived at this
agreed-on place of meeting, and be anxious about
them.

The preparations for this renewed journey had
long since been completed. A large stock of
provisions had been secured. New furs displaced the old ones. The old, worn snow-
shoes gave place to new. Their late drivers had
returned, but Ivan was persuaded by increased
pay to continue with them as interpreter. He
had proved himself a superior man for his part of
duty.

On the 5th of February, late in the afternoon
the complimentary dinners—several during the
day—were all eaten, the farewell words spoken,

and the train galloped away. The cold, clear
night soon set in. The heavens seemed ablaze
with brilliant stars. A profound stillness reigned
all around, broken only by the clattering hoofs of
the deer on the hard snow. The deer were fresh,
and, stimulated by the bracing air, were for once
fleet of foot. They whirled the sledges along,
now under the sparkling starlight over a clear
trail, now under overshadowing trees where only
the most skillful drivers could prevent them from
being dashed against the stumps or logs, and then
round the sloping sides of small elevations, so slippery that they seemed every minute about to sway
round and capsize. But all went well for awhile, and
Captain Bush dismissed his fears, and lay back for
a quiet enjoyment of the inspiring situation. Suddenly the sled swung round, the stars disappeared,
and he felt a sense of suffocation, in the midst of
dense darkness. He was not long in compre-
hending the situation. The sledge had capsized,
and he was under it, with its whole weight on his
chest. The driver had been pitched head-fore-
most into a snow bank, fifteen feet below the road.
The deer fortunately stopped at once. The driver scrambled nimbly out, righted up the sledge,
and placed its passenger into his cozy position
again. No hurt was experienced, so both laughed,
the only way they could communicate, and dashed
forward again.

After the first night's rest the train turned directly north. In addition to the usual two drivers,
a third Tungusian had been engaged with two

deer, whose sole business it was to go ahead and break a path in the snow. It proved no easy duty. But the two unladen deer, trained to the task, bravely floundered through the deepest snow.

CHAPTER XXVIII.

HOSPITABLE HALTING PLACES.

FOR two days our train had delightful sledging. It was mostly on the ice of a river down which they glided. Bush, buried in his warm furs, and leaning back in his snug place on the sledge, as comfortable as if under the robes of a fancy sleigh of a New England sleighing party, by a brilliant starlight watched the confused stumps and trees of the banks and the glowing sky above, as his noble bucks sped on over the smooth and level road. No sound but that of the clattering hoofs was heard. Nature seemed hushed in reverent silence at its Maker's revealings in the solemn grandeur of earth and heaven. The natives, imperfectly taught in God's revealed truth, yet felt his presence in all the journey. They carried, hung upon their breasts, a little crucifix. At night, ere they lay down by the camp-fire, they took them off and hung them on a branch of a tree overhead. In the morning before starting they bowed before them, and in low voices uttered their prayers and restored them to their breasts. In the darkness and the storms, and in all the perils of the way they felt safer because of the presence of the cross. They felt a little, no doubt, of the spiritual power which it symbolized.

Several mountain ridges—spurs running toward the sea of the Juggur range—were covered. On arriving on the summit of one which was especially bleak and dangerous, they found various articles of food and clothing stretched by a string between two trees. These our explorers took down to examine, which greatly surprised and offended the natives of the party. They said they were offerings made by hunters to appease the spirit of the mountains, or as thank-offerings for a safe crossing, and were regarded as sacred. Mahood corrected the fault of himself and companions in touching them, by hanging a piece of a pair of old red pants to the string. This was entirely satisfactory!

Having crossed the last of the mountains the train passed on by forced marches toward the hut of another of the Tungusian hunters, said by the guide to be in the route. The snow was deep and the traveling exhausting. One of the poor deer of the path-breakers became tired of being punched by the staff of his rider to cause him to quicken his weary steps. He deemed patience to be no longer a virtue, so he stopped and refused to take another step. The rider was, of course, provoked at this, and struck him a severe blow across the antlers, and for this assault found himself the next moment going head foremost from his seat into a snow-bank. Having remounted, he repeated his blows, and the deer, by throwing his hind feet suddenly into the air, gave his unreasonable master another gymnastic exercise over his

antlers into the snow. This was done the third
time, when the rider gave it up, and walked about,
leading the animal by the halter. But the ag-
grieved deer could not be so easily pacified. The
blows had wounded his honor as well as his flesh.
He followed meekly a few rods, and then lowering
his head he ran at his master and struck him with
such force just below the small of his back as to
half bury him in the snow. The man picked himself up, and brushed the snow from his face with
such an amazed and rueful expression that the
whole company laughed heartily.

Soon after this the train came upon a couple
of skin-tents. The dogs barked at the coming
of the strangers, and a motley company of men,
women, deer, and dogs rushed out to greet them.
The men were partly expecting the explorers, for
a messenger from Major Abasa, who had arrived
at Ochotsk, had been at the tent six days before
with dispatches for them. This was good news
so far, but as the messenger and his party had
missed them, the question now was would he soon
get on their track and return. But Captain Bush
decided to push on to the camp of the old hunter,
at whose encampment of four tents they arrived in
half an hour. As usual, their welcome was most
hearty, and their hospitality generous in the extreme; indeed, these simple people seemed to feel
that a favor had been bestowed upon them by the
strangers in accepting food and lodging. The old
hunter himself was, however, encamped four days'
journey further on the route, but his two sons sup-

plied his place in kind services, and provided deer to carry them to their father's tent.

The tents of this locality were larger than those of the kind which had been met with earlier in the journey. Our explorers had scarcely unload ed before Egory, their host, had killed one of his fattest deer, dressed it, and put it into a huge copper kettle, where it soon filled the tent with delicious fumes, giving good assurance to the hungry men of the rich feast at hand. Next to the pleasure of appeasing their own hunger was that which our men enjoyed in seeing eight or ten others squatting around a large wooden tray filled with meat. Men, women, and children thrust their knives into the meat, cut off long strips, one end of which they seized with their teeth, threw back their heads, and, having taken as much as possible into their mouths, they cut the strips off by an upward stroke of the knife, just missing their noses. The reader of our "North-Pole Voyages" has seen the Esquimo of a higher latitude eat in this way. On this occasion the whole of the savory deer was devoured, and his bones cracked for the marrow.

Our travelers had made a note of the fact that the native women were especially repulsive looking. Their high cheek-bones, narrow, oblique eyes, dark, coarse skins, and expressionless faces, would have made them a disgust but for their uniform kindness of heart. But here, eating to be sure at the large tray, were two daughters—heiresses—of the rich hunter, whose clear brunette

17

complexions, rosy cheeks, clean, new, neatly-fitting dresses showed that even among the Tungusians there were belles, who needed but the culture of a Christian civilization to shine among the best. The fancy bead-work about their dresses, and handsome, engraved silver collars showed that they had accomplishments in their way.

After a much shorter journey than they expected our train reached the encampment of the old hunter, whose sons and daughters had made themselves so agreeable. His name was Ivan. His tents were ample, his herds numerous, and his children many, a great-grandchild having been added to his family the night before. Seated in the old man's tent, the strangers were soon sipping tea and talking as well as they could considering the talk underwent several translations before the parties understood it. Swartz converted the English into Russian; Bush's Cossack, Ivan, rendered the Russian into Yakoot; Egory then translated it into Tungusian. The old man was very talkative and observing. Seeing his guests take but three cups of tea, he looked hurt, and asked if it was not good. They assured him it was excellent, but that Americans were not accustomed to take more than three cups at one time. He was surprised at this, and remarked that he often drank two kettlefuls—about six quarts—at a sitting. He then asked many questions about Americans and America. During the conversation he innocently administered a severe rebuke to our party. As they were about to partake of supper, the old man bowed his head and offered a low, brief prayer, crossing himself at the same time. Noticing that his guests did not do the same, he was sober and silent for awhile. He then inquired seriously if Americans had a God. Being answered yes, he was silent again for a moment or two, then intimated his surprise that they ate without thanking him for the food.

Captain Bush decided to stay in this pleasant encampment until Abasa's messenger, who had missed him, should strike his trail and return. This delay gave the strangers an opportunity to study the native character. A company of children one morning engaged in a game of ball, and proved by the joyous spirit in which they played, as well as by the game itself, their relation to the children of all lands. Their play was what American boys sometimes call *shinny*, the ball which was thrown up a small steep elevation, was knocked back, and so kept by their bats from coming down. The reader will recollect that Dr. Kane found this game in fashion among the little Esquimo of the far north.

We have noticed this seeming piety of the old hunter, and; according to the little light on sacred things he possessed, no doubt a sincere piety. But an incident occurred under the notice of our friends which showed how dark their light is. A man was sick in one of the tents and desired the services of a *shaman*, one of the "medicine men" whom we have met every-where in the arctic regions. Old Ivan came and asked Captain Bush if he or his men objected to the gratification of his request. They said, " No," but could not learn why he asked them. Bush in return requested peimission to see the ceremony, but was refused on Ivan's consulting the enchanter. So Bush contented himself in listening outside to the howlings. The sick man was poor, having only two deer, one of which he gave the shaman, as a required fee.

This seeking to conciliate the evil spirit, by whom they think all disease and suffering are caused, is a part of their heathen faith, to which, no matter how many prayers they offer to the Christian's God, or how often they cross themselves, they firmly adhere. How can they know much of Christ or his gospel with only the Greek priests to teach them, who seem to be satisfied with their work when by the gift of a piece of tobacco, or some little trinket, they have persuaded the natives to be baptized.

On the third day of the waiting the messenger Cossack from Abasa arrived. The major had been at Ochotsk several weeks anxiously waiting for the Bush party. The dispatch gave Bush his first news of Kennan's success, and was a new inspiration to push forward his own part of the programme of survey.

Early in the morning after the arrival of the messenger our train was on the move. Old Ivan had caused a sufficient number of deer to be lassoed and put in harness for their use. Just as the caravan had got well started, the entire herd of deer came rushing down upon it, intent upon following their companions, and it took the whole population a half hour to drive them back.

The journey for a few days was attended by intensely cold weather. It almost defied the heavy, God-given fur with which the men were well clothed. At one time the mercury went down to seventy-six degrees below zero. The atmosphere was clear and the stars at night set the heavens aglow. The mock suns, with their arches set in rainbow colors, vied with the real sun in splendor, then melted into the brightness of the heavens, and re-appeared in ever-varving arches. The grandeur was at times appalling.

The train pushed on, over mountain ridges, across rivers. until it reached a plain, or series of plains, bounded by the Juggur Mountains on the west, the Ochotsk Sea on the east, through which rivers ran to the sea, not far away. The reindeer were exchanged for dogs, and better speed was made. The huts of the Yakoots, with their cattle, became more frequent, and milk and cream were added to the daily meals. As the train neared the long-desired Ochotsk, the impatience of the men increased, and the dogs were required to do their "level best." Bush, whose team was leading, was told by his driver that the town would soon be in sight. Rushing on and straining his eyes for some time, and seeing nothing, he cast a look of reproach at the driver. The man grinned and pointed at a distant pile of burned logs, among which some log-huts and a little log-church could barely be discerned. *That* was Ochotsk, the Mecca of our explorers, toward which, since leaving the Amoor, they had been looking, and to reach which they had dared the perils of five hundred and fifty miles! The place was a disgust in their eyes after all! How like the ending of many of life's golden dreams! But driving up to a very plain, low log-hut, Major Abasa stepped out and gave them a cordial greeting. The incidents of the long jour-neys made since they parted were talked over, and, we trust, gratitude felt for dangers escaped, and for the prospective success of their great enterprise.

Ochotsk is an old fur-trading sea-port, and it was here that Bering's ships were built, and from this port he started on his famous voyages of discovery. But Nicholas, its modern rival, has stripped it of its business and its importance.

CHAPTER XXIX.

MORE DOG-SLEDGING.

THE major's present plan was to remain a month or two at Ochotsk, and to take one of the vessels which would touch here in the spring, and sail to Geezhega, where all the explorers could further arrange for the completion of the Siberian portion of the enterprise. Ivan, Bush's faithful Cossack, was well paid, some presents thrown in, and he turned his face toward the long return journey to his family at Oudskoi. A few days of the monotonous life of a third-rate Siberian village was sufficient to make our adventurers feel that climbing the Juggur Mountains, or even reindeer riding, was to be preferred. So, after three weeks of waiting, they were glad to hear their chief say that he would not wait for the sea voyage. He had decided to leave Mahood at Ochotsk, to wait the coming of the company's vessels, and to look after the interests of their enterprise in this region, and the rest of the party were to start immediately, on dog-sledges, for Geezhega. Furs were renewed, dogs, which were plenty, were selected, and early on the morning after this route was determined—a clear cold morning of the fifteenth of March—the train was dashing at a steam-engine rate over a level country, along the sea-shore. The dogs, fifteen to each sled, were fresh and willing, and fairly yelped for joy at the chance of an up-country run.* Most of the party, as do the people of the country generally, rode on uncovered sledges. But that of Bush and the other explorers were such as we have described in our ride with Kennan, a kind of coffin, on one end of which the driver sat, and into the opening of the other end the passenger slipped, leaning back and literally buried in soft bear or wolf-skins.

The first twelve hours the train made seventy-two miles! Stopping at the residence of a Russian doctor, they were lodged, fed, and supplied with fresh dogs for the early morning start. This route was a post-road, and the Russian Government not only secured good villages at long intervals, but between them constructed huts, into which travelers might go for a night, or on any emergency.

The train, after leaving the hut of the Russian doctor, made good time, and at three in the afternoon reached the foot of a mountain ridge, across which the route lay. The wind had been rising, and now blew a stiff breeze, attended by a fine, blinding snow. There was every indication of a fearful storm on the mountain, a regular native "poorga." But the major was determined to encamp for the night on the other side, a distance of about thirteen miles. He was led to this decision by the fear that the tempest would increase and

* See Frontispiece

rage until their provisions were exhausted. Once on the plain beyond they could reach a village even in a "poorga." But the drivers with one voice objected to the crossing until the storm had ceased. They had fearful stories to tell of whole trains being lost under such circumstances, which were plainly too true. The major at first hesitated under these statements and fears of the natives, and then fell back on his purpose, and declared he would go. At this the drivers rebelled, and said they would not. But the Cossacks of the party supported the major, who stormed and threatened, so that finally the drivers yielded.

The train commenced ascending the mountain in a perfect hurricane. The snow fell so fast that the leading dogs of the sleds could not be seen by their drivers, and the teams which were ahead left no track for those which followed; and, the old trail being lost, the whole train were soon floundering in the snow uncertain of the way. Those sleds which were unable to keep up were for half an hour missing altogether. Men were scattered in every direction within hailing distance of each other to find them, who by much hallooing brought them into line again. The wind howled fearfully, as if the spirit of the mountains were angry at this daring invasion of his realm. Occasionally the sleds were brought to a sudden standstill by a violent collision with a stump or a tree; again they would nearly capsize in a snow-drift. After a two hours' struggle the drivers halted the

teams, and came to a consultation. They declared that they saw no familiar marks of the way,
and that they were lost! The order was about to
be given to encamp until the storm was over, when
the wind slightly subsided. Encouraged by this
fact men were sent out in different directions to
find the trail. Soon a joyous shout came from far
away to one side, and in a few moments the whole
train was toiling up the last steep range of the
mountain. The summit was gained amid jubilant
shouts, and the descent commenced, every step of
which brought increased shelter from the storm.
There were no trees, the whole distance ahead
being a sheet of whiteness, through which the
dogs leaped with excited yelps. The descent was
so steep that the drivers thrust their driving-sticks
through the hard crust of the snow between the
runners in front of the sleds to check the speed.
The sticks tore up the snow which in a thick
cloud nearly enveloped the train, making it almost impossible to see the dangers ahead. They
soon reached a gorge, down which they would
have shot like an arrow from a bow but for the im-
peding stick grasped by steady and strong hands.
As it was they barely escaped going over a snow
precipice fifty feet in height. It was seen just in
time to bring the dogs round while the sleds were
brought broadside to its very edge. One of the
sleds had nearly escaped the danger when it went
over at a place where the fall was twelve feet, the
dogs and driver getting well mixed up in the snow
at the bottom. No damage was done, except the

breaking the sled and bruising one of the dogs
which fell under it.

The gorge narrowed as they descended, by reason of the accumulated snow on either side which
had slid from above, and in some places masses of
snow were overhanging their route and threatening
to dislodge and come down upon their heads.
While such was the situation Bush's driver entertained him with the story that a short time before
a driver and all his dogs were killed by the descent of one of these masses. But our party
reached the plain in safety and arrived at one of
the Government huts about eight o'clock in the
evening. These empty yourts were a great addition to the safety and comfort of the travelers.
Though rudely built they had a fire-place and a
small supply of wood, so that a night's rest, or a
day's halt for lunch, was made much more refreshing than a camp in the open air. In one Bush
was attracted by a small, white animal of the wea-
sel family, which made quick excursions into the
room from a pile of wood in the corner. He was
dirty and scarcely more interesting to the sight
than a common rat; but it proved to be an impe-
rial ermine, whose skin has been long known as a
part of the voluptuous dress of kings and queens.
The skin was nothing to be proud of as it appeared
in this case on the back of its dirty little owner,
though no doubt he prized it highly. The poor
people of this region pay their Church taxes in
these skins, so that at one of their halting-places
Bush bought fifty of the priest for a small sum.

The trade in them is so dull that very little pains
is taken to entrap the animal.

The next noteworthy stopping place was Tausk,
a resort occasionally of American whale ships, situated on a bay of the same name. Here they received their first letter from Kennan since the
major left him. He was at Anadyr preparing to
hunt up the stove-pipe hut and its inmates at the
mouth of the river.

From Tausk the party took fresh dogs, and Bush
secured a new driver, known as Joe. The dogs
and man were alike intolerably lazy. When well
on the trail Joe lay down on the sled and fell
asleep. The dogs, hearing no sound behind them,
looked over their shoulders, and, seeing their master asleep, gradually slackened up, then stopped
and lay down for a nap. This state of things was
not agreeable to Bush, who poked the driver with
the driving-stick, shouting at the same time in his
ear. The noise started up the dogs, but Joe
opened his eyes slowly and said, with a comical
smile, in broken English, "Big noise," and read-
justed himself to finish his sleep. It was only after
several pokes in the side and much shouting that
he roused up and drove on.

At a small settlement they met a rich reindeer
owner who, by an arrangement with the major
made on his down trip, had brought a number of
deer to sell him to be used in bringing together
the telegraph poles. The chief and his friends
listened with dignity and interest to the major's
statement of the work to which the deer were to

be put. They said they had plenty of deer, but were sullen about selling. They evidently looked with distrust on the major's enterprise. They seemed concerned as if thinking that home and country were imperiled by it. Finally one asked how near together the poles were to be placed, and, when told, the faces of the whole company lighted up. They at once sold, at a fair price, all the deer desired. They had supposed that the poles were to be set close together, making an impassable fence through their country from north to south.

An incident occurred one day which illustrates the savage character of the Siberian dog, and shows them to be own brothers to arctic dogs we have met further north. As the train was moving along, a native was seen coming along the trail with two deer. He kept near the river, hoping the dogs of our party would not see them. But the sharp sight and keen scent of the dogs could not be easily cheated. They started, at the first glimpse of them, with frantic speed and savage yelps, drowning in the tumult the shouts of the drivers. Two hundred hungry dogs were in pursuit of two frightened, flying deer, and, in spite of the sleds, which the drivers turned upside down to embarrass them, three of the teams soon overtook the deer. Twelve dogs instantly sprang on one of them and dragged it to the ground. The drivers who were on hand dealt heavy blows with their sticks, frequently laying one out in bewilderment. This timely aid enabled the prostrate deer to recover its feet and courage. Fear gave way to rage, and he drove at the dogs with his antlers, making at the same time good use of his feet by kicking vigorously. The dogs retreated, and for the moment victory was on the side of the assailed. But all the dogs had by this time come up and a renewed attack by greater numbers brought him down again, and before they could be driven off they had wounded him unto death. The native escaped with his other deer, and was afterward fully paid for his loss.

These dogs have not only the ferocity, but all the cunning and individuality which we have seen in them elsewhere. The natives study the character of the dogs in their teams, as a good teacher does the peculiarities of each of his scholars. There are the stupid, lazy dogs, which seem to think that life's great end is to eat and sleep. These they put nearest the sled, that it may be easy for the driver to poke them with the driving stick, and that those ahead may, if necessary, drag them into a run.

Next in order come the rogues—sharp-nosed, bright-eyed, knowing rascals, which are always ready for mischief. They keep their heads up and one eye over their shoulder at the driver. Their guilty consciences make them yelp if he moves in his seat; they think he is about to throw the unerring staff at them to inflict deserved punishment, and they act as if about to be killed, rushing under the bellies of the good dogs for protection. They are always picking a quarrel with their companions, and getting up fights with the dogs of other trains, but are sure to sneak off when the battle waxes hot. They cannot see a leaf drifting over the surface of the frozen snow without pretending to think it is something alive, and making an effort to chase it, and they spring at every bird which flies over their heads. They *can* pull and run with the smartest dogs in the team, but they do so only when there is a fox or deer to he caught, or a sound thrashing to be feared.

But sharply distinguished from the lazy and the knaves, are the exceptional dogs selected as leaders. You can seen in their faces their sense of responsibility, and their self-respect. They walk among their fellows with an air of conscious superiority. They are quick of apprehension and of unswerving integrity. They are directed by the driver's voice, not by his compelling-staff. They bring in the market sixty dollars, when the average dog brings ten. Bush saw on one occasion an illustration of their wit and sagacity, noticed, as we have seen, by other explorers. A fox started up and crossed the trail. Away went the rogues and drones in full chase. The leader lay back with all his might, but ten dogs were too strong for one, and they dragged him through the snow, and thumped him against the stumps until he thought that would not do. So, when his strength failed, he adopted strategy. He suddenly jumped up, pricked up his ears, looked in the opposite direction, his whole attitude expressing sudden surprise, at the same moment he yelped the startling dog-signal for fox. His com-

panions were completely sold. They followed
him after the supposed fox back into the trail,
and then unwillingly trudged along in the path of
duty.

Siberian dogs and men share alike in some very
hard times. This was seen by our travelers as they
entered another of the little sea-port towns. As
the sleds entered the town a troop of almost fam-
ished dogs came out—not rushing out, as is their
habit, but walking; from sheer weakness. Some
dried fish was on the sleds, under the loads, and
here and there a head or a tail jutted out. The
poor things seized these with their teeth, trying to
pull them out. The well-fed dogs of the train,
with their own kind of feeling for their suffering
fellows, flew at them and bit them while thus engaged to appease their gnawing hunger; but the
starved dogs only gave a feeble and piteous yelp
at the cruel bite, and held to the fish.

Dead dogs lay here and there, one of which a
hungry pack were tearing to pieces and eating.
The whole company of dogs had been unfed for
sixteen days.

On entering a hut our men were met by men,
women, and children, with haggard faces and tot-
tering limbs. They were striving to live on roots
and the bark of trees, waiting for the spring supply of fish. Such days of starvation are common
just before the spring opens, simply because the
men are too lazy to lay in a sufficient stock at
their fishing harvests, which are always abundant.
A few weeks then of work would give them food

enough for every man, woman, and child, and every dog for twelve months, yet they prefer two months of starvation to two weeks of work. It is the old story in this respect of the Esquimo of Smith Sound.

Soon after this Captain Bush's party had a night's experience which might seem rather rough, but which they appeared to enjoy. On stopping one night, the explorers pitched and crept into their skin-tents. After supper the men and dogs curled themselves up in their fur covering, and lay down under the open heavens. In the night came a gentle but deep snow, the top of which froze into hard crust. When the captain looked out in the morning only a few grave-like mounds indicated the place of the men. He gave a loud shout, and one after another they came up in their fur robes, the crust crackling as they came. But no shouts could raise the dogs, and not the slightest hillock indicated where they were. By going to the sleds and pulling on the long skin line to which they were attached, one after another was found, and a sudden jerk broke the crust and brought them out. They popped out perfectly bewildered with sleep and the jerk and shout which aroused them. Two or three kicks from the driver, a stretch and a yawn, and they were all right.

The men declared that they had breathed freely and slept comfortably in their deep snow beds.

One little incident which occurred just before the present tour ended is very impressive. The party entered one of the empty Government log-

18

huts.   As in them all, little crucifixes were nailed
against the logs, before which the drivers crossed
themselves.   Directly under one of them a swallow had in the summer cemented its nest to the
smooth log, and there had reared in assured safety
its young.   There were niches and corners all
about where a nest could have been more easily
made, but the wise bird seemed to reason that it
would never come to harm so near the cross, and
she reasoned well.   The natives of the train look
upon the nest as made sacred by its position.   To
test this feeling, Bush made as if he would tear it
down, and they raised their hands in holy horror
at so wicked an act, and it was left untouched.
Near the cross is a safe place for all, especially for
the children and young people.

CHAPTER XXX.

M A C R A E ' S   S T O R Y.

ON the afternoon of April second the explorers from Ochotsk arrived at Geezhega. They had made the journey of five hundred and fifty miles in nineteen days. Bush was four and a half months in going from the Amoor to Ochotsk, an equal distance; but then he traveled with reindeer, and our present party rode behind a dog-train. We must remember, however, in the interest of the reindeer, that his living costs the owner nothing at any time, and that his flesh is a main dependence for food of his master, and his skin gives him comforts in many ways. He can well afford to travel slower than the wolfish dog.

The major and his men found comfortable quarters in a large log-house. Scarcely had they begun to forget their toils in quiet slumbers, when they were startled by the opening of the door. Rousing up they saw before them three fur-clad travelers, their beards and hoods still white with frost. Bush suddenly grasped the foremost one by the arm, exclaiming: " Kennan, is that you!" to which came the reply, " Bush, is that you!" The fur-clad men were Kennan, Macrae, and Arnold, whom we left at Anadyr, about to start for Geezhega. There were together now of the explorers the major, Bush, Kennan, Arnold, Robinson, and Dodd. Around their blazing fire, and at the table on which steamed the odorous tea, they entertained each other for a few days with the story of their adventures since parting. We will listen to that told by Macrae:

"Having been left, as all have been informed, late in the season, at the mouth of the Anadyr, our first concern was to build a hut, and make the best provision possible for the winter. Kennan has told you how we succeeded in doing this. As we had no means of winter transportation we were under a necessity of waiting for spring when we would go up the river in our boat, or for the coming before them of a band of the wandering Chukchees who might help us to get off. Our hopes in regard to these wanderers were attended with serious fear. We had heard they were fierce and heartless savages. We were, however, armed with breach-loading carbines and revolvers.

"Soon a party of Chukchees came, led by a chief called Okakrae. They were far from being the savages we had supposed, and friendly relations were soon formed. Of course, all communication was carried on by signs. With difficulty we learned from them that their camp was twenty-five miles distant, down on the shore of the gulf, and that they would come in so many moons and take us with reindeer up the river. We tried to buy of them a deer-train, but they expressed a strong dislike to the request to sell *live* deer, but they sold us all the fresh meat we wanted.

"At other times large numbers of them came, and were always friendly. They only once stole any thing, and then an ax, a spade, and a few less valuable articles were carried off. Early in the winter Robinson and I started out on foot in search of Okakrae's encampment. We left the hut early in the morning, taking our rifles with us, expecting to spend the night with the Chukchees. We readily found the encampment, arriving about four o'clock in the afternoon. But it was entirely deserted! We were tired and hungry, for we had unwisely taken no food beyond what we had eaten, and we had no matches, and so were without fire. There was no resort left us but to retrace our steps. The cold had increased, and the wind blew in our faces. The ice of the river on which we traveled was smooth and slippery, and our steps were slow and weary. Our under clothes had been moistened with perspiration in the earlier part of the day, and they now began to stiffen about our bodies. We felt, therefore, that we *must* keep pushing forward with vigor or die. Night, dark, stormy, and intensely cold, set in, before we had made half the journey. So weary and faint were we that the slightest unevenness caused us to stumble and fall. At length Robinson threw himself down, declaring that he must freeze for he could go no farther. I took his gun and pistol, and thus relieved I induced him, with much difficulty, to struggle on. Hour slowly followed hour, while the cold rapidly increased, but by mutual assistance and encouragement we pushed on in the desperate struggle for life. We were so benumbed with cold that a sleepiness came over us almost irresistibly. We struck the land about six miles below the hut, and Robinson declared that he would lie down there and sleep until morning; but as I knew that if he lay down there to sleep he would not wake in this world, I urged him on, though not without many words and much physical exertion. About three o'clock in the morning we reached the door opening into the long, low passage-way of the hut. Our Newfoundland dog, Cook, did not recognize us and would not let us in, so we had to wait until one of the men came to our rescue. We were badly frozen, our bodies, on removing our furs, being covered with frost. We had walked full fifty miles without stopping, over slippery ice and through untrodden snow, much of the time facing an intensely cold wind. Robinson was unable to leave his bed for several weeks.

"After many weeks of weary waiting Okakrae, the chief, made his appearance, but he brought deer for the conveyance of two only of our party. I asked him about the settlement up the river, but he seemed to know but little about it, though he said there was one where there was a priest, and took from under his furs a crucifix which had been given him, and a scrap of paper on which something was written in the Russian language. Thus inspired with confidence in his statement, Arnold and I resolved to accompany him, and on arriving at the settlement to return with the means of res

cuing our companions. We took with us, to provide for delays, fifteen days' provisions. We purchased of the chief a good supply of furs, armed
ourselves well, and started. The train first went
to the bay down the Anadyr, and then followed
another river up south-west. We made provok-
ingly short days' journeys, sometimes being able at
night to see the camp left in the morning. At the
end of ten days our provisions were all eaten and
our journey but well commenced. We were guests
in a polog of Okakrae's tent, he helping us eat our
well-selected rations, and then when these were
gone, allowing us to share with him half-cooked
deer meat and soup made of the contents of a
deer's stomach.

"After weary weeks we arrived at the grand encampment of the Chukchees far south. Here was
their great 'deer-chief'—a man whose authority
over his tribe rested upon the fact of his great
riches in reindeer herds. Here we were detained
several days. Some of the natives protested against
our being carried by Okakrae through to the settlement. They believed we were spies, and that the
Russians would punish the natives who aided us.
To remove these suspicions we paraded occasionally our uniforms and showed our documents
written to the Russian officials. Yet we were an-
noyed in many ways, and at times so persecuted
that we almost decided to use our guns and pistols;
but if we had we should have been, of course, overpowered by numbers and killed. Our lives were
made miserable by these insults and the disgust-

ing mode of living to which we had to submit, but on the sixty-fourth day after we left the hut we arrived at Anadyr.   We had thought much of our companions left in the hut, and our wish to reach the settlement was scarcely less on their account than our own, and our joy can hardly be imagined when we met not only Kennan, but them also. Our long night of anxieties gave way at once to a joyous day of gratitude and hope."

During about two weeks the explorers remained at Geezhega, resting and relating the stories of their adventures, and getting acquainted with the town and its vicinity.   On the eighteenth of April Bush, Macrae, and Arnold started for Anadyr. Bush was put in command of the surveys in that region, extending to Bering Sea.   Two other explorers, Smith and Harden, of the hut company were at Anadyr.   They were to finish the survey; so well begun by Kennan, between the Ochotsk Sea and that place, set men at work cutting telegraph poles, and, when the ice left the Anadyr River, they were to distribute poles along its banks and build huts at intervals for winter quarters.

Bush started with his command, well equipped and in good spirits.   One or two incidents only of their journey we will notice, as their route was mainly that through which we have followed Kennan.

At one place they were storm-bound.   The wind drove the snow with great violence into the faces of all who ventured out, yet some small boys continued their sports as if, like the snow-birds, it was their peculiar time to be abroad. They were shooting at a mark with their bows and bone-headed arrows. Bush put a number of Russian copper coins on the top of a stick as a mark, those hitting the stick to have the coin. But their shooting was wide of the mark. About twelve yards beyond the stick and in a direct line with it were two little girls, leaning against a log-house watching the sport. One of the arrows struck a hard-crusted snowbank, glanced off, and went whizzing directly at the head of one of the girls. She had no time to get out of the way, but bowed her head, and the arrow instantly buried itself, quivering, in a soft log just above her. The explorers who were looking on felt an involuntary shudder at the narrow escape of the girl, but the little heathen shooters laughed and shot away as if nothing had happened.

Bush took the southern route of Kennan's last exploration, and, going from Penjina, struck the Myan River, which flows south into the Anadyr. They obtained an elevated position which overlooked the Myan valley, overshadowing which were lofty mountain peaks. While pursuing their journey down the valley the wizard, refraction, whose skill in arctic regions we have before seen, treated them to a few of his feats. One freak was seen very dimly. Suddenly it seemed to be brought within ten miles of them; the next moment a mighty power appeared to lift its snow and earth upwards, and before the gazers could recover from their surprise, a tower, five hundred feet high, perched upon its summit, piercing the sky with its lofty top. While the amazed observers were wondering at the sight, the tower dropped to half its height, took to itself two great wings, and as the explorers were expecting to see it take its flight heavenward, the wings became two square projections, and there was on the mountain peak an old-style parish church. This suddenly gave way to a castle, such as crowned the hills in ancient times in the old world, its turrets, bastions, angles, and wings, making it easy for the gazer to imagine the sentry pacing his rounds. Quickly the scene shifted, and the enchanter swept his rod over the whole mountain range, and vast cities and gorgeous palaces and mighty temples came and dissolved "like the baseless fabric of a vision."

When not far from the point where the Myan enters the Anadyr the train struck across the hills on the western bank of the Myan, traveled northwest, and reached Anadyr on the eighth of May, having definitely surveyed the course of the telegraph line. The major and the Russian governor had taken a shorter cut to Anadyr, and were awaiting their arrival.

CHAPTER XXXI.

WAITING.

THE month of May was now well begun, the rivers would soon be freed from their icy fetters, and the favoring time to cut and distribute poles along the proposed line was at hand. Bush and his party would meet all the help the country afforded. So the governor from Geezhega called together the inhabitants of Anadyr with their head-man, and ordered the latter to render the explorers all the aid they should require, affording them men for labor and dogs for transportation. He also placed under Bush's authority half a dozen Cossacks, at the head of whom was Koschevin, a sergeant of great influence and authority, over the natives.

Being thus able to command a force, all told, of sixty men, the captain felt encouraged regarding the results of his summer work. To obtain food for his command was one of the most difficult things to do. He had tea and sugar in abundance; but fish, the important article for the natives and their dogs, could not be obtained at all, so the Cossack sergeant was sent off with fifteen dog-trains and a supply of tobacco with which to buy deer meat of the Koraks. He was also to try to induce them to drive their herds into the Myan

Valley, where the men were to cut telegraph poles
Another Cossack was sent in a different direction
on the same errand.

While these Cossacks, with most of the native
force, were gone on their errands for deer meat,
Bush and Macrae went up the river to purchase
some of the summer log-huts which the natives
had erected on its banks. They obtained sixteen,
and arranged to have them taken down, and in
due time to have them rafted down the Anadyr,
and set up at proper distances for winter protection. They provided the expedition, also, with
vetkas, native canoes, but quite unlike those
of our Indians. The vetkas here are fifteen feet
long, and one wide. They are made of two thin
boards for the sides, a much thicker one for
the bottom, sewed together with the sinews of
deer, the cracks sealed with pitch. They are
propelled by a paddle, bladed at each end. The
canoe man sits flat upon the bottom, seizes his
paddle in the middle, and dips one end on one
side, and the other on the opposite side. A light
spear, twelve feet long, always accompanies he
vetka.

The boats of this region used for freight are
huge log " dug-outs," called *carbasses*. A carbass
will carry a dozen persons. Both of these crafts
are about as treacherous in the water as an Esquimo's cake of ice.

Another article of outfit secured for the coming
river voyage was the native summer costume.
This is made of light dressed buckskin, carefully

tanned and softened, and smoked on one side to prevent it from stiffening after it has been wet. The articles of dress into which this is made are: a shirt, closely fitting about the neck, having a hood covering the head, except a small part of the face; pants, the bottom of which are tucked into boots of the same material, except the soles, which are of bear skin; and, lastly, mits fitting closely round the wrists. Thus equipped, they hoped to defy the mosquitoes which in the warm season are as plentiful as were the flies in the Egyptian plague.

While the Bush party were getting ready for their campaign, the major and the Geezhega governor returned, taking with them Cook, the Newfoundland dog. Cook came to Anadyr with the hut party on Kennan's return from the rescue. He trotted behind a sledge, to which he was confined by a cord. While his chance of self-defense was thus put to great disadvantage, the sledge dogs took every opportunity to tease and bite him. They thought him, perhaps, one of the Bruin family, and so lawful game, or, it may be, they were jealous of his exemption from the harness. But Cook was justly provoked at these insults, and, nursing his wrath until it was very hot, waited his opportunity. On arriving at Anadyr he received the same treatment at the teeth of his very distant relatives, and, having a clear field, he fought single, or in packs, the whole village of dogs, killing one, wounding others, and teaching all of them respect for his black skin. He was, undoubtedly, amazed at their evident prejudice

against his dark complexion. Such narrow prejudice *is* astonishing! But Cook had his prejudice. He resented at first the howling of the
Siberian dogs, seeming to say, when they broke
the stillness of the night and the quiet of his slumbers with their dismal chorus : " It's a useless and
disgusting habit, and I would flog it out of every
one of them." But after a few months' residence
Cook became somewhat Siberianized, and began
to try his voice at howling. After awhile he indulged the conceit that he was the best howler in
Anadyr, having a deeper and heavier voice than
any other dog, when in fact he was regarded by
all others of the canines as a great bungler in this
line ; and with this latter opinion his friends, the
explorers, agreed ; so difficult is it for us, whether
dogs or men, to make others think of us as highly
as we think of ourselves. Yet Cook was a remarkable dog in his own sphere. Besides the
valuable service which he did at the hut, while at
Anadyr, he drew, harnessed to a sled, tubs of
water from the river, and wood for the fire. He
was a general favorite, and his departure to Geezhega was regretted by all, except the other dogs.

As we have seen, the valley of the Myan was
well wooded, while that of the Anadyr contained
no wood fit for telegraph poles. The plan, therefore, was to go in force to the Myan, and cut poles
enough for the whole route to the Bering Sea.
These could be rafted through the Myan to the
Anadyr, and thus distributed when they were
needed. So Captain Bush, without waiting longer

for the return of those sent for deer meat, started
on the twenty-second of May for the Myan. His
train consisted of ten sledges and sixteen men.
They arrived safely, and commenced cutting with
vigor. They had worked only four days when a
messenger arrived from the Cossack sergeant with
only two days' deer meat for the dogs, and bringing discouraging accounts of the prospect of the
food supply from the deer owners. This was discouraging news. To make up this lack of deer
meat a general attack was made on the geese
which inhabited the vicinity. As the night was
their flying time, the explorers strapped on their
snow-shoes, took their guns, and went out about
midnight, and took their stand at various points
around some open swamp. Soon a flock would
rise and fly within easy range, when the fire of the
gunners opened. In two hours they would have
all the game they could carry to their camp.

While the geese shooting was barely keeping
the pole-cutters and their dogs from hunger, more
discouraging accounts came from Anadyr. All
the Cossacks had returned, bringing the same story
of a short supply of meat. The laborers became
anxious about their families, whose provisions were
running low, and they desired to return to the settlement. To add to the embarrassment of the
party the geese left the vicinity, and the ice in the
Mayan broke up, the floods over its banks began to
come, and the work was abandoned. Escape while
dog-sledging was possible must be made. So all
hands promptly were off for Anadyr, where they ar·

rived after about two days of desperate exertion.

The Anadyr River was still sealed up by ice.
All nature for a few days seemed in a profound repose. The day had absorbed the night, for the
sun had disappeared only for a single hour. During
his short circuit beneath the horizon the northern
heavens were aglow with a gorgeous display of
harmoniously blended colors of gold, crimson,
orange, and purple, which cast a luster of beauty
over the otherwise cold and cheerless landscape.
The light at all night hours was sufficient for ordinary reading. At one sunset a dark cloud arose,
bordered by a glittering fringe. It rolled across
the heavens, gathering density and extent, and
darted vivid flashes of lightning, and discharged
heavy thunders. The sight and sound were un-
usual and the natives trembled while they crossed
themselves and muttered their prayers.

Though the night was not separated from the
day, yet all living things observed the usual hours
of rest. While the sun was yet high in the heavens,
hastening to his brief hiding-place, the smoke
ceased from the hut chimneys, children left their
play, and men and women their work; the village
dogs curled themselves up in the snow, hid their
faces in their bushy tails, and slept; the magpies,
with drooping tails and closed eyes, sat nodding on
the sled-bows; and in the forests of the vicinity
the wild-fowl, with their heads nestled under their
wings, were lost in quiet repose. All nature, defiant of obtrusive sunlight, had retired to rest. Nor

did any living thing awake because the sun had risen, but all waited for God's appointed time when balmy sleep had completed its work of restoration. Once in awhile a bird would break out into song midway of the lighted night, thinking it was morning, and then suddenly cease, as if ashamed of its blunder, and hide its head again under its wing. A dog would yawn, open his eyes, give one feeble bark, and subside into silence and sleep.

On the sixth of June the ice began to move in the Anadyr. Soon it dammed up the main channels, and the country was overflowed. The natives resorted with their families to the tops of their houses; only a few huts were high and dry. The wanderers with their deer herds had fled to the mountains; the rabbits huddled together on the scattered islands, where the natives in their canoes sought them and killed them with clubs; and the sea-fowl sought the upland to breed and rear their young. For a few days the ice, the accumulations of many arctic months, set free by an almost instantaneous spring, made a fearful uproar in the river. The natives, at the terrible sight, crossed themselves, repeated prayers, and fired their guns to appease the Spirit of the Waters.

19

CHAPTER XXXII.

AFLOAT ON THE ANADYR.

DURING the freshet two carbasses were completed for the explorers' trip down the river. These were for the necessary stores, and for the men when occasion required. The vetka or canoe was to do the work which the skiff does in our home waters. The log-huts which had been purchased from the natives along the banks of the river above Anadyr, were taken down, each lashed together by seal-skin lines, and made into a raft and brought to the settlement. These, ten in number, were then lashed together into one raft, but in such a manner that each hut raft could be cut loose without affecting the rest.

On the twenty-second of June the voyagers cut adrift and floated into the current. The waters were yet fifteen feet above their summer level, and rushing seaward at the rate of six miles an hour. Neither the natives nor the Americans were acquainted with the management of the rafts on which they were now sailing, and, including the windings, the distance to the Bering Sea was five hundred miles, the last three of which were through an unknown region.

The day was fine, and the voyagers swept bravely on for a few miles. Then just ahead, in mid

cnannel, was an island. The waters surged furiously against it, and then divided and rushed past on
either side. The men sprang to the "sweeps" to
keep their raft in the main channel, but her head-
way was too great, and she rushed against the
island, swung round, and became blocked in the
narrowest passage-way. The men were knocked
from their feet by the force of the collision, but
the raft held together, and no serious damage was
done; yet it could not be started from its position.
A vetka was sent back to the village, and seventeen
men came to the rescue, by whose help the raft
was started again in the main channel.

Just below the settlement the Anadyr turns
north and makes a long circuit from its direct
eastern course. But just here a "cut-off" or deep
channel opened across the bend and entered the
Myan River some distance above its junction with
the Anadyr. Into this cut-off the voyagers steered.
The whole steppe through which this channel runs
was overflowed, and from the raft no land could
be seen except that of ranges of hills on either side,
the nearest of which was forty miles. The steersman kept the channel by keeping between the
lines of tree-tops jutting from the water along its
banks.

The current now was very sluggish, and the
progress of the raft only half a mile an hour. The
men were divided into two watches, and the craft
drifted along night and day. But for the mosquitoes, which came in clouds and defied the smoke
of their fire and the canvas of their tents, this

raft-life would have been pleasant. The slow
progress of the raft enabled the men to paddle off
in their vetkas and pick up eggs and shoot ducks,
which afforded a needed supply of food. The cut-
off was fifty miles long, and it brought the voyagers to the Myan without accident. A day's sail
on the Myan brought them to its confluence with
the Anadyr. At this point the herds of wild deer
which travel north at this season swim the river.
Here were camps of natives, watching for the deer
to attempt to swim across, when they kill them
from their canoes, or so wound them that on their
reaching the shore they are speared by those
watching for them. Sometimes the deer, made
desperate by these cruel attacks, turn upon the
canoes, and then he is wisest who keeps farthest
away.

Our explorers found here some Anadyr friends
catching white fish, the first installment of their
season's catch.

Soon after leaving this point the wide, strong
current of the river swept them swiftly and steadily onward. Stretched at their ease under their
tents, our men watched the ever-varying scenes
along the banks, or lay down to sleep before sunset, and, after only a refreshing nap, arose to see
the sun well-started on its next day's circuit. The
flowers of the steppe, which were now left by the
flood, filled the air with sweet odors, and the fowls
screamed from the bushes. The skin canoes of
the Koraks occasionally joined the raft party, and
fresh meat was procured. The chief mar of this

part of the voyage was the relentless tormentors of these regions—the mosquitoes.

One day a deer was seen two miles ahead, just stepping into the water to swim across. Three canoes, in one of which was Bush, instantly started in pursuit. The natives soon left the captain far behind, their paddles flashing in the sunlight as they dipped them first on one side and then on the other, and shot swiftly through the water. The deer took the alarm and swam for precious life. He had nearly reached the bank when one of the native canoes shot in between him and the shore, and turned him back into the middle of the river. The other native glided in ahead of him again, and the two canoes kept him swimming in a circle until Bush came up. They desired the captain to spear him; but he had no heart to do so, the poor frightened animal looked so distressed, and yet so helpless and innocent. Vassilly, the native who turned him back, seeing his reluctance, raised his long, light spear, which for a moment poised opposite the animal, then it sped to its mark, and a stream of blood flowed from the deer's side, coloring the water for yards around. The victim gave a few nervous jerks of his feet, dropped his head, and the deed was done. The body rolled slowly over on its side, but was prevented from sinking by two of the vetkas, while the other went to the raft for the carbass. He was a large buck, and his meat was a timely addition to the scanty supply of the raftsmen, and, though he was reluctantly killed, he was willingly eaten

The party now came to a point of the river where a range of hills from the south terminated in a high bluff. On the opposite side of the river was a Chukchee camp. Soon two skin canoes were seen gliding toward the raft. As their men stepped aboard, a tall, good-natured looking fellow, named Yandenkow, was introduced to Bush by an Anadyr man as the chief who aided Kennan in his return with the hut party. Kennan had reached a point a few miles below this place, and all his dog food was eaten, and there was no possibility of obtaining more on the route. Yandenkow, learning his destitution, gave him twenty deer out of his winter store, without receiving the least compensation, as Kennan was utterly unable to pay. Bush told him that his good deed was known and remembered by the strangers, and as an assurance of it he gave him some powder, lead, and tobacco, with which he was delighted. He said his object in visiting the raft was to invite the party over to his camp to partake of a feast which he had prepared for them, as he had learned from a Korak of their coming.

The raft was tied to the shore, and all went to the feast. They found four skin tents pitched on the edge of the moss-covered plain. They were sheltered from the sun by a black cloud of mosquitoes which had been attracted to the spot by a large quantity of putrid deer entrails scattered in the vicinity. Four naked little children were merrily playing in the midst of swarms of these pests; the fact seemed to be that their dirt-covered skins were too much for the penetrative power of the mosquitoes' stings.

On long lines of scaffolding the carcasses of a hundred deer lay drying: twenty others lay in the water, ready to be dressed; all had been speared in their attempt to cross the river.

On entering the chief's tent our men were greeted by a dense cloud of smoke, but as it was more endurable than a cloud of stingers, they shut their eyes and dropped down upon the carpet of deer skins, and put their faces as near the ground as possible. The feast of deer-heads was served in a large wooden tray, and all helped themselves from it except those few who were repelled by the ghastly eyes glaring from the bony sockets, and the loathsome filth of the common trough.

When the Bush party returned they were presented with some nice fresh deer meat, and their dug-out was filled with jerked meat for the men. The next landing of the raft was just below the bluff, at a forsaken native village. Here the voyagers put up their first hut. They were busily engaged in this work two days, it being made tight and warm, with a fire-place and a supply of fuel, all in order for a tired, cold, winter party. At this place our men caught a good supply of luscious white-fish, and looked hopefully to the end of their drifting.

CHAPTER XXXIII.

NEWS FROM HOME.

DRIFTING about eighteen miles, they erected, on a small knoll in the midst of a level country, another hut. The next point of interest was a high bluff on the right bank. On the top of this bluff were two crosses, and the scattered remains of a Russian settlement long ago abandoned. On this hill a hut was erected by our voyagers. The next point was Telegraph Bluff, so named by Kennan, as it had occurred to him on his upward trip that it would be a good place to throw the wires across the river, and so huts were erected here.

The voyagers were now less than twenty miles from the site of the old hut, called Camp Macrae, famous for its stove-pipe and the wonderful rescue by Kennan of its men. The tide water had already been met some miles above. More than two thousand miles of river navigation had already been accomplished. The raft was now nearly extinct by the dropping off of the hut logs, and as the carbass was insufficient to carry the men and freight, Smith was sent ahead in his canoe to bring up the whale-boat from Camp Macrae. This errand he speedily accomplished, as the wind was favorable for a sail up the river. But Smith, being an old sailor, and hating mean things, was in bad humor.

He said when he left with Kennan every thing was all right about the boat. "Now," he muttered, "the bug-eating Chukchees have knocked things higher than Minots' Ledge Light-house." The rudder was unhung, the "spreet-pole" and "center-board rod" had been carried off. The house had been broken open and robbed, but Smith added: "I guess they'll get sick of breaking open houses, because I had a jug of liniment good for freezes that I left behind. That is gone too. I hope some of them will think it's American whisky, and drink it, because it's got a lot of sulphuric acid, and sugar of lead, and such stuff in it; and they carried off a can of arsenic, too, that Mr. Macrae had for stuffing birds."

The baggage and dogs were transferred to the Blue Boat, as the whale-boat was called, and Bush and Smith started off, leaving the rest of the men to come along with what hut logs remained, and the boats. The sailing was quiet and delightful, and they soon landed on a narrow neck of sand on which the hut had stood. What remained of the provisions was strewed about the sand. Beef and pork barrels had been broken open, and what was not carried off was spoiled. Blankets, left in good order, were rotting in the water. Mattresses had been ripped open and thrown out. It was not surprising that the old sailor muttered bitter words concerning the plunderers.

The rest of the party soon arrived, a hut was erected, and a tent pitched for at least a temporary home. There were thirteen men in all, but all the

provisions were exhausted. Nothing remained
but the salt pork and beef which the robbers had
left scattered on the sand. This was picked up
and washed, and the nets set in the river for fish.
The salmon had not yet begun to ascend, but a
few blue-fish were caught nearly every day to eat
with the salt pork. Geese were plenty, but our
party had no ammunition, and so could not shoot
them; but a rather mean method, though quite
as successful, was adopted to secure them. The
young were just hatched out, and the old ones
were shedding their feathers and could not fly.
At such times they huddle together on the small
lakes and ponds to get out of the way of the foxes.
One day one of the men reported having seen such
a lake covered with geese. The distance from
camp was only two miles, so all turned out on this
wild-goose chase. They took the dogs, two canoes,
two geese spears, and a good supply of clubs.
Having come near the lake, all the fowl on its shores
rushed into the water. The canoe men went softly with their boats to one side, while the rest
waited, clubs in hand, for them to drive the geese
to the shore. The dogs were frantic for the on-
slaught, and were held back with difficulty. The
canoes approached the prey, which, rather than encounter the men and dogs on the shore, suffered
them to come quite near. The goose-spear was
launched into the densely crowded flock, each time
piercing one, which was taken out of the water, its
neck wrung, and its fluttering body thrown into
the canoe. Thus pushed, the geese soon came

ashore. The shore party held in the dogs, and waited until the whole mass of them had landed. The dogs were then let loose, and the assault along the whole line commenced. The fowl headed for another pond, and many of them boldly broke through the battle-line. Others escaped by strategy—when hit they dropped as if struck dead, and were left to be picked up when the spoils were gathered, but when the charging party had passed on they jumped up and ran off in opposite directions. A noble gander enticed Macrae to a personal pursuit, whether to turn his club from his suffering companions or to exhibit his own skill in flight we know not. "Mac," with uplifted weapon, kept within four feet of the fugitive, but found it difficult to lessen the distance. On they sped, the goose for his life and the man for a dinner. Both were well out of breath and the contest doubtful, when Mac's foot caught in a tangle of the grass, and he fell. The pursuer returned to the main line of attack feeling more like a goose than did the gander.

Sixty geese were the spoil borne back to the camp.

Soon after this wild-goose hunt, the Anadyr priest, with several men, came into camp, and they most willingly aided in diminishing the supply; the geese of the vicinity, regarding the raid uncivil, left to an individual, so that the question of rations became an urgent one. To meet the demand Macrae took the whale-boat and went to the sea-shore to find his acquaintance, Okakrae, which he was fortunate enough to do, and returned with a supply of deer meat, and the pleasant assurance that all that was wanted might be obtained. The chief protested that neither he nor his people were the spoilers of the hut, but he stated that some northern-coast people had done the mischief, and that two of them drank something they supposed was liquor, one of whom had died in consequence. It must have been our sputtering old sailor's liniment; if so, its effect was no worse than the frequent effects of the liquor itself.

As the days glided away our campers improved their hut, and made their waiting for the arrival of the vessels of the company as pleasant as possible. Salmon began to go up the river, and they supplied their table with the luscious fish. One of the common amusements of the men was swimming in the river. This amused the natives, who never saw men swim before. When they plunged they watched for their return to the surface, and greeted it with an exclamation of joyous surprise. "All same as ducks," they said. One old man remarked seriously that he should not like to be at war with such people, because they would swim under the water and cut holes in the bottom of their skin canoes and sink them.

On the first of August the priest and many of the natives who had come down the river with Bush returned to Anadyr. Orders were sent by them to Koschevin, the Cossack, to send down ten or twelve dog-sleds as soon as the winter roads were open, if the explorers did not return before.

Fear began to be felt on account of the non-arrival of the vessels. Should they fail, our party must escape from this dreary region early, or have no good hope of escaping at all. Already their situation had become uncomfortable. Their under clothes were reduced to rags, and their buckskins soiled and much worn. They slept much, partly that they might need less food, and partly to pass the time away. On awaking, their first act was to look for the vessels, and it was their last before lying down. They took but one meal a day, and *tried* to be content. The summer was already drawing to a close, and the *summer* lost to the telegraph enterprise, the year was lost. On the night of the fourteenth of August our men lay down in their bunks in despondency. They were tired of looking down the river and seeing nothing to cheer them. Upon opening their eyes in the morning their hut was full of strangers. But they were welcome strangers. They were a boat-load of officers and sailors of the Telegraph Company's steamer "Wright," now anchored in Anadyr Bay, thirty miles below. Col. Buckley, engineer-in-chief of the expedition, was on board. The "Wright" was on her way to Plover Bay, two days' steaming farther up the western shore of Bering Sea, and at the southern extremity of Bering Strait, where all the vessels in the company's service were to meet. She had stopped on this occasion to take in coal left the season before. The commander had no thought of finding any person of the expedition, but had sent the boat up to leave a letter for any one who might at any time come down.

After eating a full meal from the provisions of their friends, Captain Bush stocked the whale-boat with rations, and started down the river, accompanied by the new-comers. Four hours' sail brought them alongside of the "Wright." Old friends met, and great was the joy and many the questions asked and answered. The natives were amazed, for they had never before seen a white man's ship. The elegance of the cabin, the height of the masts, the curious form of the machinery, and the immense size of the whole vessel, nearly bewildered them. When the engineer made the steam whistle scream, they were scarcely restrained from jumping overboard. When a pet black-and-tan terrier jumped among them and attempted his usual familiarity, they shuddered with fear. They could scarcely be made to believe it was a dog. They sneered at it as "no good."

When the "Wright's" steam was up, Bush sailed away in her to Plover Bay, and Macrae returned with the rest of the party up the river in the whale-boat, laden with provisions. Bush found at the bay the "Nightingale" and "Rutgers," vessels belonging to the company. In two weeks the "Golden Gate," destined for the mouth of the Anadyr, arrived, but she was another two weeks in taking in her full supply of stores and men.

While waiting, Captain Bush visited the Chuk-

chees in the vicinity. On one occasion he found
a large group of them on a rugged mountain side,
a half mile away from their village. All about
were crushed human bones. The group consisted
of men, women, and children, all talking and
laughing merrily. In their midst was a ring of
stones; on these stones some hideous-looking old
women were laying choice bits of fresh reindeer
meat, over which they sprinkled handfuls of tobacco. The women while thus employed occasionally broke out into uproarious laughter. Our
visitor, thinking they were about to offer a sacri-
fice, called one of them, named Nan-Kum, whom
he had before seen, and who spoke a few words
of English, aside, and inquired what they were
doing? Nan-Kum pointed to one in the group,
and said: "See old man—no got eyes; by-me-by
kill um."

Bush saw among the group, sitting on a rock,
an old man; but none showed him any attention,
nor expressed in any way the feeling that he had
any interest in what was going on; neither did the
old man show any concern. He was calm, and
seemed even to enter into the good cheer of the
rest; yet he and they knew that his life was soon
to be taken.

"But for what kill um, Nan-Kum?" asked
Bush.

"Old man like um. Old man plenty deer.
Last year old man son die. He plenty like um
son; want die, too. He want Chukchee men kill
um. All right. Old man pickininny no want um

kill. All right. No kill um. By-me-by last month old man want kill um ; to-day Chukchee kill um."

With difficulty Bush ascertained these facts from the above lingo. The old man had lost his only and beloved son. So, though he had plenty of deer, he did not want to live longer, and requested his tribe to kill him. The day was fixed, but his little grandson begged so piteously that the old man consented to live for his sake. But he had now renewed his request, and was about to be gratified. Nan-Kum in the meantime entertained Bush with a description of the way they performed such services. If the person was one they loved, they gave him a stupefying drug, and opened an artery and bled him to death. Some they stoned, and others they tied about the neck, and dragged them over the mountain side until dead, and then left their bodies for the wolves or dogs.

Bush showed his horror and indignation at all this, which surprised Nan-Kum. He exclaimed : "No bad. Chukchee plenty like um. All same every fellow. By-me-by me get kill um too. All same."

The party seemed reluctant to proceed in the presence of the stranger, and, after awhile, desisted altogether. The white men departed, and learned afterward that the old man was not killed. His grandson's piteous cries again prevailed, and the grandfather consented to live.

Here certainly was one of the dark places of the earth, and even its tender mercy was cruel.

On the nineteenth of September the " Golden Gate," well freighted with stores of all kinds, and with twenty-five additional men for Bush's de-partment of telegraphic work, entered the mouth of Anadyr River. She had in tow the " Wade," a little stern-wheel steam-tug.

20

CHAPTER XXXIV

CHEERFUL AND SAD THINGS.

THE steamer entered an opening of the mouth
of the river into the land which Bush named
the Golden Gate Bay. Into this bay a small river
entered, which they named Wade River; on the
sand bank at the mouth of this river they proposed
to erect a station-house, land the cargo of the
steamer, and make it the point at which the wires
should land in crossing the gulf between this and
Plover Bay harbor. Toward this point then the
vessel steamed, her flags flying and her officers
joyous with the hope that this department of the
great enterprise was now entering upon a new era
of success. But suddenly the steamer struck a
sand-bar and was brought to a stand-still. It was
not known that any vessel ever entered this bay
before, and there was no time to make careful
soundings. The little "Wade" was soon put in
steaming order, and tugged away to get her larger
companion off, but her good intentions failed. It
was five miles from the station site, and the vessel
must be lightened at once. A scow brought on
her deck was launched and loaded with materials
from the "Golden Gate," with which to build the
station house. The "Wade" took the scow in tow,
the lumber was landed, and the carpenters worked

with a will to get in immediate readiness the need
ed house. Already the herald of the arctic winter
came, in the form of a light snow which whitened
the neighboring hills. In four days every thing
intended for the station was landed except the
coal ; this was quite necessary for the station-house
and for the "Wade," as there was no wood within
a hundred miles. The "Golden Gate" was now
so lightened that she floated and came a mile
nearer the landing. Hope brightened, and the
men almost saw the coal landed, the steamer turn-
ing her prow seaward, and returning to Plover Bay.
But a part only of the coal had been landed when
the scow, heavily laden, was struck by a strong
current not far from the landing, and sunk in deep
water. Boat and coal were utterly lost. The
"Wade" and a smaller scow had to finish the unloading, which they did by the first of October.
The "Golden Gate's" steam was up, her sails
loosened, and she only waited for the boat sent
ashore with her water-tanks to return, and then
she would be off. But we have seen often in the
arctic seas how near to seeming success lies utter
failure. Before the tanks could be filled and put
aboard, large cakes of ice came down the river and
filled the bay, delaying the boat with tanks ; when
it did reach the steamer she was aground ! The
"Wade" puffed and tugged on the tow-line, but
in vain. The night came on, and the "Wade," on
which so much depended, barely escaped with life
in reaching the beach near the station, where a
sudden rush of an ice-laden current violently

beached her, high, if not dry, for the winter. The next morning ice was king in Golden Gate Bay, and sailing was as impossible as on the snow-covered steppe. The steamer was cut up by the ice and leaked badly, and her officers and crew abandoned her, taking all her provisions with them.

Here was now an alarming situation; the station party of twenty-five, with only an economical supply of food until spring, was increased to forty-six, while the party from the steamer brought only enough for themselves for two months.

Among the material brought on the steamer were five hundred telegraph poles. With these a house was made for the steamer's men, the outer wall consisting of a double thickness of boards, six inches apart, the intervening space being filled with ground moss. A store-house was made, called by the officers a *caché,* where Mr. Farnam, the quartermaster, kept his stores, such as pork, beef, sugar, and molasses; this *caché* the sailors persisted in calling Farnam's Cash.

Mirrors, chairs, a desk, and tables, swinging lamps, and berth curtains, were brought from the cabin of the steamer, and the house put on an air of home comfort, especially with the stoves aglow with a coal fire.

While at Plover Bay Bush had obtained for the entertainment of his men during the winter a hundred volumes of interesting and useful books. These were conspicuously arranged on a shelf and given out by a librarian.

A careful estimate of the provisions showed

enough with strict economy for six months, while no more could be obtained, except by specially favoring circumstances, for ten months. So each day's rations were carefully weighed and measured, officers and men sharing alike; and though the fare some days was not inviting, none grumbled. The men jocosely designated the days of the week by the article of food for each, so they had Beanday, Sugarday, Softbreadday, Baconday, and so on. Strict discipline was maintained, and, we trust, hours and days of worship observed, though they had no chaplain. Singularly enough, "a high rude, wooden cross, apparently of great age," watched silently over the place, as it must have done for many generations.

Though there was food enough for the present, the men would occasionally inquire of Captain Bush about the future supplies. Forty-six hearty men wanted no stinted stores. It was not certain that the wanderers would come this way, or that they could be found. But the latter part of October a party of our men who had been to Camp Macrae returned with the Chukchees who had called there. These came into the station shyly, as if afraid of some evil intent against them. When made to feel a little at home, they asked Bush why, if his men did not come for war, they did not bring with them their women and children. Bush told them that their women, if exposed to their cold, would wilt like flowers, and their children die off like musquitoes. The chief speaker shrugged his shoulders, and expressed a supreme

contempt for such women. *His* women faced
the fiercest storms and did the hardest of the
work.

Three days after these Chukchees left the station they returned with their families and eight
hundred deer. Bush bought for the camp a hundred and fifty, which the natives killed and dressed
on the spot, and they were piled up to be covered
with drift snow. The mercury stood twenty-seven
degrees below zero, so they were not likely to spoil.
But the wolves snuffed them while prowling round
at night, and, though they did not venture near
enough to get a dead deer, they did make a supper of a valuable dog belonging to the camp, which,
with more bravery than discretion, went out to give
them battle. These wolves were the same sneak-
ing, fierce, cowardly animals they are every-where.
Three miles back of the station on the plain was a
small lake, to which the men often went to fish for
trout through the ice. One day a man by the
name of Young was there alone, having no weapon
except an ax, which he used to keep the ice open.
While busy drawing in his trout he was startled by
the yell of wolves. Looking up he saw a reindeer
dashing across the lake within a hundred feet of
him, and on his track not far in the rear were seven
hungry wolves, pursuing with heads and tails erect
and fierce, flashing eyes. Young seized his ax
and kept quiet. His hope was that they would
not see him. But just as they were about to pass
their leader turned his head toward the fisherman,
gave the signal, and the whole pack rushed down

upon him. Young was game, for he swung his ax defiantly, shouted vociferously, and sprang toward them. The cowards paused, glared at him, and, as he stopped, they rushed at him again. The first that comes is the first to die, seemed to the wolves the language of his tremendous yell, as he swung his ax in the air and showed fight. They paused, then turned, and ran again on the track of the deer. Young hurried home, and declared, as he came panting into camp, that he was "the worst scared man in all north-western Siberia."

Now that the question of supplies was fully answered, Captain Bush determined to try to do something to further the telegraphic enterprise, though it was mid-winter weather. Taking four companions, and leaving Macrae in charge of the station, he started for Anadyr, where they arrived safely on their dog-sleds, and in good time. His purpose was to organize a party to go to the Myan, and raft down that river and the Anadyr the telegraph poles already cut. But Anadyr and the whole region were suffering with a famine. The fish of the preceding season had failed, and but few deer had crossed the river within the range of their spears. This left them dependent upon excursions on sleds over the plain to hunt the wild fowl, and find the deer herds. But, to crown their misfortues, a disease swept off nearly all their dogs.

This was an embarrassing state of things for the great enterprise. After much deliberation, Bush decided to make a trip to Geezhega, and if possible

to derive from that place supplies and men for the
Myan work.   So leaving Mr. Norten, one of his
men, in charge at Anadyr, and sending the Cossack, Koschevin, to find the deer owners, and secure from them all the meat possible for the starving people, and his own enterprise, he started for
Geezhega by way of Penjina.

CHAPTER XXXV.

A PLEASANT MEETING.

WE left the major, Kennan, Arnold, and Dodd at Geezhega, when we started with Bush for Anadyr and the trip down the river. Mahood, it will be recollected, had been left at Ochotsk, the half-way place between the head of the Ochotsk Sea and the Amoor River. Let us, while Bush is getting ready to start for Geezhega, see what those left there have been doing in his absence.

The major's party, purposing to wait for the expected arrival of the company's vessels, laden with supplies, hired them a small house, and made themselves as contented as possible. The town consisted of fifty or sixty plain log-houses, located on the eastern bank of the Geezhega River, about ten miles above its entrance into the head-waters of the Ochotsk Sea. A Russian governor lived here, and four or five merchants of the same nation. But most of its people were exiles from Russia, or their descendants. It is visited annually by a government supply steamer, and some American vessels which came to trade for furs. Our explorers found the waiting more tedious than the perils and excitement of their explorations. The people lionized them with dances by night and with calls by day. They had a fine opportunity to study their character and habits, which did not differ much from those we have seen elsewhere.

It was now June, and the ice was rapidly leaving the river. So the major sent men down to irs mouth to report the arrival of any vessel. On the eighteenth a vessel was reported in the offing, and the explorers hastened down. It proved to be the "Jackson," from Boston, with the usual carge for trade. She brought also from Petropavlovk the stores which our explorers had left there, and, what was even better, news from the great world beyond the water, the first received for eleven months. Of course, all Geezhega turned out, and there was joy in that city; but her stay was short, and the monotony even more burdensome on her departure.

The mosquitoes began now to come in clouds, and the inhabitants began to remove to their summer huts on the banks of the river, where they were less exposed by their more elevated position to their tormentors, and were at the same time nearer the salmon-fishing stations. So our explorers, except the major, removed to the mouth of the river, and took an empty government storehouse, in which to wait and watch. Many times a day, with gauze-netting covering every exposed part of their persons, and thus shielded from their remorseless little enemies, they climbed a high bluff to look for the company's vessels, and many· times a day returned to their cheerless quarters with a hope deferred which made their hearts sick. The vessels were promised for the early season, and it was now August. Winter, with arctic prohibition on out-door work, would soon come. Were they lost and forgotten to the out-s de world, or had the telegraph company abandoned the whole enterprise? Such were their desponding queries. Kennan and Dodd, tired of looking for vessels which never came, returned to the settlement, leaving Arnold and Robinson to watch. On the fourteenth, while Kennan was at work on a map of his previous winter's surveys, a Cossack servant rushed in, shouting, "A cannon! a ship!" As three cannon shots were the signal by which Arnold was to announce the arrival of a ship, Kennan ran out and listened. Soon a second shot came faintly through the distance, and then a third.

It was nearly dark when Dodd and Kennan arrived in their canoes at the mouth of the river. Twelve miles away a bark was slowly coming into port flying an American flag. Arnold and Robinson had already arrived at the vessel in a whale-boat, but it was too late for them to return before morning, or for the vessel to reach the landing, so there was another night of vexatious waiting.

Soon as the twilight of the morning showed dimly objects in the harbor, Kennan and Dodd were peering from the hill-top, almost ready to believe that the ship had, like the "Flying Dutch man," disappeared in the darkness. But there she was! and not only the ship, but near her lay a large three-masted steamer! Three boats were

rowing for the mouth of the river, and were already not far away. These were watched with
good glasses, and the long, regular sweep of the
oars of the foremost boat soon showed the practiced stroke of a man-of-war's crew. The steamer
was, then, a war vessel; but what had brought her
here?

In half an hour two of the boats landed, and an
officer in a blue naval uniform stepped upon the
beach from the smaller one. He introduced himself as Captain Sutton, of the Russo-American
Telegraph Company's bark, "Clara Bell." The
major shook his hand heartily, saying: "Where
have you been all summer? We have been looking for you since June."

The captain replied that his letters would explain.

"But what steamer is that lying at anchor beyond the 'Clara Bell?'" inquired the major.

"The Russian corvette 'Varag.'"

"But what is she doing up here?"

"You ought to know, sir," replied the captain,
with a quizzical smile; "she reports to you for orders." The facts were these: The corvette had
been detailed by the Russian Government to assist
in laying the line across Bering Strait. She had on
board a Russian commissioner, and a correspondent of the "New York Herald." The "Clara
Bell" was laden with brackets and insulators; the
ships "Palmetto" and "Onward" might be expected at Geezhega soon with commissary stores,
wine, instruments, and men. The "Wright," of

whose appearance at the mouth of the Anadyr we
have already given an account, had left San Fran
cisco at the same time with these; so the telegraph
company, though it had moved slowly, as well it
might in so vast and untried fields of operations,
was alive and full of energy. The officers of the
" Varag " were soon on the beach, chatting away
fluently in English. Our explorers, as soon as
it was courteous to do so, slipped away to read
their first letters from home.

Business with our explorers was now looking up,
and despondency fled. The " Varag " was sent
after four days to Ochotsk, with stores and dispatches for Mahood, who had been there five
months, waiting for orders, while busying himself
in learning the native language, and making surveys in the vicinity. The " Clara Bell " discharged
her cargo, took on board Arnold and, a party of
workmen, and sailed for Yansk, a port between
Geezhega and Ochotsk.

The major, Kennan, and Dodd still waited at
the old watch-tower light-house at the mouth of the
river for the two expected vessels. On the nineteenth of September the " Palmetto " arrived, followed by a Russian supply-steamer, the "Saghalin."
The " Palmetto," on which the present interest of
the great enterprise depended, went ashore near
the landing, and came near sharing the fate of the
"Golden Gate," with the loss of her precious
stores. But the officers and crews of both vessels
worked with a will, and by the first of October her
cargo was landed and she floated   Now arose a

new difficulty. Her crew were all negroes, and as soon as they learned that the major had ordered the " Palmetto " to return immediately to San Francisco, flatly refused to go, declaring the vessel unseaworthy. The major called a commission of the officers of the " Saghalin," who examined her and declared her all right. Still the negroes refused to go. Their leader was put in irons and shut up in the *blackhole* of the steamer, and at the same time the cold set in after the arctic fashion, assuring the mutineers that a winter in Geezhega would be next to a shipwreck; so they surrendered, the " Palmetto " unfurled her sails, and swept out to sea.

The major sailed at once on the " Saghalin " for Ochotsk, on his way far inland after men and horses.

Kennan started off six sledge loads of axes and provisions, and a small party of natives to re-enforce Arnold. He then set men at work in the vicinity cutting poles, and a force was organized to get ready for the wires from Geezhega, to meet Bush's line, as it came up the Anadyr, and swept over the steppe along the valley of the Myan toward Penjina, at which latter place Kennan's men arrived. If it did not now thunder all round, the lightning promised ere long to flash in every direction—across Bering Strait to Plover Bay, then through a sunken cable to the mouth of the Anadyr, and be pushed along by Bush and Macrae to Kennan, and by Kennan to Arnold, who would hand it over to Mahood, who would send it to the

Amoor. Then how easy to connect it with a Russian line already made, and with European lines
now at work, and the marvelous enterprise is done
—the earth is girdled! How grand! But let us
turn to matters of fact.

Where is Bush? was now a constant question
with Kennan. Not a word had been heard from
him in Geezhega since the major had parted from
him in Anadyr, in May. He was then planning the
expedition down the river to the sea. Had he
reached the sea? Had the company's vessel arrived
to relieve him? These were painful questions, because an answer was not given, even in the slightest whisper. So Kennan resolved to go to Anadyr
and inquire.

Five sledges were loaded with provisions and
articles for trade, six Cossacks engaged, extra furs
secured, and, on the second of November, he was
off. The snow was yet soft and the traveling
heavy; no Dodd sat by the camp-fires to break the
"aloneness" with his genial humor, and anxiety in
reference to Bush was a constant cloud; to add to
these occasions of depression of mind to Kennan,
his good-natured Cossacks returned after a few
days, and he was compelled to take an equal number of Koraks. With these shaven-headed, stupid,
sullen, savage-looking drivers he could communicate but little except by signs. They had a wonderful aptness of not doing at all what Kennan
desired, or of doing it in the wrong way. Several
times when other persuasions failed, the loaded-
pistol argument was used to good effect. They

wanted all they could eat—which was not a little—
of all the food they saw.   They were especially
curious in reference to Kennan's canned provisions.   Once he opened a tin of pickled cucumbers,
which was a new article to them, and the dirtiest,
ugliest Korak of the whole crew took a fair-sized
cucumber and began to bite it.   The rest watched
him curiously.   For a moment his face was shaded
with disgust and resentment, and with a laughable
pucker of his mouth he seemed about to spit it
out, but, suddenly assuming his self-control, he
smacked his lips with a ghastly smile, and declared
it excellent.   Being "sold" himself, he wished to
"sell" his companions, that they might not laugh
at him.   The second man took it, tasted and
passed it along with like exclamations of "Very
good," and so it went down the line to the last
man.   Then the pent-up disgust exploded.   All
spit, coughed, made wry faces, and danced about
with their mouths full of snow.   Vinegar was not
relished by them, and the pickle can was now in
no danger of being robbed.

Kennan had charged the cook as well as he
could not to set the cans of soup on the hot ashes
to warm, without first opening them.   Of course
he could not explain to him that the frozen liquid
would expand with the heat and explode the can,
and of course he did not do as was told.   So one
evening he put an unopened can on the coals, and
the Koraks all squatted around the fire, watching
the cheerful blaze in moody silence.   Suddenly
there was a tremendous explosion, followed by a

cloud of steam and a shower of boiling hot mutton.
They were too terrified to jump and run, so they
rolled over backward, with their heels in the air,
shouting, "Kammuk!"—"The devil!"—and gave
themselves up as victims of the foul fiend. Kennan's convulsive laughter satisfied them that the
affair was not quite so desperate, but from that
time they handled the cans as if they were loaded
bombshells, and they never again touched a morsel
of their contents.

When Kennan reached Penjina the whole settlement—men, women, children, and dogs—came rushing out to meet him. For six months no stranger had
been among them; to Kennan's question concerning Bush they replied that they had heard nothing.
This awakened painful fears for his safety. The
next evening there was another uproar by men
and dogs, and the Anadyr priest rode up to the
house where Kennan was sipping tea with a Russian friend.

"Where's Bush?" exclaimed Kennan, grasping
his hand.

"God only knows!" replied the priest solemnly.

"But where did you see him last? where did he
spend the summer?" asked Kennan with a beating heart.

The priest then told him what the reader knows,
that he had seen him and his command in July,
and gave him their history up to the time of his
leaving, late in·that month. Since then he had not
heard from him. The priest gave also the sad
story of the famine in Anadyr. It seemed to Ken-

21

nan that matters could not be worse, and he spent
a sleepless night. The next day he bought two
thousand dried fish, and some seal fat for dog food.
He was determined on arriving at Anadyr to get
up an expedition to the mouth of the river in search
of the Bush party. In the mean time he found a
Korak chief, who happened to be encamped near,
and, with some difficulty, prevailed upon him to
drive his herd to Anadyr and kill enough for the
present necessities of the suffering people. Two
natives were posted off to Geezhega on dog-sledges
with letters to Dodd and the governor, telling them
the story of starvation, so that provisions might
be expected from there at the earliest possible
hour.

Kennan now hasted to Anadyr, and on the evening of the second day camped at the foot of a low
mountain range, about twenty miles south of the
settlement. Having eaten and rested awhile, they
were about to push forward, scale the mountain
that night, and reach the town by morning. But
a storm sprang up and detained them. At midnight the moon struggled through misty clouds,
and they roused the dogs and commenced the as
cent. It was a wild and lonely scene, the snow-
clouds driven by a gusty wind at times shutting
out the mountain peaks which towered above
them. Panting and bewildered, they reached the
top and paused to rest, when a long, dark line was
seen moving across the summit only a few yards
away, and plunging down the ravine out of which
our party had come. Kennan looked carefully;

they must be dog-sledges, and he started in pursuit. On coming up with the train he recognized the skin-topped sledge with which Bush left Geezhega. He sprang to it, and shouted in good English, "Who is it?"

It was too dark to distinguish faces, but a familiar voice replied, "Bush!"

CHAPTER XXXVI.

HOMEWARD.

BUSH returned to Anadyr with Kennan, and
the two remained together four days, relating
the incidents of their separation, and planning for
the future. Kennan then returned to Geezhega
to apprise the Russian governor of the famine, and
to forward to Penjina such stores as were at his
own disposal. Bush posted two Cossacks off in
different directions to find the Koraks and buy
deer, but both soon returned unsuccessful. December rolled away, no supplies came to Anadyr,
the mercury went down to fifty-six degrees below
zero, and the courage of the starving natives went
down too. One day a poor, pale, haggard man
came to Bush for advice in reference to the decision of a question which greatly depressed him.
"You know, sir," he said, "that the winter has
hardly commenced. I have a wife and seven children, and seven dogs. I must support these, but
have not a pound of meat or fish to give them. I
have a few deer skins which I can boil for them to
eat, and some seal lines. These are not enough
to sustain the children and dogs too, until the
Chukchees come to trade, and I don't know where
to get more food, as my neighbors are starving."
Here the distressed man hesitated, and, with a

choked utterance, added, "If my children perish,
I will have my dogs left; but if my dogs starve I
cannot go to the Chukchees and get deer, so all
will die, and I shall have neither family nor dogs."

The case to be decided, then, by Bush was
whether he should let the dogs or his children
starve. Bush gave him provisions for his present
want, promised him more when the sleds arrived
from Penjina, to which he added a short moral
lesson on the duties of a father, for all of which
he was very grateful, especially, no doubt, for
provisions.

On the thirteenth of January Captain Bush sent
thirteen dog-teams to the station at the mouth of
the Anadyr to bring up men and implements for
work on the Myan. The natives were glad to go,
as the trip assured them for the time food both for
themselves and dogs—this food being a part of
that brought by Kennan.

Early in February eight sled loads came by the
way of Penjina from the governor of Geezhega.
As these eight teams were sent to be at Bush's disposal, and as they were well supplied with their
own dog-food, he sent them also to the station
down the river to bring up Macrae with eight
other men.

On the fifth of February the thirteen sledges
sent to the station returned after an unusually
quick and pleasant trip. Having now a good supply of dog-food, a party of eight were sent to the
Myan to commence work on the telegraph line.

The annual visit of the fur traders to Anadyr to

exchange tea, sugar, tobacco, and assorted articles
for furs was an era of much importance to the
people ; in fact, was *the* event of the year. At such
times the deer owners were the chief men of business. But the trading season and the merchants
had now come and gone, and no deer-men had
been seen. They knew that the famine prevailed,
and were afraid of the demands upon their benev-
olence. So the traders were disappointed, and the
famine still raged. A few deer only were obtained,
though our explorers made repeated and strenuous
efforts to supply both their own and the public
demand.

Macrae and his party did not arrive until the
fourth of March. They had encountered a terrific storm on their way. When about one hundred miles from the settlement, one of their men,
John Robinson, was seized with inflammation of
the bowels. He was in good health at the commencement of the trip. As soon as his illness was
known the party took shelter in one of the huts
which they had erected in the summer. The
wind was blowing with terrific fury, carrying with
it clouds of snow. It howled dismally about the
solitary hut where the stranger from a far-away
home lay dying. Rough but kind hands minis-
tered to him as well as the circumstances permitted. A fire was made in the crude fire-place, a
bed of furs spread for him, and remedies carefully
used, but without avail. The hut was closed after
his death, and the body protected from the wild
beasts until such time as his companions could

come, take it to the station, and give it a Christian burial.

Macrae was sent with additional men to re-enforce those already at work cutting telegraph poles on the Myan. In performing this duty these Myan men had from the first a fierce fight with every arctic foe which could be brought against them, among which were deep snows, intense cold, tempests of wind, and short rations. The mercury ranged between forty and sixty-eight degrees below zero. Hot drink from a roaring camp-fire froze in their tin cups unless drank with haste. Many hickory ax-helves shivered to pieces with the jar in the hands of the men when chopping. The deep snow had at times to be cleared away before the chopping commenced; at other times the men slipped round on snow-shoes. The supplies came slowly from Kennan and the governor, owing to the scarcity of dog-teams and the detention on the way by the attacks of the relentless storms upon the trains. The Koraks made stinted contributions of deer meat. A native chief, by the euphonious name of Illia, gave them kindly of his scanty supply. A few fish were caught, and now and then a fowl shot. Still the famine raged until the men were compelled to kill and eat their horses, pronouncing them good eating. In spite of all these obstacles the Myan force cut and distributed at convenient points along that river three thousand telegraph poles.

But it was now the middle of May. The rivers were breaking up, and so Captain Bush decided

to order the Myan party back to Anadyr. There
was a young man of his company by the name of
Loveman, seventeen years old. He was desirous
to be sent on this errand to the Myan. So Bush
gave him command of the teams, and he started
off in fine spirits, driving his own sledge. In four
days he returned with the Myan men, haggard,
half-frozen, and scarcely half-clothed. He had a
story to tell at which all laughed from the comical
way in which he told it, but in which there was
nothing funny in the experience. It was as follows : Soon after starting he found that his skill
in dog-driving was less than he imagined, so he
dropped in the rear of the train, thinking his team
would at any rate follow. He went on bravely
through most of the day, but coming to a thicket
of brush his dogs drew different ways, and got tangled up. When at last he got out of the brush on
the open steppe the other teams were nowhere to
be seen. The snow was hard, and they had left
no tracks, so he drove on at a venture all night.
Getting hungry, he halted to make a fire and breakfast. But to his dismay he found no matches
about his person, and his only food was a few hard
biscuit. He had not counted on traveling alone.
So he rolled himself up in his furs, started up the
dogs, and let them go where they pleased. He
slept for awhile, and, waking, he saw at a little distance a bear sitting on a ridge of hard snow, de-
liberately surveying the team. The question which
the bear was considering seemed to be whether he
should be likely, in case of fight, to eat the team,

or the team eat him. It was, certainly, well foɪ
Loveman that the bear did not take the aggress-
ive. In ten minutes they passed still nearer another bear, which, erect on his haunches, looked
defiantly at the passers-by, but did not move.
The dogs, weary to exhaustion, appeared indifferent about the bears, and refused to budge faster
than a moderate trot. Soon after this, as the sled
was crossing a pond, it broke through the ice, and
Loveman was soused into the water. Taking off
his wet furs, he put on some old ones on which he
sat, rolled himself in a blanket, and lay down. He
thought for awhile of his far away home which he
should never see again, and wished he had never
heard of the telegraph expedition. His hunger
and cold were followed by the fearful stupidity
which precedes death. What occurred after that
until the morning of the third day he did not
know. But there was One who knew and watched
kindly the boy to deliver him.

The sledges which left Anadyr with Loveman
did not miss him until they halted at night to
camp; they then searched for him, shouted, and
fired guns. Thinking he had returned to Anadyr,
they continued on to the Myan. On the return
of the whole Myan party, as they were crossing
the snow-covered plain, the weather having mod-
erated, the sleds dragged heavily, fretting the dogs,
and causing them to keep up a continued yelping.
Loveman's dogs hearing this yelping, pricked up
their ears, saw the train, and started in pursuit.
The returned party, seeing in the distance a sledge

coming toward them, were surprised, but when they perceived that it was Loveman's, without a driver, they were alarmed. Removing what seemed to be a pile of furs on the sled, the boy slowly opened his eyes and stared round, like one awakened from an unpleasant dream. A camp-fire and warm food revived him, and he received no serious injury.

The rivers had broken up early, and by the first of June they were clear of ice. The winter seemed not to glide, but rather to suddenly burst, into spring. The starving people fled to the crossing places of the wild deer, and deer meat was becoming abundant. The sleds arrived from Geezhega laden with stores, and starvation for the time disappeared.

The next enterprise proposed by Captain Bush was a trip down the river to see how the men fared at the station, and whether the expected ship had arrived. His party started early in June in three carbasses. They left the Anadyr River just below the settlement, and went through the cut-off into the Myan Here they found the natives spearing the wild deer as they crossed. Frames of poles extended along the banks filled with dried deer-meat, and the bodies of many just speared were floating near the shore waiting to be dressed. The men were jubilant over a constant feasting. They shouted to Bush, "No more starvation now, sir; plenty deer!"

As our party approached a bend in the river they saw their good friend Illia, in a brush hut on

the opposite side of the river. He had chosen as
a place to intercept the deer a gap in a bluff which
extended four miles along the river-side, so that it
was the only place in that distance where they could
land from the other side. When Illia saw his old
friends he jumped into his vetka and came to them.
While he was talking a noble buck, a pioneer of a
herd, came upon the point of land around which
the river ran, looked shyly this way and that, and
returned into the woods. Illia seized his paddle
and glided swiftly back in his skin canoe to a
place overshadowed by the bluff near the gap.
Our party hugged the shore and kept quiet to
see the fun. Soon forty or fifty deer entered the
river, and in a close column swam toward the
opening in the bluff; it was a beautiful sight, their
spreading antlers rising and falling with the waves,
and their steady, quiet, but rapid, progress showing that they were good swimmers. Illia was as
motionless as the rocks overshadowing him while
he watched them from his canoe, with his long
spear resting upon his shoulder, and his paddle grasped with a steady, strong hand. The
deer were within a few rods of the shore, unsuspecting danger, when Illia, with a few vigorous
strokes of his paddle, shot into their midst. Before they could recover from their consternation
twenty-three of them were thrust through, and the
water was stained with their blood. A few kept
on, reached the landing, and scampered off over
the plain beyond; the rest turned round and swam
back.

It was now the turn of the men in the carbasses
They met the frightened, returning deer with three
breech-loaded rifles.   At an easy range all pulled
the triggers, but the locks were rusty, the guns refused to go off, and the deer escaped.   One only
which loitered behind, received the ball of a re-
loaded gun, and fell.   The gunners were too much
vexed to take him on board, so he fell to the lot
of the spearman, who before the present raid had
taken two hundred.

Two of the carbasses were left at the station on
the Myan with a party to raft the telegraph poles
and distribute them along the river to its mouth.

Bush, with one carbass, several canoes attached,
and a small crew, floated down the Anadyr.   They
paused to give Robinson's remains, which they
found in good condition, a temporary burial, and
on the twenty-sixth of June arrived at Golden Gate
Bay.   They were greeted warmly by the station
party, who were in fine spirits.   The steamer
"Wade" had been thoroughly repaired, freshly
painted, and her engine greatly improved by her
skillful engineer.   She was better than new, and
ready for work.   The Blue Boat, as they called the
whale-boat, was also in good condition.   All had
gone well with the station party, except that the car-
penter, Charles G. Geddes, had died after a pro-
tracted illness.   Famine had not been among them,
and now wild fowl and fish were plenty.

In a few days Bush made an excursion up the
river in the "Wade," with a load of coal for a
point intended as a telegraph station.   It was the

first time the steam-engine had been heard along
its banks and over its adjoining plains. What the
sea-fowl and wild animals thought of the strange
sound we cannot say, but the Chukchees, where
the coal was landed, were amazed. They peered
into every part, touched every thing they dared to
touch, but the more they looked the more they
were puzzled. But they showed no fear when invited to go down the river in it, which they did,
with the hilarious joy of children. The body of
Robinson was taken in a neat coffin, and laid, with
an appropriate head-board, by the side of Geddes.

The little steamer made two other trips up the
river, distributing brackets, insulators, and wire for
the telegraph line. On her third trip, early in
July, she met Macrae and party with the first raft
of poles for the lower Anadyr; Mr. Mason and his
men were still on the upper waters distributing
other rafts. Macrae kept on to the station. When
the "Wade" returned she found the "Clara Bell"
in the bay. Instead of men, stores, and material
for prosecuting the great enterprise, she brought
the news of the success of the Atlantic Cable, and
the consequent abandonment of the overland line;
its work was to cease in the midst of success, and
"Homeward" was the command. The "Wade"
was sent to the Myan after Mason and his party,
and as much of the material along the line as possible. In the mean time the "Clara Bell" was
laden with the valuables in and about the station.
When the "Wade" returned, the last of July, the
whole party embarked. The Jack tars — the

sailors of the wrecked vessel—erected a board
over their abandoned house, on which was written,
"The House that Jack built," under which the essential facts of its history were stated.   A pole was
raised over Quartermaster Farnam's store-house,
on which was inscribed, "FARNAM'S CASH TO
LET."

The parting cheers were subdued by silent
glances at the graves of those who would never
return to their earthly homes.

The "Clara Bell" left our party at Plover Bay.
They waited there until September, and were carried home in the "Nightingale."

It will be recollected that Kennan returned in
December to Geezhega after his joyous meeting
with Bush near Anadyr.   The winter and spring
were full of stirring events.   The long-expected
company ship, "Onward," arrived at Petropavlovk
too late to continue on to Geezhega, so she landed
her men and supplies there, and returned to San
Francisco.   A young American, by the name of
Lewis, was sent through Kamchatka to apprise
Major Abassa of her arrival.   One day Kennan
and Dodd returned from a dog-training excursion
on their sledges, and found Lewis in their house
quietly sipping tea.   He had been forty-two days
on the way, and had traveled on a dog-sledge
twelve hundred miles.   He could not speak a
word of Russian, and his only companions were a
few natives, to which was added at Tigel a Cossack.   He had no previous experience in rough
life, being fresh from the office of a telegraph

operator. He seemed to regard the exploit as no great affair, and was ready to repeat it.

In March Kennan made an excursion to Yamsk, on Arnold's line, two hundred miles west of Geezhega. The trip was full of fearful perils, and narrow escapes of the genuine arctic kind. He met there the major for further orders for the development of the work.

On the first of June a bark from New Bedford, the whaler, "Sea Breeze," came to the mouth of the Geezhega. Of course, Kennan was soon on board eager for the American news. *The* news was soon told. The Atlantic cable was a success, and so the overland enterprise was a failure! On the fifteenth of July the "Onward" arrived from San Francisco, with orders to close up, take the men, and return home. The whole business of the Asiatic side of the enterprise stood at this time thus: The whole route of the line from the Amoor to Bering Strait had been explored and located. Fifteen thousand telegraph poles had been prepared. about fifty station houses and magazines built, fifty miles of road had been cut through the forest in Arnold's department, and a vast amount of preparatory work done along the whole line. The major had engaged eight hundred Yakoot laborers at forty dollars a year and subsistence, and one hundred and fifty of them were already at work, and the rest being rapidly forwarded. He had also purchased five hundred and fifty horses, at prices varying from fifteen to twenty-five dollars   Twenty-five Americans had come in the

"Onward," in December, to take charge of the na
tive laborers, and the field would have been taken
with a thousand men, and it was hoped that the
line from Bering Sea to the Amoor would be in
working order in two years. But "Close up" was
the command, and close up they did. The major
left soon for St. Petersburg. The "Onward"
sailed with all but four of the Americans early in
October. Kennan, Mahood, and two others, the
rear-guard, left the last of October on dog-sledges
for a journey of five thousand miles to St. Petersburg, and so round the world, home.

THE END

For EU product safety concerns, contact us at Calle de José Abascal, 56–1°, 28003 Madrid, Spain or eugpsr@cambridge.org.

www.ingramcontent.com/pod-product-compliance
Ingram Content Group UK Ltd.
Pitfield, Milton Keynes, MK11 3LW, UK
UKHW010351140625
459647UK00010B/983